J. D. Beresford

Twayne's English Authors Series

Kinley Roby, Editor
Northeastern University

TEAS 545

J. D. BERESFORD AS A YOUNG MAN
Courtesy of Elisabeth Beresford

J. D. Beresford

George M. Johnson

University College of the Cariboo

Twayne Publishers
An Imprint of Simon & Schuster Macmillan
New York

Prentice Hall International
London • Mexico City • New Delhi • Singapore • Sydney • Toronto

Twayne's English Authors Series No. 545

J. D. Beresford
George M. Johnson

Twayne Publishers
An Imprint of Simon & Schuster Macmillan
1633 Broadway
New York, NY 10019

Library of Congress Cataloging-in-Publication Data

Johnson, George M.
    J. D. Beresford / George M. Johnson.
       p.   cm. — (Twayne's English authors series ; TEAS 545)
    Includes bibliographical references and index.
    ISBN 0-8057-7039-9 (alk. paper)
    1. Beresford, J. D. (John Davys), 1873–1947—Criticism and interpretation. I. Title. II. Series.
PR6003.E73Z74   1998
823'.912—dc21   97-36418
                                            CIP

To my parents,
F. Eleanor and George J. Johnson

Contents

Preface

Although once considered a leader among the younger generation of Georgian novelists, John Davys Beresford (1873–1947) currently stands as one of the most unjustly neglected figures of the period. His first novel, *The Early History of Jacob Stahl* (1911), heralded by the *New York Times* (among others) as "one of the most brilliant psychological novels of recent years,"[1] rapidly established his reputation as a solid realistic novelist. By 1918 novelist W. L. George could argue in a very influential book, *A Novelist on Novels,* that Beresford, along with Gilbert Canaan, E. M. Forster, D. H. Lawrence, Compton Mackenzie, Oliver Onions, and Frank Swinnerton, would occupy the positions of Bennett, Conrad, Galsworthy, Hardy, and Wells in 20 years.[2] At the height of Beresford's recognition in 1924, critic Abel Chevalley reinforced George's claim by asserting that of this group J. D. Beresford is "[t]he one most equally endowed with that *intelligence* and that *imagination* of life which make good writers of fiction."[3] In that year poet and critic Gerald Gould summarized one of Beresford's particular achievements, in the realistic biographical novel; he wrote that "the writer of our generation who has carried the biographical method at once to its logical extreme and its aesthetic height is, beyond doubt, Mr. J. D. Beresford."[4] Beresford also made contributions to various other genres and subgenres, including scientific romance, speculative and metaphysical fiction, social satire, the short story, literary criticism, and reviews of books on a wide range of topics. He wrote prolifically until his death in 1947, penning a total of 49 novels, five collections of short stories, nine autobiographical and miscellaneous books, and dozens of shorter pieces. Despite the volume and versatility of his work, an underlying idealism informs and unifies it. In *Writing Aloud,* a stream-of-consciousness exploration of the creative process, he asserts, "I have but a single theme, the re-education of human beings."[5]

Beresford deserves recognition on a number of scores. In the "envoy" to the third volume of Beresford's autobiographical *Jacob Stahl* trilogy, the narrator claims that the protagonist, Jacob, "would still describe himself, in Emerson's words, as a candidate for truth" and "that earnest search of his for some aspect of permanent truth keeps his spirit young."[6] Beresford was certainly a candidate for truth whose tireless quest led him to explore an astonishing range of ideas from the disciplines of evolutionary science and mathematics to psychoanalysis and psychical research, from the philosophies of materialism, idealism, and realism to Eastern mysticism and Christian Science. An inborn eclectic tendency and his adherence to the principle of the open mind kept him from limiting himself to any one of these perspectives. Informed by his broad awareness of ideas and his sensitivity, his work, and his fiction in particular, constitutes a most comprehensive and perceptive analysis of cultural change in Britain, particularly the breaking up of the old rigid social order.

Though strongly influenced by H. G. Wells in this stance, Beresford was no mere follower; his empirical, almost scientific, approach to the minute details of human existence was modified by his idealism, mysticism, and probing of the psyche. He was one of the first and most knowledgeable of English novelists to explore in his fiction the "new" dynamic psychologies of William James, F. W. H. Myers, Henri Bergson, Freud, and Jung. His *God's Counterpoint* (1918) represents an early foray into the explicitly psychoanalytic novel. In several critical essays, he articulated more clearly than his contemporaries the strengths and limitations of the use of the "new" psychology in fiction. His second novel, *The Hampdenshire Wonder* (1911), now considered a classic of fantasy, initiated his role as critic of English society, continued in both sociological novels and the seven subsequent futuristic and fantasy novels, which deserve to be better known since they clearly retain their relevance.

Historically Beresford deserves study because he established friendships and exchanged ideas with Walter de la Mare, John Middleton Murry, Katherine Mansfield, and D. H. Lawrence (to whom he lent his Cornwall cottage in 1916). After Beresford's friend Dorothy Richardson submitted an innovative stream-of-consciousness novel, *Pilgrimage,* that was refused by publishers, Beresford championed its cause and wrote an appreciative introduction to it. From 1918 to 1922 he served as the main fiction reader at Collins and was thus responsible for introducing to the English public several novelists adept at psychological analysis, including F. Scott Fitzgerald, Vita Sackville-West, Storm Jameson, and Henry Williamson.

Despite these claims to recognition, in the latter part of Beresford's career attention to his work dwindled. Since his death his novels in the realistic vein have been almost completely neglected and his work has not obtained even a minor position in literary history. Even more surprisingly he is not accorded a single line in any of the major studies of the psychological novel, notably Dorothy Brewster and Angus Birrell's *Dead Reckonings in Fiction* (1925), Frederick J. Hoffman's *Freudianism and the Literary Mind* (1946, 1957), Leon Edel's *The Modern Psychological Novel* (1955, 1961) and Keith May's *Out of the Maelstrom* (1977). Various reasons can be postulated for this neglect, some of which are taken up in more detail in chapter 4. His position as a professional writer entirely dependent on writing for income caused him to turn out material uneven in quality, a situation that Beresford himself lamented. His large oeuvre and his versatility may have discouraged some critics. His work may also have been the victim of a change in literary taste once a modernist aesthetic became the measuring stick in criticism.

With characteristic humility (and foresight) Beresford anticipated this situation. In his 1946 autobiography he wrote, "For I do not deny that if my imaginary critic of the year 2046, were to dig up mutilated copies of some of my novels from the ruins of the British Museum, the only place in which he would be likely to find them, he would be quite unable to place them as the work of a single author."[7] As the present work, with its aim of reintroducing Beresford's thought and canon, has been published just after the 50th anniversary of Beresford's death, he has not had to wait quite so long for rediscovery. As well, some of his novels can still be found in most large university libraries, and *The Hampdenshire Wonder* remains in print to this day.

In fact, quite soon after his death Beresford did receive serious critical attention in the form of a doctoral dissertation, "J. D. Beresford: A Study of His Works and Philosophy," by Helmut Gerber. This conscientious work has proved helpful, as has the correspondence that Gerber developed with Beresford's collaborator in his last years, Esmé Wynne-Tyson, which has been preserved by her son Jon Wynne-Tyson. Gerber divides Beresford's life into five distinct phases and his writing career into three. According to Gerber, in the first phase of his literary career Beresford wrote in the vein of sociological and psychological realism (1911–1924); the second was characterized by his expression in fiction of his search for metaphysical truth (1924–1938); and in the third, as an "undogmatic philosopher," he displayed the truth he had attained.[8] While this degree of order, imposed in retrospect, may be comforting to biographer and reader alike, in Beresford's situation, at least, it misrepresents the considerable uncertainty and flux that were characteristic of his life.

The present study has benefited enormously from the insights provided in Beresford's unpublished autobiography, "Memories and Reflec-

tions," to which Gerber did not have access; a clear-sighted and elo-
quent memoir of Beresford by his son Tristram; and correspondence
with literary friends such as John Cowper Powys as well as family members that has recently surfaced. In Beresford's autobiography, which covers his development from childhood to the peak of his career in the early
1920s, the author repeatedly describes his life as "haphazard," though
he also refers to a controlling "Destiny." The record of the places where
Beresford lived provides one striking example of that haphazard nature.
He claims that the rectory in which he was raised was "the only settled
home I ever had" ("Memories," 25). Thereafter Beresford lived in a succession of boardinghouses, rented flats, houses, and later, guest houses,
in all parts of the south of England and, for a four-year period, in France.

Like many modern writers Beresford spent a life of restless wandering, in a kind of self-imposed exile from respectability and habit in his
case. The details of his early life suggest that he must have associated
that only permanent home of his with stultifying and deadening convention. Beresford also described the style of recording his life as "haphazard": "These are not intended to be any more than haphazard memories of that period of my life in which I was trying to establish myself in
an unobtrusive corner of the world of letters, and I am not attempting
to give them a literary form. They must be accepted as the garrulitie of
one approaching his anecdotage" ("Memories," 196). Nevertheless he
was very conscious in his intentions that the book not be a record of his
emotional life, as he was aware of "glaring omissions" in it. Whereas he
describes in detail his approach to the craft of letters and his relations
with more famous and enduring writers, almost with the consciousness
of one who has not attained popularity, he excludes any description of
his relations with his second wife, the mother of his four children. He
was also very self-conscious about the fictional aspects of the autobiographical form, claiming that in autobiography "[w]e are reduced, in
fact, to pretty much the same business of inventing a character as we
habitually practise in novel-writing" ("Memories," 6). Conversely,
because some of Beresford's fiction is quite autobiographical, he occasionally draws on fictional passages in order to convey something of his
life.

With these new sources I have been able to construct the most comprehensive study of Beresford's life and work to date. I have attempted
to provide a corrective to Gerber's account by acknowledging the uncertainty and struggle in Beresford's life and underlining the courage displayed by Beresford in considering, adopting, and defending new and

often unpopular ideas. For his courage, his honesty, and his humane values, I am quite frankly an admirer of Beresford the man. As a liberal Christian I appreciate the attempt Beresford made to discover the essence of his own faith as well as truths in philosophies and religious traditions other than the one in which he was raised, though I am skeptical of his ability to achieve his ideal of the open mind given the inevitable biases of that early training. I am also attracted to his probing of the psyche and have found it most appropriate to take a psychological approach in writing about his life.

I am a more selective and, I hope, discerning admirer of Beresford the writer. Though he contributed to the deepening of realism through his psychological insights, a point I emphasize throughout the book, he might have been less reticent about exploring the unpleasant and the sexual in fiction and a bolder and more vigorous writer in general. I certainly sympathize with him in an economic situation that made it necessary to write prolifically, but I also realize, as did Beresford himself, that his conscientious and mild-mannered temperament worked against him. One cannot help but wish that he had pursued further some of the experiments that he began to make in the fictional biography *W. E. Ford;* the biographies of ordinary people in *Taken from Life;* the autobiographical stream-of-consciousness book about the creative process, *Writing Aloud;* the whimsical, metaphysical short stories; and the speculative novels that were ahead of their time. Believing that these works reveal a more adventurous Beresford, I have given them more attention than did Gerber. I have not, however, attempted to deal with Beresford's voluminous essays and reviews except those that bear directly on his ideas about fiction. I have treated Beresford's novels and short stories by genre and chronologically within each genre. Since most if not all of Beresford's works will be unfamiliar to most readers, I have felt compelled to be descriptive. With the more important works I have identified some of the ideas that Beresford transformed into fiction and have entered into a fuller critical analysis. I have also tried to provide some sense of the contemporary critical reception of these works. In the conclusion I suggest some further avenues of research on this versatile, compelling, and committed writer, serious recognition of whom is long overdue.

Acknowledgments

I extend my deepest gratitude to Jon Wynne-Tyson, who graciously opened his home to me and there allowed me to examine his extensive Beresford collection, including Beresford's unpublished autobiography, and to Elisabeth Beresford for her kindness, her reminiscences, and the photographs that she showed me, some of which she provided for this book. Her children, Kate and Marcus Robertson, graciously offered their permission as Beresford's literary executors to quote from Beresford's works, both published and unpublished.

For their remembrances I would also like to thank Ann Northcroft, first wife of Tristram Beresford, and Colleen Beresford, Tristram's widow. For several grants that enabled me to travel to England, Wales, and Ontario to examine Beresford materials, I am very grateful to the University College of the Cariboo. I would also like to thank the interlibrary loan staff at said university, without whom I would not have been able to continue this project.

An earlier version of chapter 3 first appeared as "J. D. Beresford" in *British Short Fiction Writers, 1915–1945,* edited by John H. Rogers, volume 163 of the *Dictionary of Literary Biography* (Detroit: Gale Research, 1996). Thanks to the copyright holders, Gale Research, for permission to include the material here.

Finally, I am indebted to my parents for their support especially during the final year of this project.

Chronology

1873   John Davys Beresford born 7 March in Castor, a small Northhamptonshire village near Peterborough, second son of Adelaide Elizabeth (Morgan) and Rev. John James Beresford, a minister of the Church of England.

1876   Succumbs to infantile paralysis.

1887   At 14 makes his first contribution to writing.

1891   Moves to London, articled to Lacey W. Ridge, F.R.I.B.A., architect.

1897   Father dies.

1902   First literary sketches published in *Academy*.

1903   28 November, marries Mrs. Linda (Brown) Lawrence, a former actress.

1905   Begins collaborating on plays with Arthur Harvey James (stage name Arthur Scott Craven).

1907   Separated and later divorced from Linda.

1908   Begins making regular contributions of short stories and book reviews to *Westminster Gazette*.

1911   Publishes first novels, *The Early History of Jacob Stahl* and *The Hampdenshire Wonder*.

1912   *A Candidate for Truth,* second volume of *Jacob Stahl* trilogy, is published.

1913   Moves to Cornwall and (in May) marries Beatrice ("Trissie"), eldest daughter of J. W. H. Roskams of Clifton, Bristol.

1914   First son born, John Tristram.

1915   *H. G. Wells,* one of first critical studies of the writer, is published, as well as *The Invisible Event,* third volume of the *Jacob Stahl* trilogy.

1916   Returns to London in December for birth of second son, Aden.

1917   Moves to "The White House," an oak-timbered Eliza-
        bethan house in Claydon, Buckinghamshire; best male
        friend, Arthur Harvey James, is killed in World War I.

1918   Publication of first collection of short stories, *Nineteen
        Impressions: God's Counterpoint,* one of the first British
        psychoanalytic novels; serves as literary adviser to
        Collins publishers until the autumn of 1923.

1919   Third son, Marcus, born; became novelist under pen
        name "Marc Brandel" in America.

1923   Moves to France with family; lives in various locations
        there.

1925   *The Monkey Puzzle* is published.

1926   Only daughter, Elisabeth, who became a popular chil-
        dren's writer, born at Neuilly.

1927   Publication of *The Tapestry*; returns to England with
        family.

1929   Moves to Ickleford Rectory, Hitchin, Herefordshire.

1930   Publication of *Seven, Bobsworth*.

1931   Moves to Brighton.

1933   Publication of *The Camberwell Miracle*.

1934   Publication of *Peckover*.

1937   Publication of *Cleo*; in Brighton meets Esmé Wynne-
        Tyson.

1939   *Snell's Folly* is published; begins collaborating with
        Wynne-Tyson on *Strange Rival* and moves out of his
        household and then to Selsey and Oxford; thereafter
        lives transient life in hotels and vegetarian guest
        houses.

1943   Publication of *The Long View*.

1944   Publication of *The Riddle of the Tower*.

1946   2 September moves with Wynne-Tyson to Kildare,
        Sydney Gardens, Bath, to guest house run by Wynne-
        Tyson's oldest woman friend.

1947   Beresford dies 2 February.

Chapter One

J. D. Beresford:
A Candidate for Truth

Early Misfortune

In his unpublished autobiography "Memories and Reflections," follow-ing a discussion of his ancestry, J. D. Beresford begins talking about his own life by describing "the outstanding and in some sense determining incident of [his] childhood" ("Memories," 30). He writes:

> Up to the age of nearly three-and-a-half,—I was born on the 7th of March 1873—, I was a normal, active, healthy child, but in the summer of 1876, while staying with my mother in rooms at Brighton . . . the dreadful thing happened. I and my nurse had been caught in the rain, I had got very wet, and my nurse when we came in let me go to sleep on a sofa by an open window, before changing my clothes. (The name of that nurse had a place in my youth among the outstanding criminals of the century). ("Memories," 30)

Though not immediately affected by this neglect, by the third day after it he succumbed to "a severe attack of diarrhoea," and by the following morning, he claims, "I had lost the use of my left leg" ("Memories," 31). The latter condition he ascribes as "a case of infantile paralysis" with unusual features and persisting effects ("Memories," 31).

Several striking features of this description beg for commentary. First, in the description of the nurse as a criminal, one feels the intensity of emotion, which nearly bursts out of those parentheses containing it and suggests that even at the age of 74 the incident continued to arouse powerful feeling. That comment is even more remarkable since Beres-ford has stated in the autobiography that he deliberately stripped his reminiscences of emotion ("Memories," 10). Second, the description appears to have a mythical quality about it, since one wonders how exposure could be connected with paralysis. Beresford's son Tristram probably more accurately attributes the condition to an attack of polio, though as the story was passed down to him by his mother, the incident occurred when Beresford was 11, after bathing while on summer vacation.

Beresford's depiction of the incident in his first realistic and semiautobiographical novel, *Jacob Stahl*,[1] sheds additional light. I feel somewhat justified in drawing the connection since in his autobiography Beresford frequently uses his fiction to illustrate his life and at one point he says that he can no longer distinguish between his fiction and his life ("Memories," 142). Beresford varied the details, but the common thread is that the nanny, Nancy, is held firmly responsible for the disaster. The summary of the nanny interestingly links her with flaws perceived in womankind by the protagonist: "In after years she was a name to him, a name around which a legend of carelessness and neglect had been woven. To Jacob the name of Nancy Freeman stood later for all that was flippant, idle, and self-seeking in woman" (*Jacob,* 10).

The consequences of "the dreadful thing" were both immediate and far-reaching, a position reinforced by the arrangement of Beresford's autobiography, since the coverage of his childhood years consists of descriptions first of the series of doctors consulted and operations performed on his leg and then of his education, "very haphazardous" and at times unpleasant because of his physical limitations ("Memories," 35). The immediate consequence was that Beresford's leg remained weak and that he was taken to various doctors who misdiagnosed him. Nevertheless, Beresford was provided first with a machine to help him build up his wasted leg and then, at age seven, with a steel splint that facilitated his walking, only begun when he was five. The leg grew "almost normally" and, after an operation on the Achilles tendon at age 16, was only an inch shorter than the other. Nevertheless, Beresford used crutches for the rest of his life. Undoubtedly the emotional consequences were more profound, since this accident appears to have changed the dynamic of the family, to which I now turn.

"No Way without the Cross": Origins of the Beresford Family

The Beresfords can trace their family lineage back to the time of the Norman Conquest. Among their ancestors numbered many knights of the Realm and, in more recent history, clergymen of the Church of England. Of the latter were Beresford's grandfather and his father, John

James Beresford. J. J. married late, at 42, on 18 May 1864. His 28-year-old bride was Adelaide,[2] the youngest child of Thomas Morgan of Brighton, a wealthy wine importer of Welsh origin. J. J. attained the position of Minor Canon of Peterborough Cathedral just before his marriage, and the couple settled into the nearby village of Castor. Their first child, born in 1869, was given the illustrious name of Richard Augustus Agincourt, the last of these names given in honor of 12 Beresfords who survived that famous battle.[3] In the interval before John Davys was born in 1873, three-and-a-half years after Richard, Adelaide had a miscarriage from a shock received "in a railway accident on the way to Brighton where she was going to stay with her brother" ("Memories," 36). The Davys in John Davys's name derives from her Welsh side of the family.

Parents

The marriage between J. J. and Adelaide was apparently not a success. J. D.'s eldest son, Tristram, claims that Adelaide lived "virtually estranged" from her much older husband and that they "seldom exchanged words during the last twenty years of their life together" ("Portrait," 2). Though J. D. is reticent on this point, the tone of his descriptions of his parents conveys his feeling of their incompatibility and that his sympathy lies with his mother. He attempts to portray his father fairly but shows some ambivalence toward him, claiming early in the portrait, for example, that there was "very little of the authoritarian about him" ("Memories," 16) and then later that he "ruled the household with priestly authority" ("Memories," 22). Whereas he tends to focus on his father's limitations and defects, he highlights his mother's accomplishments and talents, some of which were stifled by her position as a provincial rector's wife.

According to J. D., John James, "a little man" of five feet six ("Memories," 16), was unlucky in his early years since he had wanted an active career in the army but instead was channeled into the church. At his first charge, in Derbyshire, he succumbed to fever during an outbreak. Even more unluckily, he caught a chill when playing cricket with his choristers and "developed severe sciatica of the left leg," which was mistreated and led to his limping ("Memories," 15).

However, J. J.'s main weaknesses were not physical but emotional and intellectual. J. D. claims that his father embodied "what I came to recognise as a characteristic family weakness of my generation, the shrinking from any unpleasantness" ("Memories," 16). He was a reactionary in both politics and religion, in which he was evangelically orthodox ("Memories," 20, 22). His fear of innovation extended to education, and he abhorred areligious "Board Schools." One of his most striking and telling habits, demonstrating his ascetic temperament, was his bathing in the river Nene every morning before breakfast, summer or winter, until he was 60. After that it was summers only, but he continued to have a cold bath in his dressing room, though "he often came down to breakfast in the winters with all his fingers dead with cold" ("Memories," 26).

To John Davys his father seems to have been a cold and distant figure, initially respected by the boy and later rebelled against by the young man. Though his portrait of his mother is much briefer, it is also much more appreciative. Relying on an old photograph, Beresford observes that "she must have been a handsome woman of the slightly aquiline type" ("Memories," 23). Her attributes and talents included excellent piano playing, fluent command of French, wide reading, reading aloud dramatically, voluminous letter writing, authentic wit, sociability, and organizing capability. Nevertheless, according to J. D. she apparently did not have "sufficient force of character to impress her own individuality in those surroundings," which were convention-bound and dull ("Memories," 24). She, too, was completely and unquestioningly orthodox in her religious beliefs. As well, she could display that characteristic Victorian indication of repression—nervousness—expressed through fear of horses, thunderstorms, and wasps.

Beresford's relationship with his parents seems to have changed dramatically following his accident. His father apparently viewed his second son's affliction as an embarrassment, resented the expense of years of consultation with doctors, and consequently economized on J. D.'s education. He placed his pride instead in the eldest son, Richard, whom he had educated at Oundle Public School and then at Cambridge. The Reverend Beresford's reactions seem quite bizarre given that he too had suffered lameness. However, he appears to have striven to maintain his athletic competence, perhaps suggesting a wish to deny his own misfortune. His son's affliction may have aroused unpleasant and conflicted feelings about his own perceived inadequacy. Adelaide, on the other hand, whose only outlet for her affections seems to have been her two sons, invested even more of her affection and time in her needy second son. She is the one who took him to the London specialists. Most pertinently, she evidently imbued him with an appreciation of the arts. In a striking parallel to the memory expressed by D. H. Lawrence in his poem "Piano," Beresford recalls that "I got my first introduction to Beethoven from her rendering of the Sonata Pathetique, and get a thrill even to this day at the sound of that impressive minor chord with which it opens" ("Memories," 23). He also claims to have "profited greatly" from her real gift of reading aloud the works of Dickens, whom she had heard read his own books when she was a young woman ("Memories," 24).

Psychological Response to Lameness

Beresford's own psychological response to his affliction suggests the effect of imbalance in the family dynamic and the long-ranging impact of the incident. At the age of 61 Beresford insightfully claimed in his *Case for Faith-Healing* (1934) that

> it is exceedingly probable that there still remains in my unconscious mind an association of satisfaction related to the oncoming of my lameness. One of the most urgent desires of the child-mind is that desire for attention, which probably arises from the instinctive search of the helpless for protection. In my case . . . this desire was richly satisfied by my lameness. I do not suggest that I was neglected before this thing happened to me, but afterwards I inevitably became the object of unusual care and solicitude. And, no doubt, some childish element that still persists in the strange complex that makes up the totality of consciousness . . . is still in active opposition to my cure.[4]

The "unusual care and solicitude" that Beresford received mostly from his mother must partially account for his claim that "[m]y lameness has never seemed to me the handicap that it did to other people" ("Memories," 35), at least from the retrospective view in his autobiography. Nevertheless, it seems greatly to have affected his relations with women thereafter. Aside from the anger shown toward the perceived source of his disability, his nursemaid, Beresford as a young man "believed himself to be hopelessly handicapped, from a romantic point of view, by my lame leg" ("Memories," 105). On another occasion, though, he wrote that his lameness helped decide his career;[5] and it may even have spurred him on to self-improvement.

Based on clinical evidence from active creators, psychoanalyst William Niederland claims that individuals with a "physical malformation resulting from a serious illness in childhood" experience narcissistic disturbances, develop a distorted body image, and construct compensating fantasies.[6] He observes that "through their creative acts the patients were attempting to recreate a perfection which they secretly thought had been theirs *prior* to their deformity—essentially a narcissistic wish which was transformed into a creative (i.e., re-creative) effort" (Niederland, 14). Much of this would appear to apply very well to Beresford's situation. We have seen how he proclaims that until three-and-a-half "I was a normal, active, healthy child." In his childhood he seems to have developed that introspective quality characteristic of his later years. In *Writing Aloud* (1928), he claims that

> I'm too self-conscious. I don't mean in the colloquial sense that applies chiefly to timid young men and women in society, but in the psychological sense of being endowed or cursed with a high degree of self-awareness. . . . That is partly a result of my youthful habit of introspection. My motto in those days was, "inquire within for everything." . . . I hardly knew when this habit of introspection began to grow less marked. If it had increased I should probably have ended as Nietzsche did, in a lunatic asylum. (*Writing*, 95)

Beresford also reports experiencing mystical "ecstasies" during his youth."[7] His repeated telling of his story in dozens of autobiographical novels in which a manifestation of himself is the hero who triumphs over obstacles suggests that he learned to renegotiate his experiences and conflicted feelings within the ordered and safe confines of prose narrative and the novel form. Alternately, his fantasies, notably *The Hampdenshire Wonder*,[8] demonstrate the power of his imaginative conception and show him seeking for alternative forms of perfection, whether in mental ability or in fictional worlds.

Education

Beresford's "haphazard" schooling may well have increased his capacity to use fantasizing as a means of escaping the cruelty and punishment he experienced during parts of it. By the age of 16 he had been shuffled around to four boarding schools: at Peterborough from age 8 to 12, a public school at Oundle for a year, a school at Snettisham in Norfolk for "difficult" boys ("Memories," 47) and the Peterborough King's School ("Memories," 53). Two revealing incidents occurred at the first of these. He recollected that "most of the young savages found me a tempting butt for bullying, much of it of the merely teasing variety[;] I was called Miss Beresford, but I remember being tied to an apple-tree in the playground and being pelted with chestnuts" ("Memories," 38). In the other he remembered being castigated for saying "damn" ("Memories," 39).

At Oundle he came under the strict discipline of the Reverend E. M. Eicke, "a man of violent temper" ("Memories," 42). Though Eicke never thrashed J. D., Beresford did suffer public humiliation at his hands. His stay at the third school, a "gloomy place" ("Memories," 47), was cut short by an accident during which the cart he had been riding in ran over his lame leg. It was an adventure to be boasted about ("Memories," 49).

As a day-boy at the King's school he picked up some general knowledge, but overall he claims that "I never had any interest in school subjects, nor any pride in acquiring knowledge" ("Memories," 52). However, he was grateful for "never having been drilled into the acceptable type of the Public Schoolboy" ("Memories," 53). He stresses that he was undistinguished, in contrast to someone like H. G. Wells at this age. Precociousness manifested itself in another sphere, however, as revealed by his claim that at 14 and a half he fell "deeply in love" with the resident mistress where he boarded while attending the King's school ("Memories," 50).

During those periods when he lived at home he experienced comfort, prompting his wish to remain at home, but also prompting boredom. He was stifled by his parents' strict religious observances, claiming that his father was a hypocritical Sabbatarian (*What,* 18). He found some respite in the five-acre garden, "a boy's paradise," where he played "Red-Indians" ("Memories," 27). The degree to which Beresford was sheltered in the rectory world is suggested by an incident that occurred when he was about 16. A preacher friend visited and argued against the Rev. Beresford's habitual belief in the doctrine of eternal punishment by emphasizing God's mercy and love. This view came as a revelation to the youth, who "took it for granted that Hell was the inevitable destination of sinners and unbelievers" ("Memories," 21).

Beresford's 16th year was a pivotal one for him in several regards. His general schooling came to an end when he went up to London to undergo an operation on his Achilles tendon. This laid him up for 10 weeks, spent in his aunt's nursing home on Marylebone Street. A decision about his career then had to be made, and this, too, was described by Beresford as a "haphazard affair" ("Memories," 55). By this time he knew that he did not want to enter the church and instead proposed becoming an engineer, as he had always been clever with machinery, partly because he had had to depend on various mechanical devices, including a tricycle bath-chair, to increase his mobility. His father squashed this idea, claiming that one needed one's full physical capabilities for it, and instead proposed the profession of architecture, dutifully submitted to by Beresford ("Memories," 56).

He was first articled to the local diocesan surveyor at Stamford, approximately eight miles from Castor. Two fascinating features emerge in Beresford's description of life during the nearly two years in this position. First, he focuses on the means of transport, by pony cart and train, to and from his job, and particularly on several accidents he had when driving the cart. These accidents occasioned his father considerable expense and suggest something of the difficulty mobility was for J. D. Second, he suggests that his propensity to fantasy was well developed by this time. Even when doing mechanical work he stimulated himself "by the fantasy of doing the thing, whatever it was, better than it had ever been done before" ("Memories," 61).

London

At 18, presumably with advancement in mind, Beresford started a three-and-a-half-year period of articling with the diocesan surveyor for Sussex, whose office was in Gray's Inn, London. Up to this point Beresford had lived a very sheltered life and was rather passive and conventional ("Memories," 61, 62). London changed all that.

London by 1891 had experienced some severe labor disputes and was just embarking on a decade of decadence, of absinthe and ennui. For a provincial lad far removed from politics and artistic circles it was a place of mystery, where even the legendary "pea-soup" fogs cast a spell: "I liked to be out in the worst specimens, finding it an exciting adventure in what was to me, then, the romantic and mysterious City that might reveal new wonders at any fresh exploration of its, as it seemed, endless extensions. Whenever I had been there in my youth, it had always been in my mother's company and my knowledge of it was largely confined to the neighbourhood of Oxford Street. Now I was free to explore it myself" ("Memories," 66). This he did with great enthusiasm, and he quickly succumbed to "the magic of its theatres and music halls" ("Memories," 63). His uncritical taste was "exceedingly catholic, including everything but melodrama ("Memories," 68).

Beresford's fascination with these entertainments would, of course, have been quite shocking to his parents since, as Karl Beckson claims in

his study of the 1890s, "In the minds of proper Victorians, theater people were believed to be no different from common prostitutes because of
their provocative make-up, free and easy manner, self-sufficiency, and
notorious reputation for moral laxity."[9] Beresford claims that he fell in
love with an actress but only adored her at a distance ("Memories," 68).
He also engaged in a more real and mysterious relationship at this time,
recollecting that "I had had a passionate secret love-affair, covering a
period of seven years between the ages of eighteen and twenty-five, con-
cerning which I prefer to say too little rather than too much, but it
always remained a matter of incredulous wonder to me that any woman
should have any feeling for me other than friendship" ("Memories,"
105).

Meanwhile, at work he learned the principles of building construction under the kindly supervision of Lacey W. Ridge. Sundays were often
spent with a fellow apprentice from whom he learned chess ("Memories," 63). During these years he moved residence frequently, living
briefly with relatives before adopting a transient boardinghouse life,
mainly among his social inferiors.

At one of these boardinghouses in Gloucester Terrace he met G. F.
Rogers, who started Beresford, at 21, "on the road of independent thinking and self-education," a momentous event in Beresford's life ("Memories," 74). An out-physician at the London Hospital, Rogers questioned
Beresford's fundamentalist faith and helped him throw off "[t]hose
shackles of orthodoxy . . . in a single evening."[10] Leading up to this conversion, Beresford had relaxed his moral code and had increasingly felt a
sense of duality (*What,* 20). After this revelation, he "began to take life
more seriously—and more ethically" and developed "a sense of personal
responsibility for my actions that had been lacking when I believed that
it was always possible to qualify for Heaven at the last moment, no matter what I had done ("Memories," 75). Beresford felt as though he had
emerged from a prison, and he became a convinced evolutionist. One
wonders how this news was received at the rectory, where he spent a long
summer in 1895 after finishing his stint with Ridge ("Memories," 65).

Back in London in September, Beresford reluctantly began working
for the important architect Edwin T. Hall as a draftsman at 30 shillings
a week ("Memories," 81). During "eight years of slavery" in this office,
he seems mainly to have been exposed to a broad range of expletives.
Finally he realized that the career had no future. As an escape during
this period, he continued to educate himself, reading Samuel Laing and
Darwin, among other scientists and philosophers, at the British Library

on Saturday afternoons and fiction from Mudie's lending library, notably H. G. Wells's *The Wheels of Chance* (1896). More often he "wasted" his free time playing chess or billiards, on summer weekends touring South London on his bicycle, and rowing or canoeing on the Thames between Halliford and Oxford ("Memories," 91).

He dropped chess-playing for a time after a curious experience while walking on the street in which he became obsessed with thinking that he could only make a knight's move, which would mean that he would be attempting to occupy the same space as an approaching horse-bus. He recalled: "If that had been only a passing illusion, it would not have shaken me, but I realised in those moments of hesitation just what madness might mean. For my self-control had incontinently failed. The conscious, directing self, standing apart knew perfectly well that there was nothing to prevent my moving in the ordinary way, but the rest of my personality refused to obey" ("Memories," 91). The incident suggests, perhaps, the subtle means by which his feelings of oppression and depression about the "horrid sameness" of his life found expression ("Memories," 93). Beresford summarizes himself at this stage as a "commonplace young man . . . a young man of average abilities in his profession, neither industrious nor ambitious, and undistinguished by any quality that was likely to lead to escape from the slavery of office work" ("Memories," 94).

By the summer of 1901, however, he was making "spasmodic efforts to write short stories" and humorous verse with the aim of making extra money ("Memories," 89, 93). Despite being hampered by a "habit of self-deprecation" ("Memories," 89), his efforts paid off in January 1902 when he won a one-guinea prize for "the best portrait of a street character" in the journal *Academy,* to which he then apparently contributed fairly regularly (Gerber, 18). A second mentor, Arthur Scaife, provided Beresford with his sociological education from 1902. Beresford reached another juncture when in 1903 he read the Cambridge-educated psychical researcher Frederic W. H. Myers's *Human Personality and Its Survival of Bodily Death* (1903), "a book of modern wonders that gave my mind a new twist," he later claimed (*What,* 27). Myers's descriptions of the subliminal self, multiple personalities, and mystical experiences sparked Beresford's fascination with abnormal psychology and led him, gradually, "to abandon the realist for the idealist position" (*What,* 30). Part of the attraction to the book may have been what Beresford describes as his one distinguishing peculiarity, a periodic "half-mental, half-mystical experience" of exaltation ("Memories," 95).

His propensity for fantasy had also continued to develop during this period, as is illustrated by an excerpt, dated 10 May 1903, from the first entry of a commonplace book kept by Beresford:

> The real waste of time has been when I have spent the evening alone, thinking imaginary thoughts that ended nowhere, dreams that were not controlled into the semblance of life. It has been almost a curse this imagination of mine, this power I have to drop the realities of life and substitute for them the furnishings of my own desires. This power to produce in myself the delights of accomplishment, by projecting myself into the future and, this performed, (!) to live there, to look back on achievements that became so vivid in this strange retrospect. ("Memories," 79)

Not only did Beresford begin his attempts to write for publication in 1901, but he also met his future wife, Mrs. Linda Lawrence. The "passionate secret love-affair" mentioned earlier had ended in about 1898 and Beresford's life was "singularly lacking in feminine society" ("Memories," 99) until he met several female confidantes who encouraged his fledgling aspirations as a writer. One of these, Agnes Dundas, a cousin of Beresford's, took him to bohemian parties in Chelsea, and it was there he encountered Linda in the summer of 1901.

Twenty-nine-year-old Mrs. Lawrence (née Brown), a former actress, had married an actor who deserted her, and was in the process of suing for divorce. According to Beresford, his and Linda's relationship developed rapidly, since in two weeks they "were as much engaged as [they] could be until she got her divorce" ("Memories," 111). In August the couple made the traditional visit to meet the parents, in this case Beresford's mother at Hunstanton, as Beresford's father had died in 1897. Beresford was obviously attracted to Linda's cleverness ("Memories," 113), but there was also apparently a strong physical attraction, implied in Beresford's statement that he changed lodgings so as to be able to visit Linda's rooms every evening ("Memories," 111). That arrangement cost Linda her job as secretary of the Working Girl's Club. However, the couple had to wait until the divorce came through to get married, which they did on 28 November 1903. They honeymooned in Holland, Belgium, and France. Beresford embarked on writing a play and Linda's acting contacts helped in getting it submitted to Beerbohm Tree, but it was never staged. Beresford also completed a novel, but it received a similar fate and was never published. To make matters worse, Linda suffered a miscarriage several months after their honeymoon.

Beresford had escaped the slavery of office routine by becoming an agent with the New York Life Insurance Company at the end of September 1903, just before marrying. He then found a more amenable position as editor for the bookseller W. H. Smith's first *Annual,* which appeared in 1906. Thereafter he wrote advertising copy for Smith and then briefly with S. H. Benson for five pounds per week, eventually transforming the experiences with these firms into his novel *A Candidate for Truth* (1912).[11]

Literary Life

During Christmas 1905 Beresford began collaborating on plays with Arthur Harvey James (stage name Arthur Scott Craven), who had been introduced to Beresford by Linda. Beresford describes Harvey James, who became Beresford's closest male friend, as "a man of great gifts" with "a powerful personality" ("Memories," 166). Beresford recalled that "we made a solemn pact always to speak the truth to each other, and we kept it. That is, indeed, the only safe basis of friendship; and of personal integrity" ("Memories," 179). At least two of their plays, *The Royal Heart* and *The Compleat Angler,* were produced, the former playing over 200 times in the provinces. After Beresford lost his job with Benson's, he increased his writing efforts, doing unpaid reviewing for a now-defunct monthly, *The Literary World,* and producing three more (unpublished) novels by 1907.

About this time Beresford's marriage began to crumble under the pressures of financial distress and because of temperamental incompatibility. Beresford recalled that "Linda had the temperament of an actress and enjoyed letting herself go in scenes that reduced me to the depths of misery," whereas he adopted a passive and submissive role ("Memories," 129, 155). After their furniture was repossessed to pay the rent of their apartment at St. James' Court, Beresford sent his wife to live with a cousin, the Rev. Gilbert Beresford, in Beaford, North Devon. While there she fell in love first with a young doctor and then a member, some years her junior, of Beresford's own family ("Memories," 159). Under these conditions he willingly consented to a divorce, though it took some time to obtain. She did not marry again and died in the spring of 1917 ("Memories," 159). After leaving St. James' Court, Beresford, meanwhile, had moved into a humble dwelling in Bond's Hotel off Buckingham Palace Road, where he lived lonely and undernourished ("Memories," 160).

In the midst of this personal crisis, Beresford's literary fortunes finally began to change: he published a light satirical essay in *Punch* in March 1908; and, more importantly, with the encouragement and a note of introduction from the editor of *Punch,* Owen Seaman, he became an occasional reviewer for the *Westminster Gazette* shortly thereafter. In the latter periodical, described by Beresford as "the most scholarly and literary of all the London evening papers," he also published sketches under the pseudonym of "Jacques" ("Memories," 161).

His financial distress was alleviated to some degree by a friend, R. J. Bryce, who offered him free room and board at his home in Whetstone in November 1907. In return Beresford delightedly agreed to collaborate with him on a book on socialism. Unfortunately, Bryce had succumbed to alcoholism. Beresford unsuccessfully attempted to cure this talented Scotsman and was forced to leave after a few months when Bryce revolted, but the incident, claimed Beresford, "had a permanent influence on my life, and when I read in a modern novel the constant references to drinking,—and of how few of our younger writers abstain from them!—,I think of poor Bryce and am filled with indignation against this popular pandering to a self-indulgence that may in some cases prove to be a man's destruction" ("Memories," 177). For this reason he never described drinking in his novels, though he did tell the story of Bryce's deterioration in *The House in Demetrius Road* (1914). Beresford's financial position further improved at least temporarily when he was offered the editorship at £100 a year of *What's On,* a free weekly entertainment guide to London. However, his employer dismissed him after only two months for spending too much time on his own work.

That work consisted by now of increasing numbers of reviews for the *Westminster Gazette* at four pence per line. Beresford's conscientious attitude, including his refusal to increase his remuneration by padding or indulging in "log-rolling" so impressed the editor, J. A. Spender, that in September 1908 J. D. was added to the official staff. He had moved to a boardinghouse at Swiss Cottage where his friend Arthur Harvey James and family were staying. The two budding writers often laughed themselves speechless over the humorous plays they concocted ("Memories," 182), though they had no success in getting these staged. However, the spark provided by this "daily companionship," along with Beresford's freedom "from all domestic and financial annoyances" ("Memories," 171), helped him to focus on his literary efforts, and his first short stories began to appear in the paper, including "Miranda. VI. On Idealism" (July 1908).

During 1908 Beresford also began writing *The Early History of Jacob Stahl,* a realistic bildungsroman tempered by idealism, though this novel was not published until 1911. The reviewers lauded it as a psychological masterpiece, placing him "in the forefront of modern novelists,"[12] but he made only £60 from royalties ("Memories," 340). Less than six months later Beresford demonstrated his versatility by publishing another novel (against his publisher's advice), *The Hampdenshire Wonder,* a speculative narrative about a child genius. This novel also received mainly favorable reviews, but it also did not sell well (less than 1000 copies in the original edition ["Memories," 237]) and, according to Beresford, the publishers did not make back the £25 advance Beresford received for at least 15 years ("Memories," 343). Beresford recollected that "on the whole, no neophyte could have asked for a more encouraging press or received more discouraging sales" ("Memories," 343).

These early critical successes drew Beresford from the fringe into the neo-Georgian literary circles, though he was never as well connected as someone like Virginia Woolf, for example, and was characteristically shy on first meetings. Though initially awestruck by Naomi Royde-Smith, whom he met in 1908 when she joined the staff of the *Westminster Gazette* ("Memories," 180), he became more intimate with her, attending her literary salon that lasted through World War I. There he "met such eminent writers as W. B. Yeats, Aldous Huxley and Edith Sitwell, though I was too much in awe of them to attempt to make conversation. But then, for many years afterwards, I was woefully lacking in self-confidence" ("Memories," 256). A purist in English usage, Royde-Smith taught him about the misuse of English and "was one of the influences that helped determine my attitude towards literature" ("Memories," 196, 200, 202). Hugh Walpole was another writer who helped shape Beresford's attitudes, mainly by reaction against his. In 1910 and 1911 they reviewed one another's novels and developed a cautious friendship, later hampered by differences in aim and literary method. Essentially Walpole was a storyteller in the romantic tradition of Thackeray and Scott. He relied on invention rather than experience and aimed to amuse. Beresford, on the other hand, could not write without a thesis and personal experience of what he wrote. Walpole's conservative temperament and politics could never align with Beresford's questing and questioning radicalism.

Beresford shared much more of his literary aim and method with H. G. Wells, whom he had admired as early as 1903, and whom he con-

HUGH WALPOLE
Courtesy of Elisabeth Beresford

sciously took as his main literary model. In his autobiography Beresford devotes an entire section to his rather complex feelings toward the writer whom he idolized in his early days before he realized how different their temperaments were ("Memories," 281). Through his friend Ralph Strauss, Beresford eventually got a chance to meet Wells at the Savile Club in 1913, but Beresford was too tongue-tied to make much headway. On other occasions, including weekend parties at Wells's home at Easton Glebe, Beresford never felt as though they discussed the

"really interesting things" ("Memories," 274). From Beresford's viewpoint Wells lacked "an open mind on the questions of man's origin and
destiny," partly because of his early biological training under Huxley
("Memories," 274–75, 277). Though the young writer sympathized
with Wells's "social ideals and propaganda," he could not admire Wells's
materialism or his opposition to religious ideas (Gerber, 30). Nevertheless, he wrote the first appreciative monograph on Wells in 1915, characterized him as A. B. Ellis in his novel *The Invisible Event* (1915), and
maintained his friendship with Wells and his wife, Jane, while in France
in the 1920s.

Beresford also knew the other two great realists of the Edwardian
period, Arnold Bennett and John Galsworthy, though not as well.
Beresford had enthusiastically reviewed Bennett's novel *The Old Wives'
Tale* for the *Westminster Gazette* in 1908 but was snubbed by Bennett on
their first meeting. After several misunderstandings over subsequent
reviews that Beresford penned of Bennett's novels they met again and
Bennett "was exceedingly genial" ("Memories," 240). John Galsworthy
was a disappointment to Beresford because of his philosophical stance as
a "convinced agnostic" ("Memories," 245), but, as with Bennett, Beresford greatly admired Galsworthy's best work, in his opinion, *The Forsyte
Saga.* Galsworthy for his part returned the admiration, paying Beresford
"the greatest compliment on my own work that I have ever received,"
though Beresford was too modest to quote it in his autobiography
("Memories," 246).

Beresford found more in common spiritually and psychologically
with Walter de la Mare, whom he came to know in 1911, as both
reviewed for the *Westminster Gazette.* On their first encounter, de la Mare
drew him out to recount his then as yet unpublished book *The Hampdenshire Wonder.* Thereafter they met frequently and engaged in literary and
philosophical debates. After Arthur Harvey James was killed in the war
in 1917, de la Mare became Beresford's closest friend. The two mutually
influenced one another, de la Mare for example persuading Beresford to
rewrite the second half of his fourth novel, *Goslings,* and Beresford
prompting de la Mare to rewrite a section of *Memoirs of a Midget* (1921)
eight or nine years later ("Memories," 198).

Beresford describes these prewar years, in which he approached literary fame, as "romantic" ("Memories," 200). They were romantic in
another sense as well after Harvey James introduced him to Beatrice
Evelyn Roskams ("Trissie") sometime before 1912 at his boardinghouse
in Fellowes Road, Swiss Cottage ("Memories," 165–66). Born in 1880

J. D. BERESFORD AND CLOSE FRIEND WALTER DE LA MARE
Courtesy of Elisabeth Beresford

she hailed from Clifton, near Bristol, and had come to London to work. Their relationship was based on mutual need: she fulfilled his need for attention, affection, and encouragement, and he fulfilled her desire to look after someone, especially someone who seemed needy because of his physical disability and lack of confidence. However, the relationship proved unequal in other ways. Beresford was an intellectual and she was not. He had begun the long process of questioning the principles by which he had been raised and she remained bound by convention. He no longer considered himself a Christian and she believed as she had been raised to do so.

The struggle between them began when he implored her to live with him in North Cornwall, where he retreated to write. After initially breaking her promise to go there (and, from her perspective, live in sin), eventually she joined him against her conscience, until they married in May 1913. The couple alternated between living in a rented five-room cottage at St. Merryn and going up to London. Cornwall provided the necessary solitude and inspiration for the dreamy Beresford, who set numerous fictional scenes there. However, Beatrice, born and bred in a town, and more sociable than her husband, found the place lonely and inconvenient.

Nevertheless, their Cornwall retreat proved a true haven after the outbreak of World War I in August 1914. In his autobiography, Beresford is remarkably reticent about his attitude toward the war, though he does mention in passing that "after a horrid period of trepidation in August and September 1914, I faced the future with equanimity"

TRISSIE ROSKAMS BERESFORD AS A GIRL (IN FRONT ROW), WITH HER SIBLINGS
Courtesy of Elisabeth Beresford

TRISSIE AND J. D. BERESFORD AT CONVERTED CHAPEL THEY
RENTED IN ST. MERRYN, CORNWALL
Courtesy of Elisabeth Beresford

("Memories," 183). One reason for the omission might be that Beresford's position toward war had changed somewhat, since by 1947 he
was a thoroughgoing, vocal pacifist.

Beresford's personal life also underwent a significant change in 1914,
as his eldest child, John Tristram (known as Tristram), was born on 24
February. The family stayed in their five-room cottage for less than a year,
after which they moved into a farmhouse overlooking Porthcothan bay,

CONVERTED CHAPEL IN TREHEMBORNE, ST. MERRYN, CORNWALL, LENT
BY THE BERESFORDS TO DOROTHY RICHARDSON (JUST OUTSIDE THE
GATE), WHERE SHE WROTE *POINTED ROOFS* IN 1912–13
Courtesy of Elisabeth Beresford

Cornwall, at £28 a year ("Memories," 284). They spent the "gloomy"
winter of 1915–1916 in Hampstead. Late in 1916 they removed once
again to London for the birth of their second son, Aden Noel, born on
Christmas Eve. Altogether they spent a total of about three years in
Cornwall ("Memories," 67).

Visitors to the Cornish retreats included Hugh Walpole, Middleton
Murry and Katherine Mansfield, Dorothy Richardson, and D. H.
Lawrence. Beresford had "instantly recognized" Murry's mental quality
when he came down from Oxford in 1911 to join the reviewing staff at
"The Westminster," and he occasionally contributed experimental sketches
to Murry's magazines *Rhythm* and *The Blue Review* ("Memories," 202).
Mansfield he encountered while she was living with Murry in Chancery
Lane, where the three of them discussed such topics as the qualities that
go into the making of the really great novel ("Memories," 253). Though
never on "terms of mutual understanding and sympathy" with her
("Memories," 253), they became interested in Theosophy through A. R.

J. D.'S ELDEST SON, TRISTRAM, IN CORNWALL
Courtesy of Elisabeth Beresford

Orage, the editor of *The New Age,* and attended classes together in 1922 on the theosophical teachings of Ouspensky. Beresford had come to know Richardson, the most frequent visitor to Cornwall, when she worked as part-time secretary to a dentist and both she and Beresford were reviewers. Attracted by her "splendid zest in life," he quickly developed a "rapport" with her ("Memories," 253). He had encouraged her not to give up on writing novels and had immediately seen the quality of her first novel, *Pointed Roofs*. But for him it "would have remained in seclusion," as Richardson gratefully acknowledged,[13] since Beresford was responsible for sending the manuscript to two publishers before it was accepted. He then contributed an appreciative introduction to the novel.[14] With Lawrence, whom he had met and seen frequently over the

J. D. AND TRISSIE BERESFORD AT CORNISH FARMHOUSE, CA. 1916
Courtesy of Elisabeth Beresford

winter of 1915–1916 ("Memories," 241), Beresford played the role of father. Though Beresford liked Lawrence, he claimed that "his obsession with sex bored me" and he saw him as a "young soul" in theosophical terms. Nevertheless, he helped "emancipate" Lawrence and Frieda by lending them the farmhouse at Porthcothan during that same winter and, in 1919, by helping Lawrence procure a grant from the Royal Literary Fund ("Memories," 243).

During the second decade of the twentieth century, Beresford also became friends with novelist May Sinclair. Initially he worshiped her as a "High-priestess" of literature, but their shared interests in philosophy and psychical research brought them closer together. Another friend, M. David Eder, one of the first supporters of Freud in Britain, introduced him to psychoanalysis in 1912. Though initially attracted to Freud, whom Beresford read from the perspective of psychical research, Beresford later rejected the emphasis on sexual preoccupation in Freudian theory and moved closer to Jung's position, as did Eder.

After returning to London in late 1916 the Beresfords stayed in Golders Green and Hampstead ("Portrait," 16) before moving into The

DOROTHY RICHARDSON AND ALAN ODLE
Courtesy of Elisabeth Beresford

White House, a "delightful" place in Claydon, Buckinghamshire, with room enough for their third son, Marcus James, born in 1919, and for J. D. to work apart from the children ("Memories," 284–85). On one occasion Beresford invited Frank Swinnerton up to meet him; Swinnerton recounts that the visit was calamitous because he managed to offend two women novelists also visiting, along with Mrs. Beresford. Nevertheless, he got on with J. D., and the two discussed philosophy, Beresford's architectural background, and his expertise in cabinet-making.[15]

Literary Adviser

Beginning in 1918 Beresford's work included acting as literary adviser for Collins publishers. Beresford's first connection with the firm came after his novel *God's Counterpoint* was rejected by his publisher, Cassell, on moral grounds. Gerald O'Donovan, the first reader for Collins's new modern literature division, took up the book, though he did not expect it to sell ("Memories," 204). It did, and better than any previous novel of Beresford's at 6,000 copies in the original edition. After O'Donovan left the firm, Beresford, who had ceased reviewing and was short of cash, saw an opportunity and applied for the post. Initially he was taken on as a reader of manuscripts at a guinea a piece. However, Godfrey Collins was so impressed by his insider knowledge of modern authors that he was added to the salaried staff at £350 per year. The Beresfords moved to Notting Hill[16] and J. D. attended the office two days a week. He had considerable independence in decisions on acceptance of books submitted. Collins, however, expected him to bring in his friends and acquaintances as opportunities arose ("Memories," 206–7); in return he would give Beresford's books special attention in the firm's advertising campaigns.

Though Beresford was ambivalent about the job, he believed at the outset that "such a position would give me a cachet, and add something to my importance" ("Memories," 205). It certainly increased his connections within the literary world, especially the younger generation of writers. It also kept him abreast of contemporary developments in the novel, on which he commented in such noteworthy articles as "Psychoanalysis and the Novel" (1919) in *London Mercury* and "The Successors of Charles Dickens" (1923) in *Nation and Athenaeum*. As well, Beresford helped shape the direction that the novel took by launching several aspiring writers, including Vita Sackville-West, Storm Jameson, Henry Williamson, and Sarah Gertrude Millin. One of his most important discoveries from a business viewpoint was "a first-class writer of detective fiction," Freeman Wills Croft, who was really the founder of Collins's famous "Crime Club" ("Memories," 210). He brought writers more advanced in their careers into the fold, including Eleanor Farjeon, Michael Arlen, Mrs. St. Leger Harrison ("Lucas Malet"), Rose Macaulay, Aleister Crowley, Katherine Tynan, and F. Scott Fitzgerald (Gerber, 24).[17] Several of these, notably Williamson and Farjeon, came to be numbered among his closest friends ("Memories," 218). Beresford encouraged Williamson and made critical suggestions to improve his first semiautobiographical novel about Willie Maddison (*The Beautiful Years*, 1921).

During these postwar years, then, Beresford came into his own as an established man of letters, with numerous contacts in literary circles. He could occasionally be found lunching with, and mainly listening to, contributors to *The Athenaeum*, including Middleton Murry (then the editor), Katherine Mansfield, Aldous Huxley, Edmund Blunden, and scientific journalist J. W. N. Sullivan ("Memories," 257). At select dinner and luncheon parties hosted by his friend novelist Mary Agnes Hamilton, he encountered such awe-inspiring figures as Bertrand Russell, F. H. Bradley, and J. R. Macdonald, who became Britain's first Labor Prime Minister ("Memories," 259).

Despite his critical success, with 15 well-reviewed novels to his name, he experienced a severe spiritual crisis during these years, partly rooted in disillusionment with the postwar world and partly rooted in tensions in his marriage. Ironically, this crisis seems to have been brought to a head through yet another contact made while literary adviser, with A. R. Orage, the founder and editor of *The New Age*. Orage introduced him to a powerful occultist, P. D. Ouspensky, who practiced a kind of eastern yoga, the object of which was to escape from the "wheel" of material life and the horrific possibility of repeating one's life identically in future lives ("Memories," 221). The practice involved developing a double consciousness to keep a watch on the self. Beresford abandoned the technique once he realized that it was having a detrimental effect on his novel writing ("Memories," 222). Another important consideration was his wife, who was "fiercely antagonistic to Ouspensky" ("Memories," 222). She was retreating into religious orthodoxy in the face of Beresford's explorations. Beresford was finally swayed to leave this study after a long discussion with a mystic, Millar Dunning, who impressed upon him that this approach focused solely on the self and lacked any emphasis on the power of love ("Memories," 223).

This personal crisis seems to have been exacerbated by exhaustion from having had to deal with approximately 40 manuscripts a week for five years for Collins ("Memories," 233). Beresford also felt that his role as the reader of scores of mediocre manuscripts was perverting his literary judgment and that he was running the risk of unconscious plagiarism ("Memories," 233); consequently, in the autumn of 1923 he resigned his post and decided against the "better" judgment of his wife to take his family to France ("Memories," 288). The move was made possible through the sale of *Unity* (1924) to a woman's magazine for

£500, of a novel about overcoming spiritual dividedness and dedicated
to Beresford's brother ("Memories," 211).

French Sojourn

During their four-year sojourn in France, the family moved numerous
times, but Beresford was consistently charmed by the French and exhila-
rated by the climate ("Memories," 126). The number of times that
Beresford breaks the chronology in his autobiography and reminisces
about those years suggests something of the freedom and excitement he
experienced there. On one occasion he exclaims, "I had an almost constant sense of joy in the knowledge that I was actually living in St. Max-
ims, Cannes, St. Gervais, Arcachon, St. Jean de Luz, Paris, Dinard (the
order of our itinerary), and, finally, Chateau d'Oex. I gave myself to
those places and was consciously happy in the glory of living in them"
("Memories," 67). Visitors to the writer in voluntary exile included
Upton Sinclair, Sinclair Lewis, and on one occasion Edith Wharton
("Portrait," 29). In the summer of 1925 at Arcachon Beresford encountered James Joyce, who had apparently heard of Beresford, and they "sat
and talked for a quarter of an hour almost exclusively about Arcachon
and the trouble he [Joyce] was having at his hotel" ("Memories," 256).
At Neuilly, in June 1926 Trissie, having just turned 46, gave birth to
their daughter, Elisabeth (who has become a popular children's writer).
The family returned to England in September 1927.

Aside from the excitement of living an adventure, Beresford derived
several other benefits from his French sojourn. New settings stimulated
his imagination and provided an exotic touch to his novels and short
stories ("Portrait," 29). His son claims that he "completed his emancipa-
tion from the anglicising effects of his upbringing" ("Portrait," 31). On a
more pragmatic level he did not have to pay tax on his literary income,
and the exchange rate was in his favor. His sons' immersion in French
helped them to excel in modern languages in the English school system
to which they returned ("Memories," 299). However, Trissie, who
refused to learn French, had always believed that J. D.'s decision to leave
Collins and traipse the family around France was a bad one.

Return to England

From this time on Beresford is silent about his family life in his autobiography and we must rely on the accounts of family members, and a few

ELISABETH AND J. D. BERESFORD
Courtesy of Elisabeth Beresford

letters written to writer friends that have surfaced, in order to get a glimpse of the writer in his mature years. Apparently his marriage deteriorated, exacerbated by increasing financial stresses.

The family initially lived in a boardinghouse in London (J. D. also spent some time in Canford Cliffs, near Poole in South Dorset), but by 1929 they were living in Ickleford Rectory at Hitchin, Herefordshire, from where Beresford wrote to John Cowper Powys that he worked diligently to provide for his four children. He shared an interest in mystical

ICKLEFORD RECTORY, HOME OF THE BERESFORDS FROM 1929
Courtesy of Elisabeth Beresford

states with Powys and related one or two instances of synchronicity to him. Beresford next moved the family to Brighton around 1931 to enable his son Aden to attend Brighton College as a day-boy ("Memories," 299).

There Beresford wrote methodically from nine until one and often after tea time. According to Tristram, the work had become a grind ("Portrait," 34). By this time he was churning out an average of two novels a year for an advance of £300 each without making much more in royalties. He was also reviewing and writing articles for the theosophical journal *The Aryan Path,* founded in 1930, as well as making contributions to sundry other periodicals. His prefaces to his short-story volumes and his semiautobiographical works, including *Writing Aloud* (1929), reveal his cynicism and disillusionment with the reading public. His suffering surfaces in his more personal writing, including letters to poet and novelist L. A. G. Strong. In one, from 1931, he refers to having enough suffering of his own "without seeking it in literature"; in another, dated 30 August 1933, he bitterly mentions "[t]he horrible excess of books I have turned out in the last few years" (cited in Gerber,

THE BERESFORD FAMILY (LEFT TO RIGHT): TRISTRAM, J. D., ADEN, ELISA-
BETH, MARCUS, AND TRISSIE
Courtesy of Elisabeth Beresford

43). Despite his diligence and productivity, he was forced to borrow small sums of money, mainly from his brother, Richard, but also from successful colleagues ("Portrait," 34).

Despite his rather desperate situation, he remained "scrupulously loyal" to Trissie, for example upholding a promise not to discuss religion with Tristram when father and son holidayed for two weeks in the summer of 1930 ("Portrait," 34). There were also pleasant diversions, including chess, bridge, visits to the cinema, the reading aloud of Agatha Christie, and the requisite walks along the front. Brighton brightened with visits from

Eleanor Farjeon, Beresford's journalist friend J. W. N. Sullivan, and socialist Hamilton Fyfe ("Portrait," 35).

Once again the dividedness in his life became a preoccupation. This
time it prompted him to develop an interest in faith healing, first manifested in a novel about a faith healer, *The Camberwell Miracle*,[18] published
in 1933, and then in a nonfictional book, *The Case for Faith-Healing*
(1934). The novel brought Beresford succès d'estime and numerous letters from people fascinated by the subject as well as practitioners of faith
healing, such as Dr. Maude Royden in Kensington ("Portrait," 36). Max
Plowman was one of those compelled to write to Beresford; the two
then met and developed a strong sympathy.

Probably through his contact with Plowman or possibly Dick Sheppard, Beresford, who had always had the temperament of a pacifist, was
drawn more actively into the peace movement. His was one of the early
signatures on the Peace Pledge Union, he supported the Peace Ballot,
and he was offered the editorship of *Peace News* but declined it because
he felt that he would be a bad editor ("Memories," 265). Of those
involved in the movement, he was closest to Dick Sheppard, who wrote
a preface to *The Case for Faith-Healing*, but he also worked with Gerald
Heard, Vera Brittain, and his old friend Middleton Murry.

In the summer of 1935 it was time for another holiday with Tristram,
and the two stayed for the season at a gate-keeper's lodge in Nanceal-
verne, Penzance, both working on novels that they were writing. The
visit marked a high point during this period of Beresford's life, especially
since he was "deeply moved" by his son's writing ("Portrait," 40). It also
marked a reprieve from a still-deteriorating domestic situation and an
increasing sense of isolation.

Two years later Tristram married and moved on, and J. D.'s close
friend J. W. N. Sullivan died. In letters to Powys from 1937, one catches
glimpses of Beresford's condition when he mentions "having a lot of
trouble with my eyes for the past few months"[19] or suggests how humor
saves him from being angry at the world: "I haven't told you all my
troubles, and don't intend to. I do not kiss the gods' feet, but I can
laugh. You know there comes a point at which a redundance of misfortune becomes humorous. One smiles and says, 'Oh! go on, Go on,' and
waits for the next thing whatever it may be. And it really does not matter much so long as one can keep one's mind clear."[20] Despite his misfortune, to others, including his brother, Tristram's Cambridge friends
("Portrait," 43), and fellow writers like Frank Swinnerton, he had the
qualities of a sage. Max Plowman, for instance, wrote in August 1937,

"I share something with you I haven't with any other man living. What it is I hardly know, but I've only to think of you to have a unique sense of one who has 'overcome the world'."[21]

Collaboration

Beresford's fortunes started to change and he truly found help in overcoming the world when, probably late in 1937, he met Esmé Wynne-Tyson.[22] From 1936, she had been living with her son, Jon, on the same street, Chesham Place, in Brighton on which the Beresfords lived, and the two became acquainted through their children, Elisabeth, by now 11, and Jon, 13. Wynne-Tyson was a novelist and journalist, and she had been a child actress, and friend and collaborator of Noel Coward. Though their mutual vocation would have been a factor in bringing them together, Beresford and Wynne-Tyson were drawn to one another much more deeply once they recognized that they were on a common spiritual quest. According to Wynne-Tyson, "He was deeply and absolutely in love for the first time in his life—at 65."[23] Apparently he was attracted physically to this woman, 25 years his junior, and to her vivacity and charm ("Portrait," 47). Nevertheless, Wynne-Tyson, who had separated from her husband in 1930, refused to be dragged back into the "bondage" of sexuality, and their companionship developed platonically.[24]

Wynne-Tyson, on the other hand, was attracted to Beresford partly out of compassion for him in his downtrodden state and partly because of his wisdom. She described Beresford when she met him as being ground down by a routine of writing for profit about subjects that did not really interest him. He would rather have continued writing about metaphysics and faith healing but was blocked by opposition from his wife.[25]

Wynne-Tyson referred to the relationship as "heavenly," and it does seem to have been a marriage of true minds. Wynne-Tyson lent him a copy of Mary Baker Eddy's *Science and Health* (1875), and Beresford found in it and through their discussions an integrated model for living based on the main element of love. Significantly, though, neither one ever became members of the Christian Science Church, Beresford remaining a determined eclectic to the end. His intellectual beliefs in divine guidance and faith healing, based on reasoning, gradually gave way to a full inner conviction of their practical operation. The two then became determined to communicate "the truth to all who may desire to know" and on 15 April 1939 began collaborating on a novel, *Strange Rival*.[26] In order to find the peace necessary to continue collaborating, Beresford moved out of his household and into a service flat around the corner in Chichester Terrace in May 1939. In four months they had completed the novel together, though it was published only under Beresford's name for contractual reasons.

However heavenly the relationship, it certainly made the lives of all affected by its development "humanly difficult." According to Beresford's factually detailed but emotionally reticent diary, he and his wife had "finally agreed" on a separation as early as February 1939.[27] Nevertheless, Trissie understandably saw Esmé as a temptress and felt devastated and abandoned when Beresford left the household, though he conscientiously continued to provide financial support. Beresford apparently broke down shortly after leaving his wife. Wynne-Tyson argues emphatically, though, that his departure and their relationship was the best for all concerned. Beresford's health improved and through increased productivity he was able to provide for his dependents. Though Trissie always regarded herself as the injured party, she benefited from the separation, too, a point on which their son Tristram concurs, by achieving independence; she earned her living by running a club, something she had always wanted to do but could not have done while raising a family. It is less easy to evaluate the emotional costs, especially with regard to the children involved.

Nevertheless, there is no doubt that the collaboration was very fruitful. Beresford published 14 books in the last eight years of his life, 12 of which were novels; produced two unpublished works, an autobiography and a large novel about peace; and worked on the background for a philosophical book, *The Unity of Being,* eventually written and published by Wynne-Tyson. Wynne-Tyson collaborated on at least 11 of these books, although on only 3 was she credited as joint author, since Beresford needed to supply one "solo" book per year to fulfil his contract with Hutchinson's. Wynne-Tyson mainly contributed fresh ideas for novels, though she also supplied some characters and scenes.[28]

In addition to this work, Beresford continued to write short stories, sketches, articles, and regular reviews for the *Manchester Guardian,* the *Times Literary Supplement,* and *The Aryan Path.* Moreover, he wrote stories and sketches for the B.B.C. radio, some of which he himself broadcast, and gave a number of public lectures to an assortment of organizations, including the Chester Society, the Shirley Society, and to students at Morley College.

Despite this extraordinary productivity, he made time to meet with friends, occasionally visiting them while on motoring tours with Tristram. In 1938 Tristram drove him over to the Francis Brett Youngs, where Hugh Walpole was staying for the weekend. In August he made the trek from Tristram's home in Warwickshire to John Cowper Powys's council house in Corwen and shortly after visited the Black Mountains, Tintern, Gloucester, and Tewkesbury. During this year he met Storm Jameson and Frank Harris for the first time.

After Beresford moved out of his household in the spring of 1939 his lifestyle became even more transient. He lived at no less than eight addresses following his separation from Trissie until his death. Most of these were residential hotels and vegetarian guest houses where Esmé and her son stayed as well. From Brighton, J. D. moved just after the outbreak of war on 3 September 1939 to Selsey, where Esmé had a bungalow. J. D. stayed in a nearby hotel. On the advice of Esmé's air force husband, who feared an invasion, they moved inland a year later, first to Oxford, and then further into the west country. At least two of their moves—to a hotel in the Wye Valley in October 1942 and to Holt, near Trowbridge, Wiltshire, in June 1944—were made so that J. D. could be closer to his son Tristram. Jon Wynne-Tyson meanwhile moved out on his own early in 1943. J. D.'s last residence was a guest house in Bath, where the pair moved in September 1946. Their transient lifestyle was perhaps appropriate for a couple for whom worldly possessions now had little meaning, but it was also necessary since if they had officially cohabited they would have had to obtain divorces from their spouses, and in any case their relationship would not have been understood, let alone condoned, by most in the Britain of the 1940s.

Though Beresford became more isolated from his literary friends and acquaintances during the last years of his life, he did maintain a correspondence with his oldest friend, Walter de la Mare, as well as with Henry Williamson, L. A. G. Strong, Mr. and Mrs. Kenneth Richmond, H. M. Tomlinson, and Eleanor Farjeon. His main aim, though, was to communicate to his public something of the spiritual synthesis that he had achieved.

Eventually the strenuous pace of his work started to take its toll. Wynne-Tyson noticed that Beresford began to tire late in 1944 while writing the latter part of their final collaboration, *The Gift* (1947), but he persisted and wrote a solo novel, *The Prisoner* (1946). Both Wynne-Tyson and Tristram advised him against writing this autobiographical novel because they saw it as dangerous for him to dwell on the past, and the evidence suggests that he suffered both physically and emotionally while writing it in 1945. He then embarked on the factual autobiography that has been used here as the main source about his life to the 1920s, the period that it covers. The writing came slowly, and on some days he could only write five lines or so. Although the book was never published because of his wife's opposition, he completed all of it but a final section on religion, perhaps appropriately for a man who continued searching out the truth and never claimed to have the last word on it. Following a stroke and a short illness of one week, he died in his sleep in the small hours of 2 February 1947. Jon Wynne-Tyson, who came up from London to attend him, claims that he witnessed a kind of mystical experience just before Beresford died, in which J. D. suddenly sat up in bed and started talking, though he had been unable to speak for several days.

Summary

How can any human being be summarized, let alone such a complex individual as J. D. Beresford, who underwent so many transformations and continued growing and seeking until his death? Beresford would be the first to acknowledge the impossibility of this, as numerous references to the hopeless inconsistency of human beings in his autobiography illustrate. At the outset of that work he makes the very prescient point that in any autobiographical writing, "[w]e are reduced, in fact, to pretty much the same business of inventing a character as we habitually practise in novel-writing" ("Memories," 6–7). After having constructed such a character for 300 pages he returns to this point, claiming that "[t]here are, indeed, so many 'selves' that all one can hope to do is to dissociate those that we—mistakenly perhaps—believe to be the most representative" ("Memories," 318). That is the most I can hope to do here as I attempt to gather a few strands of Beresford's personality at the multiple remove of time and place and as biographer.

Beresford seems to have been closer to his mother than any person in his life, and she remained a powerful presence long after her passing. Following his bout with poliomyelitis she made a particular emotional investment in him and closely nurtured him. In all probability she implanted in him a love of language and story through her dramatic readings, a talent that Beresford himself cultivated with his children ("Portrait," 27). Her voice persisted as the voice of conscience within him and, as is typical, his relations with her conditioned his subsequent intimate relations with women. He tended to idealize the women in his life, particularly their physical beauty, perhaps seeking in their physical perfection compensation for his own physical imperfection. That imperfection made Beresford dependent on women both emotionally and in the practical matters of life, and the women who were attracted to him tended to have a strong need to nurture and support. His relations with women contrast to his relations with men, conditioned by his rather distant relationship with his father, against whose conventionality and dogmatism he rebelled so strongly. Because of these qualities Beresford does not seem to have considered his father a rival, and neither, apparently, did the father consider his crippled son a threat, but more of a disappointment. Strikingly, Beresford developed a number of warm friendships with men, notably Arthur Harvey James, Walter de la Mare, John Cowper Powys, J. W. N. Sullivan, and his own son Tristram, that were marked by a lack of rivalry. With men Beresford seems to have been much more reticent about any difficulties he might be experiencing. Aside from his physical disability, however, Beresford did share at least one anxiety that haunted his father, over financial matters ("Memories," 263). We also see J. J.'s influence in Beresford's interest in alternative methods of education, Beresford following his father's lead in educating his children largely outside the regular system, and in Beresford's characteristic fastidiousness.

How did these relations bear on Beresford's role as a father? Though we get glimpses of him playing with his children, or making wooden blocks for his son ("Memories," 252), and of his willingness to be interrupted occasionally from his work ("Memories," 285), he seems more often, and increasingly, to have been harried and pressed by financial stresses necessitating long working hours ("Memories," 263). Nevertheless, he was conscientious about his children's education, a subject to which he devotes an entire section of his autobiography ("Memories," 297). He was also proud of his sons' success at achieving what to him was the cachet of a university education. His conscientiousness extended to keeping the increasing conflict between him and his wife hidden from his children. Both of the children who have left any written record of him—his eldest son, Tristram, and his only daughter, Elisabeth—speak admiringly of him.

As a social being, Beresford was hampered by a lack of self-confidence and intense self-consciousness. Over and over again he describes disastrous first meetings with fellow writers. That lack of self-confidence does not seem to be related to a negative self-image of his appearance.

By his own admission, claims Tristram, "he cut a dash as a young man" ("Portrait," 6). He stood a full six feet tall, had a Grecian physique, a face striking for its suggestion of deep contemplation, and piercing blue eyes. Perhaps it had more to do, even unconsciously, with his physical disability, as I have suggested in describing his beliefs about his undesirability as a lover. Beresford's self-consciousness and his placid temperament made him a better listener than a talker, a role that he consciously acknowledged.[29] He was also a man who made time to help others, especially younger writers, in relation to whom he frequently saw himself in a fatherly role.

Increasingly as he matured he found the basis of his friendships in spiritual affinity, and there is no doubt that the spiritual nature and destiny of mankind became Beresford's main concern. His progress along this path, however, was slow. As a youth he does not seem to have been particularly interested in spiritual beliefs, but he always seems to have been a detached dreamer who delighted in fantasy and to have possessed a questing spirit. He does speculate that "I must have been born with the eclectic tendency, although owing to the cramping of my mind by early associations and education, the tendency did not manifest itself until I had come of age" ("Memories," 355). Once he had been released from the mental prison of his parents' rigid belief system at 21 and had escaped the alternate prison of materialism, he began to see himself on a quest for truth. Above all he tried to keep an open mind about new knowledge presented to him. As Frank Swinnerton noted, "He wanted to know whatever men thought. His thirst for such knowledge was unquenchable."[30] Not until late in life did the truths that he had come to accept intellectually become convictions expressed through mysticism.

Nevertheless, even in 1946–1947, when Beresford wrote his autobiography, a tension is evident in his worldview between his reliance on reason, expressed in his continuing interest in realism, and his attraction to the romantic conception of a guiding providence. His realist tendency prompts him to comment repeatedly on the haphazard nature of life and the recording of it ("Memories," 133, 264), but he also alludes to the concept of Fate or Destiny, or what he at one point refers to as his "fastidious daimon" directing his life ("Memories," 162).

Beresford's fastidiousness is another important element in his constitution, also no doubt conditioned by his strict upbringing. Though I will return to the great and perhaps crippling impact of this characteristic on his writing, it is worth mentioning here that he frequently speaks of a censor hovering above his shoulder while writing ("Memories,"

264). Nevertheless, any tendency to priggishness that this might have produced was held in check by a constant and highly developed sense of humor, which was appealed to both by Michael Arlen's *The Romantic Lady* ("Memories," 216) and more fully by Wodehouse's tales of Bertie Wooster and Lord Emsworth. Significantly, the professional and personal disappointments that Beresford experienced did not squash that sense of humor but rather shaped its nature, and Beresford developed a wry and ironic sense of human foibles and weaknesses.

Many of these characteristics are captured in the fleeting glimpses provided by those who wrote about him as they viewed him in his last years. In 1936 his friend of 20 years Frank Swinnerton described his thoughtful but melancholy face before adding, "But if, normally, his spirits are low, he is not therefore a gloomy person. He is merely a man to whom a miracle has not happened. He is all *piano;* but his humour is constant and his interest in the doings of his compeers is as free as possible from envy or destructiveness. I never saw philosophic resignation so clearly expressed" (Swinnerton, *Autobiography,* 292). Mary Agnes Hamilton, in *Remembering My Good Friends* (1944), claimed: "He was at all times a grand person to talk to about writing and very generous. . . . At a time when he was professing the most radical doubts about moral values and their sanctions, his conduct was invariably of the most sensitive goodness; so was his loyalty to friends. He had suffered much—not only through being a cripple, but in spirit; pain was incised deep on his fine austere face, with its beautiful eyes, nobly cut features and real sweetness of expression."[31] His son Tristram adds that in those last years he had become a detached but not indifferent recluse who had achieved some mastery over his life ("Portrait," 59).

For dramatic and narrative purposes it is tempting to suggest that by the time of his death Beresford had permanently secured that mastery, but the evidence suggests otherwise. Most significantly, according to Tristram, he never completely overcame his remorse over the breakup of his family.

In succeeding chapters I will consider J. D. Beresford's achievement and success in a more worldly sense as a thinker and writer in various genres, but in this chapter we have been concerned with his achievement as a human being. Despite the flaws and shortcomings that made him human, one cannot help but feel inclined to agree with Esmé Wynne-Tyson in her summation of Beresford, with the recognition of its inevitably subjective nature: "Therefore, if success means to succeed in doing that on which our innermost heart is set, J. D. B. was a successful man, for he not only discovered those spiritual values for which he had so long searched, but he also achieved a degree of personal non-attachment to things visible, rare among his sex. But, put more simply and comprehensibly, perhaps I should say, he was a truly successful man because he was a truly good man,—a success, I think, that comparatively few enjoy."[32]

Chapter Two

"Listening In to the Broadcast Thought of Humanity": Influences and Experiments

Is it possible that the so-called inventors of plots are gifted with a "subconscious" that has the power of listening in to the broadcast thought of humanity? (*Writing,* 30)

J. D. Beresford was a voracious reader and a prolific writer in many genres, and his oeuvre constitutes a comprehensive and perceptive analysis of cultural change in Britain in the first half of the twentieth century. In this chapter I want to provide some indication of the main influences on Beresford and particularly to convey something of the astonishing range and depth of Beresford's reading, especially in the areas that had the greatest impact on his fiction writing: idealism, psychical research, the "new" psychology, faith healing, and mysticism. Beresford gave expression to many of the ideas and beliefs that he developed from this reading and from his own experience not only in the short story and the novel but in numerous essays and longer autobiographical works as well. He left a detailed account of the growth of his knowledge of matters psychological and spiritual, notably in *What I Believe,* which I have drawn upon. Though an assessment of his voluminous book reviewing and literary criticism is beyond the scope of this study, I will also touch on some of his most important contributions to literary criticism. This chapter concludes with a summary of Beresford's literary experiments, works that fall in between genres, focusing on Beresford's extraordinary autobiographical stream-of-consciousness "novel" manqué, *Writing Aloud* (1928).

Early Influences

In an article explaining the effect of psychoanalysis on novelists, Beresford asserts the relative importance of learning on the writer, an acknowledgment rather uncommon in his vocation. He claims that

it must be remembered that while the novelist's best material undoubtedly comes from his personal contacts, almost infinitely extended by his
powers of entering with an emotional sympathy into the experiences of
other lives either presented or recounted, he cannot entirely neglect the
precedents afforded by learning. Such precedents may only serve him as a
test and a formula for correction, but should he overlook them altogether
he will be liable to fall into the error of regarding his personal equation as
a universal standard and generalise from the atypical.[1]

Beresford was also rather uncommon among writers in that he came
to his vocation quite late, after having read a great deal in diverse fields.
As he admitted, he was not a "born writer." He first penned a badly told
story in a homemade magazine at 14 ("Memories," 318).

During his teenage years Beresford devoured Dickens, Charles
Reade, Harrison Ainsworth, and Marie Corelli's *A Romance of Two Worlds*
(1886) ("Memories," 323, 346–47; "Discovery," 133). By 1891 he had
discovered Samuel Richardson's *Pamela* and the works of Charles Kings-
ley, and shortly after arriving in London that same year he read Plato's
dialogues in an English translation ("Memories," 71).

However, after his "conversion" from fundamentalism to independent thinking in 1894, Beresford began to read more systematically. His
first tutor in print was the agnostic Samuel Laing, whose *Modern Science
and Modern Thought* (1885) and *Human Origins* (1892) introduced Beresford to the study of biology and physical evolution.[2] For the next nine
years, he mainly read works that supported the materialist, positivist
theory of evolution, including Darwin's *Origin of Species* and *Descent of
Man* (*Jacob*, 256). The influence of this reading can be felt in Beresford's
fiction through his empirical approach to his subject matter and
through the emphasis he places on the importance of heredity in shaping character. At some point after 1897 he also became interested in
progressive education, including the ideas of Froebel and Johann
Herbart (*Ford*, 21).[3]

Idealism, Psychical Research, and the "New" Psychology

Beresford reached another major turning point in his self-education
when he read F. W. H. Myers's *Human Personality and Its Survival of
Bodily Death* (1903).[4] It introduced him to the new science of psychology,
to a less dogmatic view than the traditional one of the possibility of sur-

viving death, and to the concept of the "subliminal" self, the nonphysical aspect of personality (*What,* 27–28). Beresford eventually preferred the subliminal, which he characterized as "at once wise and ignorant, immoral and beneficent, uncontrollable," to Pierre Janet's conception of subconscious or to Freud's unconscious, the latter of which he described as "hopelessly misleading" (*What,* 28). The cases of multiple personalities cited by Myers also vividly illustrated to Beresford that the subliminal was not necessarily a single entity. Most important, Myers's work activated Beresford's dormant imagination and led him, gradually, "to abandon the realist for the idealist position" (*What,* 30). Throughout his life Beresford continued to examine the findings of the Society for Psychical Research and to demand scientific evidence. Though he remained a skeptic about survival, he became convinced "that many strange phenomena, at present beyond the range of scientific enquiry, do occur, phenomena that illuminate some of the astonishing potentialities yet undeveloped in the great mystery that is man" (*What,* 31). His reading of Ernst Haeckel's *The Riddle of The Universe*[5] in 1904 temporarily dampened his enthusiasm for his new pursuit but eventually caused him to question even more closely the materialist explanation of life it argued.[6]

In succeeding years, his practical idealism evolved, based on reason. Foremost, Beresford held that this is a spiritual, not a physical, universe (*What,* 118) and that mankind was developing "an increased spirituality, a deeper, fuller consciousness" (*Writing,* 118). This position reinforced his tendency toward introspection. He also believed in an immortal principle residing within every man (Gerber, 50) and in the ideal of unselfishness (*Writing,* 119). His reading of Henri Bergson's *Time and Free Will* (translated in 1910) and *Matter and Memory* (translated in 1911)[7] along with his knowledge of the then recently developed theory of relativity helped convince him that "[t]ime, in fact, [is] a function of motion, and in a static universe in which all movement and therefore all change has ceased, the conception of time has no meaning" (*What,* 57). Beresford later found confirmation of this hypothesis in W. J. Dunne's *An Experiment with Time* (1927) with its "theory of humanity's power to enter another dimension in which the cross-section of time that is all we can realize in this three dimensional state, becomes a line" (*What,* 57).[8] Dunne's theory used the dream state to show that, "freed from the illusions of matter, we may live for an instant or so in what we, here, regard as the future, and occasionally retain the memory of the anticipated experience in the message of a fugitive dream" (*What,* 57). Both time and space, then, are illusions of the senses (*What,* 57). That dreams also illustrate the process of rationalization, as does the problem of posthypnotic suggestion, caused Beresford to question the reliability of the reasoning faculty, on which he had placed such emphasis up to this point (*What,* 58–59).

In addition, Beresford's personal experience of mystical moments demonstrated that the materialistic hypothesis did not account for all the facts of experience. During the period of his apprenticeship as a writer (1901–1908), he attended parties at which there were psychics and was told by one of these "psychometrists" that she saw him "always with a pen in [his] hand" ("Memories," 99, 162). Regardless of how seriously Beresford took this prophecy, psychical research and the new developments in psychology that threw doubt on the materialist hypothesis had become of prime importance for Beresford as he began to write his autobiographical novel, *Jacob Stahl,* in 1908. Nevertheless, he had not discarded his belief in the importance of heredity in shaping character, as the analysis of the novel in chapter 4 illustrates.

The next major advance in Beresford's knowledge of the new psychology came with his introduction to psychoanalysis in 1912 through his friend Dr. M. D. Eder. Beresford interpreted Freudian psychoanalysis in the light of the findings of psychical research, and sought in it further information about the soul, but was disappointed. He viewed the Freudians as dogmatic, found that their "uninspired" geological terminology distorted the functions of the mind, and argued that their paradigm failed to explain the moral sense. Like Eder, Beresford came to favor Jung's psychology, finding it more inclusive and probable.[9]

What psychoanalysis did offer to Beresford was confirmation of the power of unconscious or subconscious processes and of the inadequacy of the mechanistic theory of man's being (*What,* 37). Along with psychical research, psychoanalysis helped Beresford develop a new, less rational, more symbolic technique of thinking, about the mind in particular (*What,* 33). Beresford's reaction to psychoanalysis also provoked further investigation into the source of man's religious tendency and the nature of soul and psyche. In the second decade of the century, he continued to argue in articles that the most enlightened approach to these enigmas occurred in the work of the Society For Psychical Research. He deplored the sensational craze for spiritualism of the previous five years in "More New Facts in Psychical Research" (1922)[10] and praised the continuing scientific investigations into psychical phenomena of researchers such as Dr. Gustave Geley in *From the Unconscious to the Conscious* (1920), to which Beresford had contributed an introduction. He also mentioned that he had "never in [his] life either consulted a medium or attended a spiritualistic seance" ("More," 477).

Theosophy

Beresford had been introduced to Theosophy by G. F. Rogers, his first mentor who had "converted" Beresford to independent thinking. Theosophy had been revived through the founding of the Theosophical Society in 1875 by Madame Helena Petrovna Blavatsky. Among its claims are that all religions stem from the same ancient wisdom deriving from a supreme, absolute deity. Though Beresford claimed that he had never read any of Blavatsky's works, he did read Rudolf Steiner (the founder of the Waldorf School movement) and he attended theosophical meetings in a studio in West Kensington ("Discovery," 134). His interest waned while he explored the materialist stance, but it revived after 1904 under the guidance of his close friend Arthur Harvey James and through reviewing books on the subject.[11] Another phase of interest began when he was introduced to the teachings of Gurdieff, as expounded by P. D. Ouspensky. He practiced these teachings for a time in the early 1920s until it became clear that the degree of self-awareness necessary to follow this practice was having a detrimental effect on his novel writing. Beresford seems on the whole to have maintained a certain detachment in his approach to Theosophy and was aware of the "dangers of occultism" ("Memories," 253).

Faith Healing

Continuing spiritual and psychological turmoil led Beresford in the 1920s to turn to mysticism and faith healing as he renewed his quest for truth. These concerns are treated in works of the early 1930s, notably his novel *The Camberwell Miracle* (1933) and in *The Case for Faith-Healing* (1934). Beresford was prompted to write the latter work after he realized that *The Camberwell Miracle,* featuring a healer who relied on "the power of a purely unselfish love" (*Case,* 21), had fallen short of the truth of what had actually been accomplished by faith healers. *The Case for Faith-Healing* draws on a number of Beresford's personal convictions, including the idealistic account of the world. He outlines the premises of that account early in the work: "The first is that God, immanent and transcendent, is the great creative spirit and the only reality. The second that what we know as matter is a transient and largely illusory presentation of spirit in a temporal, three-dimensional complex. The third that the means of communication between matter and spirit is by way of that minor trinity, understanding, sympathy and love" (*Case*, 20). Beresford argues that these premises should be acceptable to people of all religious persuasions so long as they do not hold the materialistic view of the world. He thus pleads for religious tolerance. Faith healing itself depends upon the complete integration of the self and the overcoming of habit, Beresford goes on to postulate. In his reasoned account he draws on studies of hypnosis as well as historical evidence, notably Christ's miracles, which he claims are based on natural law. This readable book has implications for the nature of faith in general. In the preface, the Reverend H. R. L. Sheppard called the work "a valuable contribution to Truth."

Literary Criticism

Beresford's career as a literary critic began as an unpaid book reviewer for the *Literary World* and then as a paid reviewer with the *Westminster Gazette*. He continued to review books during most of his life, at some points reporting on as many as 10 books a month (Gerber, 263). Beresford claimed that his "early training in honest criticism" always prevented him from falsely praising any book even if written by a friend ("Memories," 179).

Though Beresford began writing longer literary essays as early as 1908 ("Memories," 178), among the most significant are those that assess the shifting impact of the new psychology and especially psychoanalysis on the contemporary novel: "Psychoanalysis and the Novel" (1919) and "Le déclin de l'influence de la psycho-analyse sur le roman anglais" (1926). In the first of these he argued that psychoanalysis would give a new mystery to the human mind, suggest the necessity of a freer morality, and provide unworked complications of motive for the novelist. However, he was critical of opportunist novelists who grasp psychoanalysis intellectually and superficially and who apply it arbitrarily and mechanically. By 1926, when Beresford wrote "Le déclin de l'influence," his optimism about the merits of psychoanalysis for the novelist had completely dissipated. In this article, Beresford locates the most significant influence of psychoanalysis on the English novel during the years between 1918 and 1922. He then distinguishes three categories of novels: those that would have been written had Freud never existed; those in which the influence is subconscious rather than intellectual; and those "based on the principle that the repression of thought and those infantile tendencies can reappear during the course of adult experience in the form of a perversion or of a 'complex' " ("Déclin," 257). Beresford focuses on the third category, the most striking examples of which are Beresford's own *God's Counterpoint* (1918), Rebecca West's *The Return of the Soldier* (1918), and May Sinclair's *The Romantic* (1920).

According to Beresford, the rapid decline of the psychoanalytic stimulus in fiction can be accounted for by three factors: British critics suspicious of the new and of "unhealthy" themes; the censorious and hypocritical British public; and writers who realized that Freudian theories with their focus on abnormality run counter to the novelist's aim of presenting representative types ("Déclin," 261–64). Consequently, Beresford concludes "that there cannot be a future for the psychoanalytical novel" of the third type ("Déclin," 465). Though Beresford was well aware of the various psychological influences on his own fiction, one reason that he proclaimed the decline of psychoanalytic influence in particular has to do with his own experience when he focused almost exclusively on applying Freudian theory in his two novels *God's Counterpoint* (1918) and *An Imperfect Mother* (1920) as discussed in chapter 4.

H. G. Wells was an important literary model for Beresford, and in 1915, two years after having met his mentor, Beresford penned the first monograph-length introduction to Wells's work.[12] He admired Wells for his empirical approach to his subject matter, his pragmatism, and above all for his detached standpoint unfettered by the bonds of convention. He esteemed Wells's romances most highly and concluded his avowedly personal reading by claiming that Wells's "chief achievement is that he has set up the ideal of a finer civilisation" (*Wells,* 116).

Beresford made numerous other contributions to literary criticism. Among the most noteworthy is his response to Virginia Woolf's polemic "Mr. Bennett and Mrs. Brown," titled "The Successors of Charles Dickens."[13] In defending the Edwardian novelists, Beresford claims that they present human beings that satisfy "our sense of probability; inasmuch as they are, like ourselves, composite, full of irresolutions, often self-conscious, and apt to change their minds" ("Successors," 487), whereas the Victorians tend to highlight one feature of a character.

Literary Experiments

Beresford made a number of experiments in prose throughout his career—the three that fall outside the normal conception of the novel are discussed in this section. From the beginning of his career Beresford blurred the distinction between the forms of biography and fiction, types of experimentation the ramifications of which literary theorists have only recently begun to address. In *W. E. Ford: A Biography* Beresford, along with his collaborator, psychotherapist Kenneth Richmond,[14] created what Beresford refers to as an "experimental biography," a fictional biography of a pioneering educationalist. According to Richmond's wife, Zoe, the biography is based mainly on Richmond's life and views,[15] but it is also revealing of Beresford's life and views. Beresford is responsible for the first part, "A Personal Impression," and the last, "A Few Notes on Ford's Philosophy," both written in the first person. In the former he begins with some interesting comments on biography. Whereas most biographies recount the lives of successes, this one tells of "a man who was completely unknown to the general public"; his biography is justified because his ideas have subtly percolated into society (*Ford*, 5). Ford's ideas have helped bring about the change "from a negative to a positive attitude towards God; from a morality that depends upon repression to one that depends upon the liberation of impulse" (*Ford*, 7). In the second chapter Beresford presents himself as a shy but "egregious young ass" eager to impress Ford on meeting him in 1897 but carrying the knowledge of his own incapacity (*Ford*, 16–17). Ford suggests that Beresford's "scattered education" had saved him from intellectual vices that typically arise from a single dogmatic method (*Ford*, 21), a suggestion similar to one that Beresford made about Wells's education. Ford's insights and selflessness cause Beresford to worship Ford as a "towering hero." For his part, Ford praises Beresford's *The Hampdenshire Wonder* because it "satisfies innumerable instincts," "leaves the moral to be inferred," and achieves "a certain half contact with the illimitable" (*Ford*, 39). Also of interest is Beresford's psychological explanation that World War I arose "from individual and national inhibitions" (*Ford*, 11). The final part of the book presents Ford's philosophy, loosely labeled as a form of Vitalism or Idealistic Monism (*Ford*, 259). Ford postulates consciousness as a universal property of matter and speculates that "the degree of realisation necessary for the understanding of what we speak of broadly as consciousness, is proportionate to the degree of reciprocity between the units of consciousness" (*Ford*, 269). This accounts for the phenomenon of group consciousness, for example. Inhibition of thoughts into consciousness is the great danger in Ford's view. According to Beresford, "Where there is no fear there is no danger, was one of Ford's *obiter dicta*" (*Ford*, 291). Ford's ideas have implications for the understanding of genius: the man of genius is one who is able to access and interpret the primitive urge and thus reveal some fraction of the universal content of mind (*Ford,* 299). Beresford's essay reveals his ability to synthesize the ideas of diverse thinkers including Bergson, Nietzsche, William James, Maeterlinck (*Life of the Bee*), Clutton Brock (*The Ultimate Belief*), Freud, and Jung.[16] In using a fictionalized account of a life as the vehicle for progressive, socialist ideas the work also suggests an indebtedness to Wells. The *Bookman* reviewer called it a "great book" and claimed that "[t]he originality of its conception and execution cannot be denied. Though its chief merit is its enormous garrulousness."[17]

Beresford's next experiment in biography, *Taken from Life* (1922), similarly presents a socialist critique of society, though Beresford claims that it did not begin as such. This time Beresford collaborated with prominent photographer E. O. Hoppé to present seven biographies of actual, though unknown, people, in both visual and narrative form (this combination of genres is also only now being explored by literary theorists). The portraits are of "a tramp; a Cabman; a Drug-fiend; a Pedlar; an old Countrywoman; a Courtesan; and a Charwoman."[18] Beresford's lively and informal accounts demonstrate characteristic psychological insight and touch on the influences of heredity. In a few instances he attempts to extrapolate from the lives of his subjects to show that they represent a type. His connection with these people is also described. The radical nature of these portraits stems from the fact that the majority of these subjects would be considered "failures" from society's viewpoint. Of two "successes," economic necessity forced one to sit on the box of a cab for 40 years though "he was a thinker and a maker" (*Taken,* 209), while the other lived her entire life below the poverty line.

In a concluding lengthy and wide-ranging essay entitled "Relatives," Beresford draws some inferences from his subjects about society at large and socialism as a means of transforming some of the ills described. He begins with a fictional biography of a man named William who threw over his unthinking acceptance of tradition while at university, nearly took up anarchy, and instead settled for Fabianism. Although to Beresford the chief aim of Fabianism "to substitute State for private ownership, as a preliminary means to the establishment of a greater equality" seems above criticism, he shows that William falls into the trap of making the Webbs's brand of socialism into a religion (*Taken,* 175). Beresford uses this case to illustrate his main point, which is the relativity of seeming absolutes, based on an application of the mathematical theory of relativity. Other examples of the misapplication of socialism and the 10 commandments serve to drive home this point. Although Beresford proclaims himself "a convinced believer" in socialism, he does not believe that it would work in practice. Instead of supporting a system, he advocates increased awareness of our limitations and honesty with ourselves in not setting up our abilities as the standard against which to measure mankind. As well, he strongly advocates training children to look at life with an open mind (*Taken*, 213). The essay is revealing in its focus on the personal as the root of societal ills, and it provides insight into Beresford's values. His ideal is not riches "but the opportunity to live a quiet, orderly life, with just so much responsibility as would be entailed by my duties, whatever they might be, as a servant of the community; and a sufficiency of leisure to do the work I liked best" (*Taken*, 205).

Perhaps the most fascinating of Beresford's literary experiments, however, is his unique combination of stream-of-consciousness novel manqué and autobiographical work-in-progress, *Writing Aloud* (1928). In this "formless" book, Beresford generally allows the characters he has conceived to guide him as though he were writing automatic script (*Writing,* 53, 79), but he also includes his opinions on diverse topics, as well as autobiographical information supplied in the third person in square brackets. Beresford reveals in it the very pragmatic concerns and attitudes about handling psychological influence that arise as he is in the process of developing a novel.

Though as an idealist Beresford admires the principle of psychoanalysis—"the winning of self-knowledge and a free mind by the eradication of deep-seated habits of thought" (*Writing,* 148), he is well aware of the tendency to apply it dogmatically. He thus approaches it selectively, discounting, for example, the Freudian interpretation of dreams when it does not fit the evidence. He desires to go deeper than the Edwardian realists and convey something of his "characters' inner life that could never be expressed either in action or speech" (*Writing,* 117). However, several forces combine to thwart this desire and "to compel him to misrepresent humanity in fiction . . . [by] making it far too consistent" (*Writing,* 144). Beresford repeatedly criticizes the tastes of the general reading public, who constrain his fascination with experimentation since he does not have economic independence (*Writing,* 141). The general reading public, or "GRP," as he refers to them, wants recognizable types that come from other books rather than from life (*Writing,* 42, 142), does not care to know about the influence of heredity on behavior (*Writing,* 14–15), and in general lacks interest "in learning anything new about themselves or the human mind in general" (*Writing,* 174). The

GRP's response to psychoanalysis in fiction is particularly "shallow," some even arguing, for example, "that because Dickens never wrote of anything approaching a passionate relationship between mother and son, the 'mother-complex' either does not exist or is not a proper subject for a novel" (*Writing,* 33, 34). They are joined in their aversion to the application of psychoanalysis by the critics.

Beresford attempts to resolve the dilemma by proposing to disguise the influence. At one stage in his hypothetical novel, a mother, Emma, comes into contact, after 19 years of separation, with her illegitimate daughter, tentatively named J. J. Emma recognizes that the girl is confused about religion and will play the role of psychoanalyst without knowing it in order to help her achieve clarity about her feelings (*Writing,* 133). As Beresford develops the idea, he supplies Emma with a motive for helping J. J., which "will distract, I hope, the reader's attention from all comparisons with the methods of the clinic" (*Writing,* 135). After struggling for some time to incorporate this conception, Beresford comes to the realization that, in the interests of making the action more natural and the characters more probable to the reading public and critics, he will have to discard any parallels with psychoanalysis (*Writing,* 173–74). Furthermore, although all along he had intended to write from the point of view of the stream-of-consciousness of his heroine, "the psychical history" he has designed for her—including complex and revelation of unconscious motivation—would make that direct method unacceptable, and perhaps impossible (*Writing,* 178). Instead, Beresford decides to try and make it a "purely objective book," but he concludes that it will likely relate his own experience in a semiautobiographical mode, as he has done in most of his previous novels (*Writing,* 202).

Thus, *Writing Aloud* records with considerable candor some of the very practical pressures influencing the novelist as he or she writes. Beresford reveals both his fascination with psychoanalysis and with the obstacle it presents, his impulse to probe the deeper mysteries of human conduct in his work, and the checks to that impulse. The extent to which Beresford dared to follow through with this impulse, to challenge the conventions of the novel, and to overcome the constraints placed on him, can now be assessed over his career by considering his fictions.

Literary Taste: A Summary

Beresford was an extraordinarily eclectic reader and thinker. As a young man he read extensively in evolutionary thinking, materialism, and ide-

alism. He gained an even more extensive knowledge of the literature on
psychical research and psychology and was perhaps more knowledgeable
than any other of his novelist contemporaries in these fields, with the
exception of May Sinclair. He also devoured books in the fields of science, socialism, mysticism, faith healing, and philosophy throughout his
adult life.

Though Beresford's earliest reading in literature included both
romance and realism, throughout his maturity he favored the realists in
the genre of the novel. However, he also understood that realism took
many shapes and forms and that the realists frequently drew on the elements of romance. In fact, for example, he seems to have found James
Joyce's *Ulysses* unreadable because it lacked romantic motives in its
treatment of realism (*Writing*, 23).

His chief test of a novel was that a writer should know what he or she
is talking about ("Memories," 70). The writers that Beresford felt knew
their materials best, and had the greatest impact on Beresford as he
began his novel-writing career, included H. G. Wells ("Memories," 185)
and William de Morgan (both of whom Beresford directly acknowledged as models), Samuel Butler, Arnold Bennett, and John Galsworthy, among others. As his career developed he encountered and
esteemed highly the psychological realism of Dorothy Richardson, May
Sinclair, and D. H. Lawrence. However, he also held very highly the
mystical novels of John Cowper Powys and the fantasies of Walter de la
Mare and Eleanor Farjeon ("Memories," 217). Near the end of his career,
Beresford asserted that "[m]y favourite authors are Shaw, Aldous Huxley, H. G. Wells, Sinclair Lewis, and Upton Sinclair, all of them determined critics of our present day social system."[19] Among poets, Beresford admired Shakespeare, Donne, Blake, Keats, and Francis Thompson
(Gerber, 261), and he frequently paid tribute to them in the epigraphs
to his later novels. In his later years Beresford continued to review the
next generation of novelists, including Walter Allen, Louis Bromfield,
Joyce Cary, Daphne Du Maurier, Aldous Huxley, J. B. Priestley, G. B.
Stern, Evelyn and Alec Waugh, and others.

Beresford's awareness of and openness to contemporary currents of
thought and new directions in fiction writing prevented him from
"regarding his personal equation as a universal standard." Nevertheless he
developed a unique vision and distinctive perspectives in his remarkably
varied fiction, a vision that will be examined in the following chapters.

Chapter Three
Short Stories: Experimental Outlet

Beresford began his writing career by attempting short stories and brief *contes*, and he continued to explore these forms throughout his career, publishing five volumes of short stories and numerous uncollected pieces in literary periodicals and magazines ranging from the *English Review* and *Harper's* to the *Woman's Home Companion*. Though he aimed at supplementing his income with the stories he penned both at the beginning of his career and toward the end, many throughout reflect the enjoyment that he found in writing them. They frequently capture inspired moments that could not be sustained in the grind of producing the longer novel form year in and year out. For this reason the neglect that they have suffered at the hands of critics is perhaps more unjust than the similar neglect of Beresford's large and uneven canon of novels. Beresford himself probably did not help to engage critical inquiry, as he points out in increasingly bitter prefaces to several of his volumes, in typically self-deprecating fashion, that these volumes include stories that "meant nothing" and to which he turned his attention in order to make money. He distinguishes these conventional and sentimental tales from those briefer ones written to amuse himself, but we can identify quite a range, from short whimsical *contes* to romance to mystery to psychical stories, many of them containing rare psychological and spiritual insight.

His dominating theme, though, is to show the reality of the spiritual, transcendental world and the inconsequence of the material world. Typically, characters living mundane lives come into contact with a higher plane of being, which radically alters their perspectives. Frequently fate or destiny precipitates these encounters. The tone toward these situations ranges from persuasive to skeptical to playful, with a vein of irony that grows significantly in the course of his work. With Beresford's background in architecture it is not surprising that place, whether it be houses, towns, or even the stage, often plays a significant role, especially in evoking atmosphere. Other stories have a less precise, more symbolic setting as a vehicle for allegorical development, though this type thins out in his later volumes and is replaced by more narrative and plot-based psychological mysteries. Yet another group of stories are character-based. Beresford's protagonists are typically men in early middle age from the lower middle class who are living narrow, circumscribed lives. They tend to be introverted or at least introspective. He also focuses on extraordinary individuals, such as writers, a criminal, a scientist, a doctor, and a musician.

Occasionally Beresford turns his attention to psychological types, such as the introvert or the extrovert. However, these last mentioned, along with narratives drawing on the case study form of the psychical researchers, sometimes suffer from didacticism, a weakness that appears in all of the genres essayed by Beresford. As well, in a few of the stories the plots creak, or the skeleton of the structure obtrudes, or the ending turns a little too neatly or sentimentally. Nevertheless, he usually more than compensates for these flaws by his willingness to experiment with ideas, sometimes playing with them in imaginatively concrete ways, by his capacity to engage his readers with his own sense of wonder at the larger spiritual realm elusive to the five senses, and by his acute psychological understanding. A brief chronological survey of the collected short stories and some of the more striking uncollected short stories will illustrate the development of these characteristics and show the flawed aspects within their context.

Beresford's earliest attempts at short fiction, published in *Academy* in 1902, were really sketches (that demonstrate his social conscience).[1] His first short stories proper, including "Miranda. VI. On Idealism" and "A Test of Friendship," began to appear in the *Westminster Gazette* from 1908 on.[2] According to Helmut Gerber, "All these stories favour an idealistic attitude, all have a subdued humorous tone, all have a touch of sentiment or pathos, and all use the stylistic techniques we label realistic" (Gerber, 21).

Nineteen Impressions

By 1912 Beresford seems to have hit his stride in the genre of the short story since he thought highly enough of a half dozen published that year to include them in his first collection, *Nineteen Impressions* (1918).[3] The volume demonstrates clearly Beresford's interest in psychical research, psychoanalysis, and idealism, particularly in Henri Bergson's idea that "[t]here is neither time nor even succession in space" (used as the epigraph to one of the tales). In an introduction written as a response to friends' requests for explanations of several stories, Beresford suggests that the "impressions" of the title refer to moments of awareness of "something bright beyond, something that shines" (*Nineteen,* ix). Many of these symbolic stories deal with uncanny or transcendental experiences in which fate plays a role and time collapses, leading to a new perspective on the world.

By way of contrast, the opening story seems to present an allegory for a materialist's view of the world, using the narrator's visit to "Cut-Throat Farm" (the title of the piece) in what appears to him to be "The Valley of the Shadow of Death." His horror intensifies as one by one the starveling animals disappear, victims of the knife of the predatory farmer, who sizes up the narrator at the close. The irony lies in the suggestion that the narrator, one of Beresford's writer characters, is working on a story involving cannibalism. The following story, "The Power O' Money," takes another stab at the materialist's view by suggesting that those possessed by hopes in the material world are victims of an illusion.

In contrast to these, one of the best uncanny tales, "The Criminal" (June 1912), concerns two reporters' attempts to satisfy their curiosity about the appearance of "the arch-criminal, the very creator of crime" (*Nineteen,* 26), who has been brought to a trial in camera in order to simulate fairness. Since both reporters have open minds, they do not join in the "great cry for revenge" voiced by "the whole civilisation of Christendom" (*Nineteen,* 28, 26). Everyone else has a stake in the execution of the criminal because he has caused universal suffering. That revelation, along with the statement that the number of deaths for which he is responsible is incalculable, suggests that he represents the evil within all of us or within the collective unconscious. This possibility is strengthened when the reporters obtain strongly conflicting reports of the criminal's appearance from those who are admitted to the trial. Eventually one of them gains admittance and takes photographs secretly. Beresford effectively invokes a supernatural element when the two discover that no trace of the criminal appears in the pictures, though the surroundings turn out perfectly on the film. Beresford rather harshly commented on the tale in a letter to Sir Edward Howard Marsh (14 February 1918): "The Criminal was an abortive attempt to pose the suggestion that crime was a figment of the imagination, and that the arch criminal merely presented some force antagonistic to our own tendencies, and hence that we see him as the negation of some pet ideal of our own. I had not read a word of psychoanalysis, when I wrote it, but I see now, that many of Jung's theories are implicit in my idea."[4]

"Flaws in the Time Scheme," a series of three stories following "The Criminal," deals more didactically with the effects of psychical phenomena on people. In the first, "An Effect of Reincarnation," a skeptical narrator gives offhand advice to a friend, Tommy Birch, to join the Theosophical Society to discover his past reincarnations. After Birch does so and reveals that he had been a martyr during the English renaissance, his friends dismiss him, especially after he decides to become a lay missionary in China. Another friend remarks that "it wasn't in the scheme of things that he would be killed twice for the same offence" (*Nineteen,* 49); the detail that Birch wasn't killed during a mass slaughter at an uprising is presented without comment. In "A Case of Prevision," Jessop hallucinates a landslide while walking with his friend Galt along the Cornish coast. Galt attempts to cure him using posthypnotic suggestion but later reads of a cliff accident in which Jessop perished. In the less didactic "The Late Occupier" the narrator listens to a house agent's monologue and is struck by the repetition of the word "occupier." He slips out of time and experiences the tale of a man obsessed with occupying the house after his wife dies and he no longer can pay the bills. The narrator images the unfortunate end of the man before returning to the present and abruptly leaving the affronted house agent. A note explains that the story is a draft of "The Lost Suburb," which is presented later in the collection. In that version the narrator becomes obsessed with finding the house because of an "unplaced memory," a moment of unity with life experienced when viewing the building in childhood, although he later believes that he has an older association with the place. The dimension of memory and time passing adds to the depth of mystery in the piece. In "Force Majeure," place similarly exerts an obsessive influence. In this case the protagonist's rooms have a sinister impact, causing the protagonist to defenestrate his dead lover's dog and then to jump from the window himself after sounds of the lover and the dog persist.

Several other stories imbue place with a larger and even symbolic significance. In "The Little Town" the narrator visits St. Erth, Cornwall, where he feels the presence of "unseen creatures" before attending a crude puppet show at the "Kosmos" theatre. Obsessed by the ineptitude of the operator, he confronts him, only to find a serene and wise old man with no visible connection to the "tottering figures" below. The piece may well be an allegory of God's relation to mankind, but it is not limited to this interpretation. "The Empty Theatre" opens with a narrator wearily listening to a cockney clerk posing as a well-off resident of a resort town as they sit on the parade watching a storm approach. Finally left to himself, the narrator is "shut . . . in to a little world" by a wall of rain (*Nineteen,* 150). As he slips out of time he hears "the awakening voice" of an "actor" who has posed both onstage and off. He recounts the supreme, pride-filled moment of his existence when he plays "the greatest of parts in a great theatre" (*Nineteen,* 153), only to discover during the performance that his audience does not exist and that he stands naked, exposed in the great, dark theater. After the storm rages and passes, and the narrator finds himself "alone in a deserted world," the possibility arises that the King Lear-like performance described has been another rather chilling, moral allegory of God's perspective on man's pride. At the close the narrator realizes, "Within an hour the curtain of cloud would be lifted and the play begin again" (*Nineteen,* 156). "Powers of the Air" also features a storm, though in a less distinct setting. An older person attempts to warn a "blind youth" of "the forces that have power in the black time," but the youth ignores him and braves the elements, returning filled with exhilaration and new knowledge. If this story, written in 1915, reflects at least the mood of the early war years, "Lost in the Fog" (1916), placed at the end of the volume, represents a more defined allegory of the conflict. In an attempt to escape the fog of London, the narrator leaves by train but takes the wrong line and ends up in a village where a mortal feud is taking place between the Turtons and the Franks. Wondering whether he should help, he finds relief in returning to the world he *knew,* but closes with the pointed questions: "Is it conceivable that out there in the little unknown village—for ever lost to me in a world of white mist—men are fighting and *killing* each other? Surely it cannot be true?" (*Nineteen,* 226). Beresford's transformation of the conflict of nations into a local conflict effectively makes the horror more real and immediate.

Another group of stories focuses more precisely on individuals whose visions expand, alter, or retract, often because of escapes from time or merely its passage. In "The Escape," for instance, an office clerk beset by "steadily accumulating" worries has an out-of-body experience in which he views the vast panorama of the earth and its position in the universe. Afterward, realizing he is "only just awake," he attains peace, and daily routine seems insignificant. "The Misanthrope" presents a bleaker view of humanity. Beresford immediately piques the reader's curiosity by having his narrator claim that if he believed what he has experienced he would know himself to be some kind of human horror but would not know exactly what kind. The narrator then relates that he decided to visit the island where a reputed madman lives in isolation, only to discover that the man, William Copley, is sane but has become a misanthrope because he can perceive the moral defects of individuals when he looks back at them over his shoulder. With the aid of a mirror he has also discovered his own flaws. As the piece closes he glances back at the departing narrator, who shockingly views the man's face transformed by disgust and loathing and is left to wonder why. The title of "The Man in the Machine," one of Beresford's tales that seems to symbolize God's relation to His creation, refers to its protagonist, who barely escapes death from a fall. Under morphine he enters into the "Great Hall" of his vision and experiences the body as machine in which the man at the controls seems "hopelessly distant" (*Nineteen,* 212). In contrast, "The Instrument of Destiny" offers promise for the future of mankind. Adrian knows that he will be the instrument of destiny and, just as "the fog of his material life began to thicken," his vision contracts "into an urgent desire for expression," which he finds through a sexual encounter, after which he is abruptly killed (*Nineteen,* 200). However, a child is born of that moment of ecstasy, "and he may be the saviour of mankind, or at least a link in the long, long chain of man's transcending destiny" (*Nineteen,* 205).

Two other brief tales deal with vision over generations. "The Great Tradition" centers on a legend of marmalade making and amusingly deflates the sacredness with which some traditions are held. "The Contemporaries" climaxes with a moment of unspoken communion, suggesting a collapse in time, between the youngest and oldest at a gathering of five generations.

Many of these cryptic contes effectively create uncanny, otherworldly atmospheres and provoke ontological questioning. The ambiguity of situation and philosophical dimension gives these stories a rich texture, marred only occasionally by didacticism. The reviewer for the *Times Literary Supplement* judged that "they are, on the whole, very successful adventures in the uncanny. A few may be rather too mechanical to be convincing and too trivial to be interesting; but most of them one reads eagerly, convinced, and, to a certain degree, thrilled. They do convey genuine impressions of strange flights of the mind (as we may for convenience term it) into the past, into the future, and more especially, under the surface of appearances."[5]

Signs and Wonders

Beresford continued his experimentation and preoccupation with altered perspectives and psychical phenomena in his second volume of stories,

Signs and Wonders (1921), the third volume published by the esteemed Golden Cockerel Press.[6] A brief prologue in dramatic form, "The Appearance of Man," sets the tone by placing a mundane conversation between a woman and two men against a backdrop of images (described in stage directions). These images depict the beginning of the world through to the end and include a procession of brontosauri, a civil war, and the bursting of the universe into flames. The ironic treatment of the repeated phrase "The world's a very small place" implies the blinkered vision of mankind and plays with the idea that all time can happen in an instant. Reviewers responded diversely to this experiment: the reviewer for the *Saturday Review* dismissed it as "tedious" whereas his counterpart at the *London Mercury,* Edward Shanks, found that it "approximates to the level of great poetry and is probably, length for length, the finest thing he has ever done."[7] Both of these opinions are too extreme, since the piece playfully serves as a concise and clever introduction to Beresford's main theme of man's ability (or lack of ability) to apprehend the signs and wonders of the larger forces at work in the midst of his mundane existence. In the title story the narrator has a transcendental experience and sees a procession of "signs and wonders" across the sky before returning to reflect on humanity's preoccupation with "the miserable importance of their instant lives" (*Signs,* 14). In "The Cage" the narrator, while riding the "Tube," envisions an encounter between himself and a primitive man. He benevolently reveals to the primate the distant future featuring escape from the cage through imagination, but the primate recoils in terror at the glimpse of commuters reading "little black-dotted white sheets" (*Signs,* 19). The disturbed narrator is left wondering whether "the distant future might not seem equally unendurable to me?" (*Signs,* 19). In "Enlargement" the narrator escapes from a modern-day cage, the air-raid shelter, and feels liberated as he approaches the "Cleopatra's Needle" monument in London. Beresford vividly creates the atmosphere of the deafening bombardment, but even more shocking is the vision of a procession of elephants, which causes the narrator to feel that "he had pierced the veil of the commonplace" (*Signs,* 24). Later his landlady reduces the experience to a comic sight when she reports that elephants had escaped from the " 'Ippodrome." Though the premise seems implausible, Beresford's main interest is in the enlargement of perception that his protagonist experiences.

Several stories deal with various spiritual and psychological types, occasionally rather too didactically. "The Perfect Smile" traces the development of Douglas Owen's gift of smiling to avoid punishment until, finally, that gift fails during his sentencing for murder. "The Hidden Beast" tells of one of Beresford's outsiders, who is attracted more to the wild in man than to the restrained. Beresford carries through the image of the primitive in man in "The Barrage: A Study in Extroversion," the title alluding to this type's forceful, attacking voice and the complete confidence with which extroverts express their opinions. Though the quizzical narrator feels wonder and admiration at his acquaintance of this type, he implies that their barrage must be louder in our modern relativistic age. Both this tale of extroversion and its companion piece, "The Introvert," deal too didactically with those psychoanalytic types, though it is interesting that Beresford presents the latter more favorably, especially as introverts make up the majority of his protagonists in his novels. "The Barrier" similarly deals with a type, the glutton, whose spirit is imprisoned by his indulgence in physical satisfactions.

Most of the remaining stories deal with visions of the future or of the immediate past, notably the trauma of World War I. "The Convert" treats subject matter similar to Beresford's novel *Revolution* (1921)—the possibility of revolution in England—but from the viewpoint of a detached, self-absorbed historian whose reputation is based on his claim that the "English temper" would never permit revolution. On the night of the outbreak a forthright young woman bursts into his house. Once she discovers his identity she confronts him with the fact that he has been responsible for the revolution. In wrenching him from his detachment, she voices the very modern idea that "we've pretty well scrapped history now" (*Signs,* 63) and converts him to the cause as adviser to the rebel "Youth League." However, his transformation is too abrupt and not entirely believable. The consciously Wellsian tale "A Negligible Experiment" presents a more apocalyptic vision of the future, a cosmic collision, in which the earth and its inhabitants appear to be a negligible experiment, a view ironically underlined by the framing device of a young sculptor's abortive attempt to model man in plasticine. In "The Miracle" a wife reclaims her comatose, shell-shocked husband through an out-of-body vision, with an echo of the Orpheus legend. In "Young Strickland's Career" Strickland obsesses about the future of his son until he views in a crystal ball a live scarecrow digging turnips. This fragment of his past transforms into horrific reality when he searches for his son on a battlefield in France after the war. "A Difference of Temperament" contrasts the boastfulness of Royce, who leaves a business to experience a life of "romance and wonder," with the reserved character of his long-time associate Bunnett, who seemingly has remained at his mundane job with the firm. Royce fails to notice, however, that Bunnett has lost his arm, presumably in the war. "Reference Wanted!" is a more light-hearted story of a possibly shell-shocked man who claims to have been caught plagiarizing the works of European writers; at the close the narrator has the impression that he has heard *this* story somewhere before. Also written in a mildly humorous tone, "As the Crow Flies" focuses on a novel of that title supposedly written by George Wallace but never found by the publisher after Wallace dies in the Boer War. Ironically, the reputation of the unwritten book outlives him.

The collection closes with the longer story "The Night of Creation," which is based on a weekend at H. G. Wells's in Easton Glebe and is consciously presented in the form of a Society For Psychical Research case ("Memories," 281). Despite a pedantic opening, Beresford manages to develop dramatic tension through two characters: a skeptic and rationalist, Harrison (loosely based on Wells), and a psychical researcher, Vernon. After the apparition of a woman in white appears in the garden during a house party, Harrison sets out to show that it was Phyllis Messenger, rejected by her lover and suicidal, who had appeared in a trance state. Harrison triumphs over Vernon, but an anomalous piece of evidence that he had suppressed bothers him and leads to the shock of discovery that the woman in white was Phyllis's friend who had committed suicide several weeks earlier. Though for a moment Harrison has a sense of uncanny activities, the question of whether he is converted to the psychical researcher's view by his mystical experience is convincingly left open at the denouement.

Beresford's development in speculative stories in *Signs and Wonders* of his dual interest in psychological states and in signs "of the coming of the new age—the age of the Spirit" is most compelling when not overtly didactic (*Signs*, 112). Despite appearing in a British edition limited to 1,500 copies, the volume was generally well received, more than one critic recognizing Beresford's capacity and talent for presenting a "sudden flash of the unexpected."[8] At least one modern critic, Brian Stableford, has rediscovered this talent, claiming about Beresford's first two volumes that "[t]he vignettes are ahead of their time in their methods and preoccupations. They are surreal and oblique, playing with time and space in a manner that was not to become fashionable for many years. Their interest in psychological theory and in the peculiarities of man's existential predicament was virtually unprecedented in English fiction, though not in Russian or French short stories" (Stableford, *Supernatural*, 459).[9]

The Imperturbable Duchess

Beresford published his third collection of stories, *The Imperturbable Duchess and Other Stories,* with Collins as his stint as their literary adviser drew to a close in 1923. He signals a change of tone in the preface, entitled "Author's Advice," in which he describes the economics of writing for young writers aspiring to financial success. With some bitterness he recounts how he began with an obsession for originality in subject and treatment in his contes but was forced to abandon them since they did not pay. Instead he turned to "the writing of short stories that meant nothing."[10] The title story, dating from 1913, and "Reparation" (1919) represent his original aim, whereas others deliberately avoid obscurity and are written in a condensed and polished style, necessities for commercial success. Though the volume does vary more in quality than earlier ones, Beresford was perhaps being too hard on himself, since the collection does cohere around significant themes, including the ascendency of life over art. Possibly because of his own frustrating experiences, Beresford shows fate playing a larger role in these stories than in previous ones. He typically implies that it is an ancient and powerful force not to be dismissed or trifled with by modern man with his pride in scientific accomplishments. Fate connects man with his primal roots and shocks him into recognizing the limitations of his materialist view of the world. Most of the stories feature alienated or obsessed outsider figures and probe the intervention of fate in their lives, occasionally through uncanny circumstances.

"The Grand Style" picks up on the dilemma outlined in the preface, featuring an artist who scorns to please but who nearly succumbs to the persuasions of a commercially minded theater manager to write him an "art" play after they view a vile performance by a worn-out troupe. The poet is impressed that the actors perform with nothing to gain until fate intervenes and he finds out from one of them that they were playing up to the manager. "The Whole Truth" similarly builds a story around the stage to comment on the relationship between art and life.

Life outdoes art in the title story, one of the best in the collection, and one of several focusing on unusual relationships. Class-conscious writer Cunningham Black affronts the "Imperturbable Duchess" Valetta, Duchess of Tottenham, on a train only to discover that they are both guests at the same weekend house party. He seizes the opportunity to humiliate the ignorant but dignified Valetta but is not entirely successful until he vindictively transforms their contretemps into a variety of fictional genres, which successively move further away from the truth. Having fulfilled his "obsession" "to prove that cleverness was more than the air of the aristocrat" (*Imperturbable*, 21), he attempts to make amends to the by now infamous and exiled duchess, whose single dignified comment, "insufferable," exposes the gulf in class once again.

"The Successful Marriage" treats class differences from the opposite perspective. In it a shabby narrator exposes the prejudice and snobbery of an aristocrat by recounting to him the tale of a successful "mixed" marriage between a carpenter and the daughter of an earl, before neatly revealing his identity as the suitor of their daughter. In "The Awakening" the atypical feature of the relationship portrayed is age. In it a mature man who adopts a girl eventually attempts to murder her seducer before acting on his submerged desire for her. "The Sentimentalists" also deals with awakening desire. A depressed doctor with a nonentity of a wife develops an attraction for a delicate patient with an alcoholic husband. Fate intervenes at predictably regular intervals despatching both spouses, but readers' expectations are subverted and desire is deferred permanently when the couple eventually realizes that their unspoken desires had "bled internally, and the life had gone from them" (*Imperturbable*, 52).

"The Looking-Glass" explores an almost uncanny relationship between Rachel Deane and her elderly aunt of the same name. On visiting the aunt, Rachel realizes how strongly she resembles her, even down to her facial expressions, but is shocked when she discovers that she has become a mirror for her aunt, who maintains her youth through the strength of her obsession with her resemblance to her niece. Once that idea is shattered by a glance into a mirror, the aunt shrinks and abruptly dies.

Beresford probes other types of obsessions in the remaining stories. In "The Deserter," written in 1914, a soldier obsessed with deserting ironically stumbles across a Frenchman spying for the Germans, which nets him a promotion, though he recognizes in the Frenchman the same cowardly impulse that he attributes to temporary insanity in himself. Only fate separates him from the Frenchman's ignominious end. Correspondingly, "Paul Hickson's Return to the Wild" shows a civilian stepping far beyond the bounds of expected behavior. The protagonist's obsession with a holiday turns into resentment against authority when his holiday is canceled because of a heat wave that afflicts his coworkers. This tale of the office worker who snaps, transgresses, and becomes a fugitive in the wilds seems quite modern. The suggestion is that the man's primal instincts have emerged, but society prefers to explain away the disturbing incident by claiming that the man is "just another victim of the heat-wave" (*Imperturbable,* 155).

Both "Reparation" and "Expiation" deal with resolving guilt complexes. In "Reparation," the more dramatic of the two, Angus Whitely undertakes an amazing odyssey to fulfill the dying wish of his boss to make reparation to a young woman whom the boss believes he had impregnated. After first ceasing the quest and then continuing because he feels haunted, Whitely finally catches up with the ungrateful woman only to find that she has not been ruined, though she takes the gift of diamonds anyway. "Expiation" deals with the still-topical issue of euthanasia from the perspective of the person who has assisted in the death of his terminally ill friend. "No Defence" contains a less psychological and more definitely supernatural element as a crime of passion is very nearly repeated in a haunted house, though evidence of supernatural interference cannot be introduced in the consequent divorce proceedings.

The stories in *The Imperturbable Duchess* are less experimental than those handful in his earlier volumes that treat existential themes using symbolic settings. These ones rely instead on straightforward historical narrative, though they do contain some subtle emotional and psychological analysis, as the *Times Literary Supplement* reviewer noted. The weakest of the stories, such as "The Awakening," suffer from too much compression, and they too cleverly and obviously rely on the closing "click" that Beresford describes in his preface. The best, including the title story, "The Sentimentalists," and "The Looking Glass," are paced better and resolve with unexpected and occasionally uncannily refreshing endings. As the *Times Literary Supplement* reviewer astutely observed, "the story called 'Paul Dickson's Return to the Wild' in this collection shows that he can present a psychological case in an exciting manner when he chooses."[11] The various angles presented on the role of fate and the relations between life and art give the volume coherence and depth and demonstrate that it has a modern self-consciousness.

The Meeting Place

The "Conclusion" to Beresford's next volume of short stories, *The Meeting Place and Other Stories,* published by Faber and Faber in 1929, belies his increasing frustration with the commercial constraints placed on the genre and, underlying this, his own increasingly precarious financial situation. Beresford reiterates his criticism of the control exerted by American magazines with their demand for sentimental and romantic conventions. He also reveals the boredom that he had to overcome in trying to address the average man or woman and the immense labor involved in constructing such artificial tales. As in previous volumes, one can identify stories written for the magazine market as well as those shorter pieces written to indulge his own taste, but there is a range between these two poles. Some common themes emerge in the different types of stories. Most significantly, several stories deal with the intrusion of fiction—and the emotions expressed through it—into reality, through developing relationships between writers and their readers. In most Beresford continues to be preoccupied with encounters or moments at which "the hand of God" enters; "You may call it Fate, Luck, Coincidence, anything you like, but I sometimes wonder if they are not just different names for the same thing," claims one of his narrators.[12]

By far the most striking are those speculative and quizzical tales reminiscent of his first two volumes. The first of these, "The End of Phipson," lightheartedly touches on the theme of the writer's position in society by playing with the idea of a shrinking reputation. Celebrated novelist Phipson, "afraid that too much praise might spoil his work," escapes to France (*Meeting,* 38). However, at the "Splendid Hotel" he goes unrecognized and begins to shrink physically until he is trod on and the "very little mess" left is swept away (*Meeting,* 42). More reflective than speculative, "Justice: An Impartial Comment" conveys a very disturbing portrait of a justice system at the mercy of questionably motivated jurors. In the Wellsian story "The Man Who Hated Flies" a scientist, taking up the suggestion of his son to eliminate flies, inadvertently destroys other insect forms crucial to the existence of plant and animal life. Ironically his son discovers an immune fly to restore the balance, as the story offers a wry commentary on tampering with providence. "The Wind and Mr. Tittler," as brief and imaginative as "Phipson," deftly and amusingly portrays a timid and thoroughly conventional man with no vices who is "carried away into the depths of space with all the other rubbish" by an unnatural wind (*Meeting,* 221). "The Marionettes" presents an allegory of the inception of creation reminiscent of "The Little Town" in *Nineteen Impressions* but from the perspective of the weary artist attempting to banish the "shadows" of negative memories before he can begin arranging his characters and creating once again. In "The Devil's Own Luck" we encounter another struggling artist, this time an alcoholic journalist, Wallace Edgar. The first-person narrator engages in "a contest of the Spirit" with Edgar but to no avail. Only a severe crisis of identity, touched off when Edgar cannot see himself in a café mirror and believes he has gone to hell, begins a spiritual rebirth within him. The narrator constructs the incident as a miracle, omitting to reveal to Edgar that the broken mirror had been replaced by a very realistic painting. In the narrator's mind the incident does ironically and finally stand as a miracle since it counters the superstition about breaking mirrors, unless "it was the devil's own luck that had been bad" (*Meeting,* 268). Another ironically presented miracle lies at the center of "Common Humanity." In this story two doctors experiment "for the good of humanity" on a drunken derelict, a specimen "of common humanity" brought into the hospital by a policeman. The man's dreams reveal his former powerful and honorable status as advisor to an emperor. The doctors are of course oblivious to these dreams, but the more sensitive of the two does sense that the man "*has* got something of an air about him" (*Meeting,* 279). Their jest that the miracle of saving him is a calamity bears on the issue of euthanasia, as did "Expiation" in *The Imperturbable Duchess.* "The Trap without a Bait" offers a mocking indictment of the middle class by portraying a visit to a materially perfect but empty town, symbolic of the artificiality and soullessness of this class. In the ambiguous but powerful "Illusion," during a party of profligates at the Pandemonium, Stanley has a vision of an endless procession of unemployed surging forward to overwhelm these wasters. In "The Summary," wryly positioned as the concluding story in the volume, a novelist asked to write out the whole truth at Judgment Day finds he has learned nothing on the subject during his lifetime. The only futuristic story in the volume, this fantasy calls into question the succession of time as well as the life events and accumulation of knowledge typically so highly valued.

The bitterness of this allegory does not reflect on a smaller cluster of stories that might be termed psychological mysteries or thrillers. In the well-constructed tale "Ways of Escape" a psychological novelist, Mrs. Holmleigh, becomes interested in the eccentric behavior of a neighbor, Mrs. Trevarrian, who she believes has a complex involving a longing for a domestic servant. In reality, Mrs. Trevarrian awaits a signal from her convict husband that will indicate his escape, for which he will be disguised as a servant. When another convict turns up at her isolated cottage on the moor, claiming that her husband has "turned pious," she reluctantly helps the fugitive. However, Mrs. Holmleigh later informs her that in order to make his escape, one convict had murdered another

(Mr. Trevarrian), and the novelist unwittingly expresses her opinion that "it must be a lucky escape for his poor wife, whoever she may be" (*Meeting,* 217). Beresford wisely does not elaborate on the stricken wife's response. "The Artificial Mole" is another slick psychological mystery involving an escape and disappearance, with just a touch of mysticism about it.

Two others of this type, "The Clever Mr. Fall" and "The Last Tenants," make ironic comments on the relationship between literature and life. The former resembles "The Imperturbable Duchess" in its depiction of class conflict generated by an unfavorably portrayed writer's contact with those above him in class. In the latter a novelist discovers two distinct collections of books left at the house he has rented, one set that is repulsive to him and one, which includes his own books, that was owned by someone with the initial "J," whom he romantically imagines to have been a woman named Judith. This intuition uncannily proves true. These longer stories feature most of the conventions of this genre, notably the twist at the close, though thankfully in "The Last Tenants" Beresford stops short of describing the reunion between the novelist and Judith after he discovers that her drunkard husband is now dead.

Several other tales focus more centrally on the psychology of various relationships, at the worst contrived and unbelievable and at the best unusual. Two of the former, "The Meeting Place" and "Laughter and Tears," continue the theme of the meeting place between one's dreams and one's life, between fiction and reality, and lead to revelations of love between novelists. More refreshingly, "The Air of Paris" features a quiet, habit-bound bachelor with an unlived life on his first business trip to Paris. His rather comic encounter with a passionate Frenchwoman, which is driven by miscommunication, leads to his new vitality and resolve to marry a woman attracted by him back in England. Also with a somewhat sentimental ending, "The Three Cases" deals with the rather interesting idea that two people can be out of sync with one another over a number of years before being ready and appropriate for one another. In contrast, "Verity" recalls "The Sentimentalists," as a long-standing attraction does not come to fruition. In "Love of Youth" a mother falls in love in a timeless moment with the suitor of her daughter, once the daughter realizes that "he loves young things, all young things" rather than her in particular (*Meeting,* 183). The story demonstrates unusual insight into mother-daughter relations as well as subtly suggesting a slight uncanniness at the fringes. "The Indomitable Mrs. Garthorne" turns the lens on a domineering mother who unsuccessfully attempts to block the marriage of her son to her ex-husband's adopted daughter, a talented but impecunious violinist.

"The Hands of Serge David" falls in between this type and a final set of stories that focuses on extraordinary individuals. A violinist overcomes a psychological block with the aid of a woman who forces back into his consciousness the memory of a trauma that she had caused, after which revelation the couple marries. "The Gambler" tells an amazing tale of a gambler's turn of fortune, while "The Champion" narrates what turns out to be an unreliable tale of how an accident ended a "champion's" brilliant billiards career. In "Tops and Bottoms" a grocer amusingly proves his tenuous connection with the " 'ighest in the land." "Professional Pride," called "capital straight farce" by one reviewer,[13] focuses on a "reformed" burglar who is really a kind of artist, at least as concerned as one about his press notices. Professional pride motivates him to tell of how he turned himself in to thwart his "furriner" victim's insurance scam.

Though the reviewer in *Punch* admired Beresford's range in this collection,[14] fewer of these tales show the inspiration or originality of earlier volumes, a trend that unfortunately continues in Beresford's final volume, *Blackthorn Winter,* published in 1936.

Blackthorn Winter

In a preface more cynical than earlier ones, Beresford states in *Blackthorn Winter and Other Stories* that instead of trying to trick readers by interspersing "unpalatable" stories with sentimental magazine-market ones, he has separated them honestly.[15] Most of the first 16 stories are relatively conventional and lightweight, though many are linked by a theme of mistaken identities and deceptiveness of appearances. The title story is representative, showing how a young woman's fantasies about a novelist nearly lead to her deception by another writer with a similar name, until she is romantically saved by the actual novelist who writes under a pseudonym. "Allied Interests," "The Lift," "Love is Blind," "Two Romantics," "A Scrap of Paper," and, most notably, "The Two Sirens" similarly depict initial misperceptions or mysteries leading to love relationships. "Reality" convincingly conveys a vain young woman's awakening to love, which is brought about by her reluctant participation in a poor family's crisis. Beresford deftly handles the image of "The Open Door" in a story of that title, which shows the transformation of a relationship between a peevish, spoiled wife and her long-suffering husband. "With Modern Effects" deals with another kind of transformation as a family overcomes conflicts and feels the Christmas spirit despite the children's obsession with the modern material trappings of that season. "Ailing Mary" features an arrogant magazine editor who is brought down a few notches by the failure of the car about which he has boasted. "The Other Way" vaguely recalls stories such as "The Hidden Beast" that deal with the animal nature in man, but in this one the two characters in conflict transcend their brute instincts. Beresford closes this section with two mysteries, "The Coincidence" and "The Beck Lodge Case" (the latter far more compelling), and one of his rare forays into the world of politics and espionage in "Number 10," based on an actual incident in which the publication of an alleged letter from Communist Grigori Zinoviev to British Communists led to the defeat of the Labour government in 1924.

In the remaining 12 brief contes Beresford sketches a range of incidents from the trivial and humorous to the significant, all of which have a transforming quality about them. In "The Bitter Look," for instance, a personable pig's penetrating stare before being slaughtered mortally affects his owner. The transformation in "Dreams, Idle Dreams" is to a state of disillusionment and confusion because of a misperception of fate.

"The Philosophy of Mr. Punch" presents a disturbingly eerie allegory of the artist's relations to his ideas, reminiscent of "The Marionettes" in *The Meeting Place* but darker. Mr. Punch assesses four figures—Judy, a beadle, a flaccid executioner, and a clown—that represent the remains of his ideas of love, justice, death, and joy, before killing each one of them by beating them with a stick. Nevertheless, he perceives this act as a liberating one, claiming, "I regret none of my killings. Once the thought has been crystallized into expression it must inevitably die inch by gradual inch. And if I had clung to these old notions of mine, I, too, should have suffered a slow paralysis" (*Blackthorn,* 318). At the close pride reasserts itself and he steps out "to seek a new idea and kill it" (*Blackthorn,* 320), unaware that the clown, though dead even before he had belabored it, has revived and is following him. Is Beresford the artist suggesting that, despite its repeated slaying, the joy of life persists and continues to prompt him to seek out new ideas? This optimistic reading must be tempered by keeping in mind Beresford's use of the metaphor of killing to indicate his treatment of ideas. "The Irrational Quantity" is a more playful piece and probably the most imaginative of this group. This conte portrays the narrator's encounter in the bathtub with a fanciful figure, the "Root of Minus One," who is the victim of mathematical imprecision.

However by far the most intriguing and perhaps revealing story is "A Feat of Alchemy" in which the narrator throws a catholic selection of novels into a cauldron and boils them down until only the following contents remain: "1. A few really beautiful crystals of idealism; 2. Some crystals—feathery things—of romance; 3. A lot of grey powder, slightly bitter, which must have been realism; 4. Some unanalysable stuff, probably humour; 5. Two or three handfuls of detritus—the bulk of the residue—very light in weight and almost colourless, which I judged to be practically worthless" (*Blackthorn,* 280). This allegory can be read as Beresford's rather bitter commentary on his profession or his hypercritical analysis of his own contribution. If the latter, then his assessment is surely too severe. Though this volume did not receive as much attention as earlier ones, the *Times Literary Supplement* reviewer astutely observed that Beresford's "sincerity and humanity" redeem the commercial stories and claimed about the sketches that "their tonic effect of satire and sly fun-poking is very salutary."[16]

Beresford's best stories reflect his humane values in their sensitivity to the unseen, their penetrating psychological insight, and their philosophical and ontological questioning. Only occasionally are these tales marred by didacticism. Many of his finest stories were written early in his career before financial pressures forced him to succumb to more formulaic writing, betrayed by the bitterness of tone in the introductions to later volumes.

These early stories owe only a slight debt to Beresford's major English predecessors. Beresford shares Kipling's fascination with the unexplained and supernatural, but he does not rely on exotic settings or physical violence and suffering as did Kipling. Beresford avoids the patriotism and occasional heavy-handed morality that date Kipling and treats characters much more introspectively as well. In common with H. G. Wells, Beresford explores lower-middle-class characters and the awakenings undergone by them. While some stories by both writers demonstrate a fablelike quality, others read as incitements to change, betraying Wells's and Beresford's mutual concerns about social development. Nevertheless, whereas Wells focuses on the transformative powers of science, Bereford emphasizes spiritual transformation.

Among his contemporaries Beresford also has a distinctive niche, though to his credit he shares with the modernists a self-consciousness in his stories about writers and writing as well as the themes of disillusionment and the isolation of individuals. As with Joyce and Katherine Mansfield, Beresford tends to use the episodic tale, but his stories are not nearly as particularized or as symbolically dense as these two modernist masters. Both Joyce and Mansfield probe ordinary characters and everyday events, whereas Beresford's interest lies with extraordinary characters and unusual, spiritually transcendent events. In common with that more ambiguously modernist writer D. H. Lawrence, Beresford frequently demonstrates fascination with personal and family relations (though he does not share Lawrence's obsession with sexual relations); both also tend toward the fabulistic, partly through their use of abstract titles (e.g., Beresford's "The Criminal" or "The Misanthrope" and Lawrence's "The Man Who Died" or "The Woman Who Rode Away"). Beresford's early stories, though, are not nearly as conventional in structure and plot as D. H. Lawrence's, and Beresford's forays into the psychical tale precede Lawrence's by a decade or more. Beresford's psychical tales have more in common with his friend Walter de la Mare's in their whimsicality and concern with metaphysical issues and the enlargement of inner vision, though, unlike Beresford, de la Mare's province tended to be children's experiences of the unexplained.

More than any other of his contemporaries Beresford developed the conte, or brief, oblique, abstract impressionistic story that frequently has allegorical overtones. These tales, with their spiritual and ontological questioning, constitute Beresford's main contribution to the short story. Critic Brian Stableford captures the potential of these mainly early innovative tales, claiming that "it is probable that modern readers, familiar with the fiction of Jorge Luis Borges and Italo Calvino as well as the surreal fantasies of Nikolai Gogol and Franz Kafka, would find more in these stories than contemporary readers could have" (Stableford *Supernatural*, 459). Beresford's primary concern with presenting awakenings or transformations of various kinds, from sentimental to speculative, makes these stories seem as relevant and necessary today as when they were first penned.

Chapter Four
Early Psychological Realism

J. D. Beresford's main claim to historical recognition is as a novelist of psychological realism. During the first two decades of his career he achieved considerable critical acclaim for his thoughtful and probing analyses of character, perceived as somewhat daring in their questioning of the conventions of Victorian morality. From the late 1920s on, he received less critical notice, and since his death he has been largely ignored.

There are numerous factors that can account for such a radical shift in critical opinion, and it is difficult to assess their relative importance. In his rather large oeuvre of 49 novels Beresford tackled an array of subgenres, including various types of realism, such as the autobiographical "life-novel," the sociological novel, and the psychoanalytical novel, not to mention his essays in fantasy, the futuristic and visionary tale, scientific romance, supernatural novels, and sentimental romance and detective potboilers. Although this versatility underlines his talent, it also contributed to his neglect, as his work tends to fall between the categories of genre constructed by critics, many of whom, Gerald Gould among them, found it impossible to label him (Gould, 18). The use he made of the "new" psychologies and psychoanalysis in particular is a second factor that contributed to contemporary critical attack and subsequent obscurity. His impulse to deal with what were referred to as the more "unpleasant" aspects of human pathology in his fiction was often viewed as an unfortunate aberration. Despite his general praise of Beresford, Gould called the psychological novelist in Beresford "wayward" and "truant" (Gould, 29). A. St. John Adcock spoke for many of Beresford's severest critics when he claimed that "one deprecates his [Beresford's] excursions into eccentricities of psychology."[1] A third and slightly more justifiable reason for the tepid retrospective response to Beresford is that some, but not all, of his novels from the late 1920s lacked the imaginative penetration of his earlier work and became increasingly didactic. Notable exceptions include *The Camberwell Miracle* (1933), *Peckover* (1934), and *Cleo* (1937). A less justifiable but important reason for his neglect has to do with changes in the criteria of assessment.

Although contemporary critics occasionally referred to Beresford as an "experimenter," as a realist he was certainly left in the wake of the wave of modernism that swept over western culture after World War I. Given the significance of this last reason, it is necessary to examine how Beresford conceived his approach to the novel, to assess him in light of the realist project in which he participated, and not to judge him solely according to the modernist aesthetic that continues to influence critical thinking.

As indicated in chapter 2, Beresford was strongly influenced by H. G. Wells in his thinking about fiction, especially at the beginning of his career. Drawing on Wells, he was not content to "present a slice of life, neatly dissected and displayed" but invariably worked an implicit thesis into his novels (*Writing*, 79, 49). However, he was no mere imitator of Wells, because his empirical approach to the minute details of human existence was modified by his idealism, probing of the psyche, and, latterly, mysticism. As early as *Jacob Stahl* Beresford articulates through his protagonist a modification of strict realism:

> [F]or the best construction of dream-pictures, certain practical knowledge was required. "If one had to write that story, now," reflected Jacob, "it would be necessary to know many things. I am so vague in my dreams. I must study detail. I must learn construction." He had a choice between two corollaries. One must study detail for the purpose of writing romances, or one must write only of what one knows from experience. Jacob inclined to the belief that there was a possible compromise which included both alternatives. (*Jacob*, 276)

Beresford was never so naive as to believe that he was making a transcript of reality in his fiction. In *Writing Aloud* (1928), Beresford makes a number of statements revealing the modifications he has made to the empiricist's approach to realism. He acknowledges the role of imagination and selection in constructing "reality" and claims that "[r]ealism does not depend so much upon the facts treated as upon the treatment of the facts" (*Writing*, 57). He was astonished when reviewers like Dixon-Scott accused him of "dressing up the old romantic material in realistic clothes. What a remarkable discovery! As if any realistic novelist had ever done anything else. Or tried to. What material has he to clothe in realistic form but that old, old stuff about birth and development, love and hate, decline and death?" (*Writing*, 23). But his most perceptive critics, such as Gerald Gould, recognized his method. Gould wrote about the *Jacob Stahl* trilogy that "[r]ealism is idealised into reality. Not that the most accurate observation would by itself suffice for that— Mr. Beresford not only sees details, he sees them in their due priority and place; he makes them 'compose.' And this, I think, is the secret of his delightful descriptions" (Gould, 52–53).

Beresford was not content with selecting details and blending romance with realism. Though he praises a number of contemporaries "who have honestly attempted to draw humanity as they have known it," including Wells, Galsworthy, Bennett, Frank Norris, Upton Sinclair, Theodore Dreiser, and Sinclair Lewis, he claims that "my desire is to go even deeper than any one of the admired novelists I have selected. I am not content to picture the doings and sayings of typical humanity; I want to know *why* they do and say these things, which is a mistake from the artist's point of view. That is work for the clinic. Unfortunately, these clinical dissections absorb me because they are an aspect of the everlasting search which is my one true object of study" (*Writing,* 143). Beresford was well suited to attempt this deeper probing of psychological reality because of his introspective habit, analytic mind, and extensive study of the new dynamic psychologies of William James, F. W. H. Myers, Henri Bergson, Sigmund Freud, and Carl Jung (discussed in chapter 2). The degree to which this fascination overtook his artistry will be considered in the discussion of individual novels.

In his novels from the mid-1930s on, Beresford moved even further away from a Wellsian version of realism, from depicting "the doings and sayings of typical humanity" to showing the reality of the unseen world, of the ideal and spiritual, a view that he had always experimented with in his short fiction. Nevertheless, even at the end of his writing career he continued to refer to himself as a realistic novelist, though he applied the term in a very broad sense to distinguish those novelists who use their own observation of life from those who rely on imaginary characters derived from fiction ("Memories," 1).

Elements of Beresford's Fiction

Beresford's fascination with psyche and spirit typically caused him to emphasize character over plot in his realistic novels to the mid-1930s. Although accused early in his career by Hugh Walpole of being more interested in ideas than people, Beresford claimed that "characterisation is the basis of all my better books, and I have let it guide me both in the detail and the development of the story" (*Writing,* 53). Critics like Walpole failed to recognize that characterization is inextricably bound up with Beresford's central theme. He states in *Writing Aloud* that "I have but a single theme; the re-education of human beings. That theme has always enthralled me. Has it not been the theme of my own life? Even in such deliberately constructed books as *The House in Demetrius Road, The Jervais Comedy* or *The Prisoners of Hartling,* the essential has been the re-education of the principal character through an emotional experience. All the ramifications of plot have been nothing but a setting for this" (*Writing,* 53).

Beresford's conception of character and the aspects of it emphasized continually evolved. He treats his characters more gently than Wells and never pillories them, as his mentor occasionally does ("Memories," 272). At the outset of his career, influenced by naturalist writers like George Moore and by late-nineteenth-century positivist psychology, Beresford emphasizes the hereditary forces and habits that shape his characters' behavior. However, he seems ahead of his time by also portraying the fluidity and inconsistency of characters, though in *Writing Aloud* he claims that he felt constrained in his impulse to do so by the "General Reading Public's" desire for consistent characters based on recognizable types from other books (*Writing,* 42, 142). He increasingly gives access to characters' dream lives and reveals the influence of subconscious processes on their actions. He typically approaches characterization from a developmental perspective, assigning great importance both to crucial traumatic events in his protagonists' lives and to moments of illumination that may either block or facilitate growth into individuation. This growth is figured most frequently as a quest for truth about identity, vocation, and love.

Beresford drew the majority of his characters from his own life, though he most often altered his sources by fictionalizing only certain aspects of a person, by combining several people into one, or by transforming details of their lives such as their professions. At the beginning of his career he drew most heavily on his life before 1911, when he had established himself as a writer. He continued to rely on his youth as source material in the postwar world partly since, as he claimed in 1930, "I remember very clearly that in the years immediately following the War I often felt that for such non-combatants as myself there was little left to write about."[2] Not until the mid-1930s do his protagonists turn from reexamination of their past to the future (Gerber, 196). Given Beresford's strong autobiographical impulse it is not surprising that the vast majority of his protagonists are male, though he tends either to idealize their experience or to emphasize flaws that he may or may not have possessed. There are only four female exceptions, in *Unity, The Next Generation, Cleo,* and in the novel sketched out in *Writing Aloud.* One of the reasons for this dearth may be that he felt it "presumptuous to attempt the telling of a whole story through the consciousness of a young woman," a worry expressed in *Writing Aloud (Writing,* 48). All of the females suffer from dividedness and seek spiritual unity, which is initiated through their contact with males in these stories. Typically, Beresford's male protagonists are quite introspective, self-doubting, somewhat weak physically and psychically, sensitive and effeminate, but also intellectually courageous and adventurous. Intent on overcoming the dogmas of their upbringing, they value open-mindedness a great deal but find themselves in frequent conflict with those limited by prejudice, and thus they are, or become, outsiders. Like the females, these central characters are also deeply divided, often on more than one level. To their own disadvantage, they tend to rely too heavily on intellect, lack passion, and instead seek maternal comfort. If their sensitive mothers have not died in the early stages of a novel, the mothers often meet this need, but these figures also quietly exert powerful and binding influence over the protagonists. Their jealousy of the protagonists' burgeoning relationships with women temporarily thwarts the protagonists' psychological growth. The young women who are the object of the heroes' quests are typically initially distant and idealized and are frequently of a higher class than the protagonist. As the shy protagonists painfully cross social barriers and make advances toward intimacy, these women are revealed to be more conventional in attitudes towards religion, marriage, and sensuality than the protagonists. Beresford tends to deal with sexuality obliquely. The heroes are generally rewarded in their quest but achieve only partial success in converting their women to their less conventional views. They may be approaching marriage, living together, or be married as the novel closes. Other women in more minor roles make sacrifices, suffer from hysteria, or, less commonly, rebel as protofeminists, are sexually loose, or function as seductresses. Fathers and symbolic representations of them in institutions like the church are depicted as authoritarian and are restraining forces, though they also display the weakness of wishing to avoid unpleasantness. Fathers are often clergymen or failed writers, and they frequently die early in Beresford's novels.

Beresford's thorough immersion in the ideas of psychoanalysis, first fully expressed in *God's Counterpoint* (1918), generally helped to clarify and focus the approach to character that had been shaped by his earlier studies in psychical research. He shifts attention from studies of so-called normal, or typical, characters to abnormal ones, although the normal and abnormal become increasingly difficult to distinguish. As an influence, heredity slips into the background and is replaced by psychosomatic symptoms indicating repression. Moments of illumination are imaged more as the cathartic release of repressed impulses. Though Beresford rarely used symbolism in his early work (Gerber, 197), he begins to employ Freudian symbolism to reveal subconscious attraction and conflict. Finally, psychoanalytic influence emerges in later works as characters either undergo talking cures, initiate self-analysis, or employ literature as therapy.

From the late 1920s on Beresford increasingly saw "humanity as a vast herd of highly trained, performing animals" (*Writing,* 27) and correspondingly more strongly emphasized his theme of reeducating humanity, which occasionally becomes overly didactic. When he does highlight individuals he is less interested in their abnormal psychological complexes, focusing instead on protagonists possessed of supernormal spiritual powers, such as prophecy or faith healing. These protagonists have the capability of influencing the herd if it could recognize the importance of the spiritual rather than materialistic values that they live out without proselytizing.

Beresford's main contribution to characterization in the novel was in his probing of the psyche and spirit of his characters more precisely and less moralistically than many of his predecessors, drawing on insights gained from his intensive reading of psychical research, psychology, psychoanalysis, and mystical writing. He also experimented with expanding conceptions of character by developing buildings as characters, which he does tentatively in *The House in Demetrius Road* (1914) and more fully in *Seven, Bobsworth* (1930), where the technique is used to a satirical end.

With the exception of *Writing Aloud,* Beresford did not, however, experiment with presenting his characters through narrative viewpoint. Most often he employed the omniscient viewpoint with access to the private incidents in the lives of his characters, but he limited this stance by not allowing himself more insight into the thoughts and secret impulses of his characters than he had with people in ordinary life. In *Writing Aloud* he provided a rationale: "This means that I must refrain as far as possible from guessing what their thoughts may be, because if I do guess in the person of the novelist it will be assumed that I always guess right; and in fact I do not" (*Writing,* 179). Less frequently he turned to omniscience limited to one person, a technique particularly useful for probing the psyche of his protagonists, and one he used in his psycho-analytical fiction, notably *God's Counterpoint.* Despite the strong autobiographical vein in Beresford's fiction, he rarely employs first-person narration, claiming, "Technically, I find it an easier method, but it always involves a denial of realism, for which I have an innate distaste, in any record of dialogue. No one could be supposed to remember the *ipsissima verba* of a long conversation; and yet, unless it is reported in *oratiorecta,* all the finer shades of character and individual turns of speech would be lost" (*Writing,* 49). Nevertheless, he did essay the technique in part of *The Hampdenshire Wonder,* in *Housemates, Love's Pilgrim, Love's Illusion,* and in an altered form in *Seven, Bobsworth.* But unlike Dorothy Richardson and May Sinclair, Beresford avoided transcribing his own responses to life in them, though he does admit that the protagonists "must have represented some germ that I found in myself, a germ that I abstracted and cultivated in new surroundings of my own imagination, and nurtured into the passable likeness of a true species" (*Writing,* 47–48).

Although Beresford typically allowed his characters to drive his novels forward and did not give priority to his plots, he did believe that some development and shape involving selection of details were necessary. His plots range from traditional in his detective fiction to episodic in his later fiction, including *Quiet Corner* and *Men in the Same Boat.* Most of his serious realistic fiction comes closer to presenting an arranged and selected slice of life infused with a problem or complication that is not resolved at the denouement. Typically Beresford leaves his protagonists on the threshold of a new experience or task, as he does at the close of the *Jacob Stahl* trilogy. One of Beresford's protagonists, Wilfrid Hornby, muses that story writing is a far less precise art than architecture, and yet numerous critics and novelists, including Mary Agnes Hamilton and Frank Swinnerton, praised Beresford's careful construction and superb craftsmanship (Hamilton, 141; Swinnerton, *Georgian,* 241).

Another element of that craftsmanship was Beresford's style, about which he was quite particular on a minute level. He developed a precise attention to choosing exactly the right word in order to convey the most subtle nuances of realism (Gerber, 247). Nevertheless, he frankly admits in his autobiography that he "was not endowed by nature with either a literary style or a literary method" ("Memories," 338). Early on he realized that he "was incapable of the grand manner" of stylists such as George Meredith and Maurice Hewlett, and he decided instead to model his style after the "easy, go-as-you please manner" of William de Morgan and, in particular, H. G. Wells ("Memories," 181, 272, 338). Beresford's "ambition was to be clear, direct and, if possible, forcible" ("Memories," 272). He found that his style varied considerably, even in his first two works, *Jacob Stahl* and *The Hampdenshire Wonder,* and in retrospect he stated that "if I have a literary style, it is so adaptable to the needs of the kind of story I am writing that it does not possess the representative individuality found not only in the masters but in many living authors ("Memories," 344). This adaptability could be both a strength and a weakness. It demonstrates Beresford's versatility and enabled him to avoid the kind of irritating mannerisms that in his opinion disfigured the later novels of Arnold Bennett ("Memories," 347), but what Beresford refers to here as lack of individuality seems to have been perceived by several critics as lack of color and emotion in his novels (Swinnerton, *Georgian,* 241; "Memories," 341).[3] Beresford used imagery effectively but not strikingly, and his novels were not highly allusive (Gerber, 248).

Essentially, all of the elements of fiction are subsumed to Beresford's main aims—dealing with life honestly, and speaking the truth in the spirit of education and reform ("Memories," 324). The following analysis of Beresford's realistic fiction emphasizes the main developments in both technique and subject matter employed to attain those goals and evaluates his achievement (according to this criteria as well as from an overall aesthetic viewpoint).

Early Psychological Realism

The Early History of Jacob Stahl (1911), Beresford's first published novel, was not the first he had attempted; two previous ones were not published. He began writing this unheroic picaresque adventure of modern life as a means of relaxing in between reviewing for the *Westminster Gazette.* The opening chapter, he claimed, was "a frank imitation of the method of William de Morgan in *Joseph Vance*" ("Memories," 180), but "after a chapter or two, I began to feel myself into the adoption of a representative narrative style, which differed so markedly from that of de Morgan that when the book was finally finished, I had to go back and entirely re-write the original, purely imitative chapter" ("Memories," 181). Despite Beresford's feeling that he had discovered a narrative voice while writing *Jacob Stahl,* it very nearly suffered the fate of the first abortive attempts once it was refused by Methuen on the rather questionable grounds that it was old-fashioned ("Memories," 340). Only his wife's insistence that he send it to another publisher, Sidgwick and Jackson, brought it into the public light, since they decided without hesitation to publish it. According to Beresford he did not receive an advance for it and made only about £60 on the British and American editions over the next few years ("Memories," 340).

This first volume is most appropriately considered along with the two others, *A Candidate for Truth* (1912) and *The Invisible Event* (1915), comprising the *Jacob Stahl* trilogy. Together they confirm that Beresford did not adhere slavishly to his chosen mentors but that he deepened realism in the manner of Wells and Bennett by attending to unconscious motivation and the spiritual quest. These "semiautobiographical" novels ("Memories," 6) depict the circuitous evolution of the introspective protagonist, Jacob, into awareness and to the profession of novelist. We can also identify a certain evolution in Beresford's technique of revealing the psychology of his characters. Beresford conveys more of their subconscious desires, ambitions, and conflicts over the course of the three novels. He does so increasingly by making readers privy to characters' unconscious reveries, rather than spelling out from an objective viewpoint their logical trains of thought. In this respect, his technique is analogous to the stream-of-consciousness method. His introduction of this technique corresponds with his exposure to psychoanalytic thought.[4]

In the first volume, *The Early History of Jacob Stahl,* Beresford traces the primary forces that shape Jacob's character: his growth into manhood, the breaking up of the original mold, his dissipation, the process of his intellectual discovery, and his marriage to and separation from the egotistical Lola Wilmot. The novel closes on an optimistic note, with Jacob, having had a vision of eternal values, now fully prepared to enter the next stage of his life.

Beresford's psychological orientation is suggested at the outset of the novel, since he focuses on the temperament and habits of Jacob's mother and his nursemaid Nancy; these aspects of personality help explain why the first of the incidents has profound emotional consequences for Jacob. His mother's habit of procrastination, indirectly, and Nancy's negligence, directly, result in Jacob's fall from a pram at seven months. He becomes permanently lame. Beresford also stresses heredity; Jacob inherits his Irish mother's imagination and laziness as well as his father's conflicting tendencies. Nevertheless, Beresford does not neglect the importance of Jacob's early environment. Since his father is authoritarian, distant, and possessed of "unsteady desires" (unbeknownst to Jacob's mother, his father is unfaithful to her), the young Jacob seeks comfort in his mother, thus initiating a pattern in his relations with other women. By skipping over external events of Jacob's life in order to bring into bold relief the second traumatic event of Jacob's youth, Beresford confirms his primary interest in the psychology of his protagonist. When Jacob is 14, his mother dies from typhoid. Though initially Jacob "unconsciously" adopts the adults' attitude of resignation, his first recorded dream represents the reality for him: "But in the night he dreamed of his mother, and when he awoke the bitter tears, the desperate longing, the agony of desire for her presence, were all intensely real; and the reality stayed with him" (*Jacob,* 32). Jacob's practical, confident Aunt Hester then takes up where his mother left off.

Beresford also shows the role that Jacob's love and sexual relationships play in shaping him. His attraction to the opposite sex begins in adolescence at a "moment of tensity," "subconsciously noted" by Jacob as he gazes at a 14-year-old girl (*Jacob,* 52). She turns out to be Madeline Felmersdale, the daughter of an aristocrat, and thus far above him in class. There is the oblique suggestion that Jacob eventually makes love to her (*Jacob,* 126–27), only to discover that she is not as innocent as she has appeared to him, having had an earlier physical relationship (*Jacob,* 115). In renouncing her, Jacob also rejects the upper-class standards that she represents (*Jacob,* 159) and is provoked into deciding to explore life (*Jacob,* 125). Several years later, after a night of debauchery in London, Jacob has a blatantly sexual dream (*Jacob,* 195). Beresford also implies that Jacob's Aunt Hester is more like a lover than a substitute mother to Jacob, since she feels superseded by Madeline. The aunt feels "jilted" and her life is shortened because of bitterness and grief when he leaves her for London (*Jacob,* 228).

Occasionally, Jacob's thoughts are shown to have emerged from his subconscious (*Jacob,* 124, 241, 359), and Beresford confirms the consequence that characters are "disgustingly inconsistent" in real life. At several points, Beresford suggests why Jacob would be of interest to an anonymous psychologist (*Jacob,* 215, 256). In his attitude toward Jacob's stressed condition following the deterioration of his marriage, Beresford sides with this hypothetical psychologist—viewing Jacob as a pathological case—over the philosopher of human nature, who would find Jacob culpable on a priori grounds (*Jacob,* 349). Beresford claims that "Jacob must not be judged by the philosopher's index, his case was pathological. He had come to believe in his own incapacity, and, mentally, wrote the story of his failure" (*Jacob,* 358). This view is reinforced by the glimpse Beresford affords us into the darker side of Jacob as he contemplates suicide (*Jacob,* 358) before he takes hold of his life and begins anew.

The sequel, *A Candidate for Truth,* develops the spiritual dimension of the protagonist. Jacob becomes attracted to the ideal of self-sacrifice under the influence of the charismatic preacher and social worker Cecil Barker. A "superman," completely devoted to self-denial, Barker takes on the case of Jacob's soul and provides him with a job as his personal secretary until he realizes that Jacob takes the approach of a dilettante to his spiritual growth (*Candidate,* 128). While working for Barker, Jacob finishes his first novel, in the realistic genre. Once again, dreams convey Jacob's motivation or longings. One that "possesses" him while alone in a restaurant suggests the burgeoning artist's bisexual nature and may well draw on Nietzsche's conception of the artist, since Nietzsche is mentioned in another context in the novel (*Candidate,* 356): "Within him was conceived the story of a man who longed passionately for love, sympathy, and admiration, but who was dumb to express his longing; who by some twist of fate was unable to attract love or admiration from either man or woman. The secret lay in the fact that the man had a feminine soul imprisoned in his masculine body, a soul which expressed itself in the manner of a woman" (*Candidate,* 101–2). Following his break from Barker, Jacob enters the advertising business, is unsuccessfully pursued by a sexually repressed widow, and falls in love with Betty Gale, the woman who runs the boardinghouse at which he lives. At this stage Jacob finally rejects Barker's ideal of self-sacrifice and renunciation (*Candidate,* 357), courting Betty even though he has not been able to obtain a divorce from his estranged wife. All of the issues touched on are treated realistically, including love. We are told, for example, that initially Betty "was not desperately in love with Jacob" (*Candidate,* 359). By the close of the novel, they express their passion openly in a park and declare their independence as lovers from the world's opinion (*Candidate,* 402).

However, not until the third volume, *The Invisible Event,* do they actually put that declaration into practice by living together. This decision is reached only after a painful struggle on Betty's part to defy her upbringing as a clergyman's daughter. Recalling that psychoanalysis confirmed for Beresford the necessity of a freer morality ("Psychoanalysis," 426), we can speculate that Beresford's exposure to the new science while working on *The Invisible Event* was at least one factor in enabling him to defy still-current moral convention.[5] Several subtle allusions to repression and neuroses strongly suggest that Beresford had by this time begun to assimilate some ideas of the "new" psychology. While in Cornwall awaiting Betty's decision, Jacob gives vent to his suppressed Celtic strain, which urges him to seek out places of wild and isolated natural beauty, though he fears his response as "something to be ashamed of, something that must be repressed" (*Invisible,* 127). After Betty's arrival, Jacob becomes aware of her tendency to repress her qualms about their present relationship: "He had a queer picture in his mind of all those inhibited thoughts being thrust down and growing malignantly under the surface" (*Invisible,* 188).

In this third volume Jacob's reveries continue to be explored more fully and his increasing awareness is reflected through the image of waves succeeding and "overleaping" one another (*Invisible,* 241). On one occasion, as he sits and watches these waves, "his thought began to emerge in an effortless, unconscious process—thought that seemed to have a greater intensity and reality than life itself" (*Invisible,* 241). More than once he realizes that he has undergone such immense inner change that his younger self is like a completely different person who has died and been replaced (*Invisible,* 123–24, 241). This new awareness of his shifting and even disjunctive self emerges in the next novel that he conceives. To Betty he confides, "It's slightly fantastic . . . an allegory of sorts, I suppose—and yet the fundamental idea comes out of my own experience. The theory is of a man who reacts so tremendously to his circumstances that he is a different person altogether in different conditions. It's an enlargement of the Jekyll and Hyde business in one way, but treated realistically, you know. There would not be any romantic potions or spells" (*Invisible,* 275). The idea for this novel, "The Creature of Circumstance," is of course only a slight exaggeration of the history of the development of Jacob's fluid personality. In an ironic twist, after his divorce, Jacob must persuade Betty to marry for the sake of their first child. At the close of *The Invisible Event,* however, he continues to refuse to accept dogmas, instead renewing his search for that permanent truth that "keeps his spirit young" (*Invisible,* 388). He upholds the principle of the open mind so that he will not "fall into the habit of fixed opinions," claims Beresford, with a William Jamesian emphasis on habit.[6]

While Beresford's use of the new psychology is neither extensive nor revolutionary in the trilogy, its influence does help to set the tone of the work by providing language and concepts, and generally by giving scope to his own psychological impulse. The trilogy reveals that subtle incorporation of psychological ideas can convincingly increase the psychological complexity of character. Beresford's assimilation of these ideas goes a long way toward explaining why the trilogy was recognized as a psychological masterpiece. Perhaps the highest praise came from Gerald Gould:

> But the writer of our generation who has carried the biographical method at once to its logical extreme and its aesthetic height is, beyond doubt, Mr. J. D. Beresford. In the Jacob Stahl trilogy he has traced a full life, not adventurous in the obvious sense, not startling, but rich with varieties of intellectual and emotional experience; he has never come near a formula; he has blended creation with recollection; and in consequence has produced what will live, not as a picture of the times (which it never pretended to be), but as an almost unique revelation of one adventuring soul. (Gould, 51)

After rereading the work in his old age while working on his autobiography, Beresford himself was less complimentary, claiming that it lacked balance and that what once had seemed daring, now seemed a "model of circumspection" ("Memories," 341).

Beresford exercised more control over the selection of details in *The House in Demetrius Road* (1914), despite its similarly (but even more flagrantly) autobiographical genesis ("Memories," 272).[7] The story is based on Beresford's friendship with a young Scotsman, who has political aspirations and an alcohol problem, R. J. Bryce, whom Beresford lived with briefly in late 1907. Bryce had invited Beresford to collaborate with him on a book on socialism. Along with Bryce's sister-in-law, Miss Angus, Beresford administered a treatment to Bryce that he eventually resented so much that he expelled Beresford from the house.

The novel is, in Beresford's words, "a romanticized version" ("Memories," 177), mainly, it would seem, because of the love interest that he added between the fictionalized version of himself, Martin Bond, and Bryce's sister-in-law, called Margaret Hamilton. As well, Beresford attempted (not entirely successfully) to create a character out of the house in which the events occur, Garroch, with its atmosphere of gloom and restrictiveness. In the novel Bond's poor impression of his prospective employer, named Robin Greg, almost causes him to turn down the job of helping Greg write a book on socialism, but his attraction to Greg's sister-in-law, Margaret, and his revulsion at Greg's treatment of her persuade him to accept. Initially he does not understand the "double personality" of the house until he discovers Greg drunk on the stairs one night and then realizes the source of the tension there. Bond helps Margaret persuade Greg to take a cure for his alcoholism, at the end of which Greg announces his engagement to Margaret. Crestfallen but not defeated, Bond increases his intimacy with Margaret, who is determined to sacrifice herself to keep Robin from destroying himself. However, once the perceptive Greg realizes the nature of the relationship between Bond and Margaret he dismisses Bond and tells him to take her along. By this time Greg is back on the bottle, and the novel closes unsentimentally. Frank Swinnerton found this fiction, whose sales were destroyed by the outbreak of war, to be Beresford's "most vigorous novel" of the period (Swinnerton, *Autobiography*, 292), and Gerber praised its "excellent construction" (Gerber, 80). The novel is typical in its opposition to the slavery of habit, its idealized treatment of the woman figure, and its questioning of the ideal of self-sacrifice.

The House in Demetrius Road also anticipates an important theme in Beresford's canon in its discussion of socialism, a discussion made more central in *The Mountains of the Moon* (1915).[8] This novel originated as a four-act play written in collaboration with Beresford's best friend, Arthur Harvey James. Harvey James supplied the scenario, and Beresford wrote out the dialogue, probably in the summer of 1907. It was never professionally staged but was put on by Beerbohm Tree's Dramatic School shortly before Harvey James was killed in 1917 in the war. Beresford transformed it into a novel in 1915, hoping that it would be a financial success in the United States, but it was not ("Memories," 163). Dedicated to Captain Arthur Harvey James, the novel features the practical idealist Arthur Grey, author of "The Mountains of the Moon: An Essay in Sociology," who believes in the need for every man to earn his own living and who opposes the aristocratic idea, whether based on inheritance or money. He thus struggles with his conscience about revealing his identity as the true heir to the Downham title while visiting the family for the purposes of his sociological research. Eventually he does accept because of a love interest in Tempe, the daughter of the Downhams, and because of a desire to use his wealth to finance an educational project, the latter reason a characteristic ambition in Beresford's novels. This novel is also the first of several that deals with the issue of inheritance, revealing both the desires and conflicts that arise in people because of it. Through Grey Beresford articulates his beliefs in a collective purpose and the possibilities for humanity's development (*Mountains*, 60).

In *These Lynnekers* (1916) Beresford turned to the autobiographical family novel, with some critical success.[9] According to Annie Russell Marble, "As a group picture, *The* [sic] *Lynnekers* excels in distinctness of individuals."[10] It has a special interest from a biographer's viewpoint because Beresford claims that he came nearest here to a description of the Beresford family, although, he adds, "the central character is far from being autobiographical" ("Memories," 14).

The novel traces the development of Dickie, a younger Lynneker son, who is determined to break through his family's "web" of religious orthodoxy and tradition threatening to crystallize him before his growth is complete. Dickie's self-education includes study of the intricacies of higher mathematics, Samuel Butler's *Erewhon,* and Herbert Spencer's *Principles of Ethics.* In striving to obtain knowledge necessary to refute this orthodoxy, Dickie comes to inhibit thoughts about sexuality "almost automatically." Like other Beresford heroes, Dickie has an overly close relationship with his mother, resembling that of a lover's relationship, but he does not find release for his repressed thoughts until they are triggered by the lewd remarks of novelist A. B. Ellis (based on H. G. Wells), as Dickie and Ellis observe the beautiful Sibyl Groome.[11] Not surprisingly, Sibyl becomes the object of Dickie's desire (*Lynnekers,* 421). Nor is Dickie's spiritual nature neglected by Beresford. Dickie occasionally experiences flashes of vision. On one such occasion, he reaches his personal solution that no stage in his life or in the progress of humanity "must be judged as an absolute. . . . Behind all progress and all life was this permanent spirit of endurance, of resistance, of power: endurance to maintain the truth of independence to all material pains and changes; resistance to demonstrate the transience of the image; power to prove that while the symbol may be changed, the spirit shall endure inalterable to find ever new forms of expression" (*Lynnekers,* 447–48). This novel subtly conveys considerable psychological insight, especially in its use of the idea of sublimation.

Beresford's insights are applied to a larger canvas in *Housemates* (1917), in which a wider variety of individuals and classes is represented.[12] Even so, compared to *These Lynnekers, Housemates* is a much bolder and more intimate account of the mental odyssey of the protagonist, facilitated by its first-person viewpoint. The theme of Wilfrid Hornby's growth into independent thinking is quickly made explicit using the metaphor of a shell hatching the chick. Wilfrid confides that "the history of my hatching, so far as I can trace it, is written in my consciousness. I admit that I am quite unable to explain the impulse to germination" (*Housemates,* 4).

Indulged and protected by his parents and governess in his youth, Wilfrid emerges from his shell only after he breaks his engagement to a woman who typifies the conventional world and becomes otherwise engaged in life at the slightly disreputable boardinghouse where he begins his practice of architecture. The plot coheres around several incidents taking place at the boardinghouse that force Wilfrid to overcome his dividedness and fear of humanity and to assert his independence. His success is measured by his marriage to the woman who is appropriate for him.

In such a bildungsroman, the protagonist's conception of his "self" is important and revealing. Wilfrid believes his to be fragile, insubstantial, and deeply divided, and Beresford shows that it became so following his suppression of grief at his father's death when Wilfrid was 17. At this time, as Wilfrid details to the doctor the events leading up to his father's death, "below all the ebullition of my excited chatter, another personality, reserved and timid, held itself aloof, occupied with some general impression of things that had little relevance to all this apparent preoccupation with the new experience I was suffering. When I look back now I see that rather fair-haired callow youth of seventeen from outside. Memory recalls a picture of him and the sound of his voice, but nothing of what he felt" (*Housemates*, 26). Wilfrid does not recognize his duality, emanating from this divorce from emotion, until a cathartic moment at the boardinghouse. One Saturday night, the landlord attempts to evict one of the boarders, Rose Whiting, for her activities as a prostitute. She strips off her clothes while screaming that the landlord can turn her out naked. Though a relatively weak and fragile creature, in "the recklessness of her passion" she dominates and intimidates the brute opposing her. Wilfrid admires her for this passion and because "she was at that moment, a single and powerful personality" (*Housemates*, 133). The vision of Rose inspires the following revelation in Wilfrid: "I struggled then as if I were fighting for the control of my reason. I was very much aware of my duality; and presently, as I began more successfully to defend myself against the invasion of the single image which had nearly obsessed me, my visions took another shape. I remembered the night of my father's death and my walk home with the little deformed doctor through the moonlight; and more particularly I recalled the clearness of my recognition that there were two Wilfrid Hornbys" (*Housemates*, 142). His recognition releases him to begin to overcome the division, and he admits to himself that he is in love with another boarder, Judith.

As Wilfrid emerges into awareness, Beresford makes the reader privy, far more frequently than was the case in *These Lynnekers,* to his protagonist's subconscious motivations and feelings. In one instance, Wilfrid confronts the man who has swept away the fiancée for whom his attraction was waning anyway: " 'You infernal ass!' was the unspoken comment of my bubbling subconsciousness" (*Housemates*, 123).

The protagonist's developing sexuality is also more candidly conveyed than in *These Lynnekers*. Beresford links the religious emotions and conversion experienced by Wilfrid at puberty with his sexual awakening: "But the true characteristic of my conversion was associated with those sexual yearnings which had just begun to find queer forms of expression" (*Housemates*, 15). As a young man, Wilfrid has sexual relations with a loose woman, Nellie Roberts, before becoming engaged to his cousin Gladys, who does not attract him physically at all (*Housemates*, 52, 77).

Once again, Beresford demonstrates his sensitivity to the role that the mother-son relationship plays in his protagonist's relations with women as an adult. Following his engagement at 27, Wilfrid finds it inconceivable that he would be separated from his mother and "wonder[s] whether she [his mother] was not divided between her love for me . . . and something that can only be called jealousy" (*Housemates*, 77–78). Beresford very astutely implies the further consequences of this overdependence. While arguing with the admittedly shrill "feminist" Mrs. Hargreave, Wilfrid realizes that "in my experience the bullies had all been women. Gladys had nagged me; my aunt had kept Uncle David in subjection by the constant threat of her ill-health; Miss Whiting had delighted in her power to intimidate Pferdminger [the landlord] and myself; and this woman now cross-examining me was the very type of an autocrat" (*Housemates*, 159).

Beresford also explores more fully here than in *These Lynnekers* the secular soul, the mystical nature of his protagonist. Wilfrid refers to "these transitory flashes of ecstasy," experienced from his youth on, as the state of "being exalté" (*Housemates*, 7, 8). They involve his most intimate self and have been kept secret, even from his mother (*Housemates*, 8). His "first great experience" concerns one that significantly occurs as he is reunited with his parents upon returning from a traumatic episode of being bullied at boarding school. He catches his first glimpse of his home:

> And the sight of that rich colour, outlining the beauty of form that was so sharply picked out by the direct light of the high sun, stirred me for a moment to a higher consciousness of being. I hovered for an instant, with a keen sense of expectation, on the edge of some amazing adventure. It was as if I had discovered some pin-prick in the world of my reality, a tiny hole that let in the dazzling light of a richer, infinitely more beauti-

ful world beyond. It seemed to me that if I could but hold myself intensely still, I might peep through the curtain of appearances and catch one glimpse of something indefinable that was the fountain of all ecstasy. (*Housemates,* 6)

In these moments, so strikingly similar to the ones Virginia Woolf would later evoke in her fiction, Wilfrid surmounts feelings of anxiety and dividedness. Unlike in *These Lynnekers,* Beresford touches on the supernatural in this novel, although he referred to it as "ultra-realism" (*Writing,* 49). The night that Rose Whiting is murdered at the boardinghouse, Wilfrid is in a "condition of nervous exhaustion which so often gives us the power to transcend our physical limitations" (*Housemates,* 293). Her cry may have reached his subconscious or his response may be attributable to "a supernatural agent" (*Housemates,* 253, 305). Though never conclusively determined, it is appropriate that Wilfrid should be linked psychically to Rose, since her earlier impassioned action opened his consciousness to his dividedness.

Finally, mental illness lurks in the shadows of this novel. Aside from his nervous exhaustion, Wilfrid experiences paranoia and becomes obsessed with the idea that Helen, Judith's close female friend, is a female devil, because of her attempts to thwart the advances Wilfrid makes toward Judith. Wilfrid admits that his "mental processes were all a trifle abnormal about that time" (*Housemates,* 172), but Helen does eventually betray her hysterically jealous response by offering herself sexually to Wilfrid in an attempt to divert his attention from Judith (*Housemates,* 248). In the epilogue, Wilfrid labels her a monomaniac and claims that, subsequent to the period covered in the novel, she had a serious nervous breakdown (*Housemates,* 349). He himself suffered shell shock. Beresford's astute suggestion that through writing Wilfrid effected his own therapy and cure seems very forward-looking. Wilfrid confesses that "when I began this book in January, I did it in order to forget. I was in danger of becoming insane then and I found relief by plunging myself back into the past" (*Housemates,* 347).

Thus, in its representation of the struggle to overcome dividedness and achieve individuation, and its concern with sexuality, the mystical, and mental illness, *Housemates* contains many of the elements, some in embryo, that were to preoccupy Beresford in his future writing. Like several other of Beresford's novels, notably *The Hampdenshire Wonder,* *Housemates* is also a type of compensation fantasy since, in Beresford's words, Wilfrid Hornby "had the abilities as an architect that I lacked and a greater intensity of purpose" ("Memories," 96).

Chapter Five

Psychoanalytic and Mystical Novels: 1918–1929

Psychoanalytic Novels

In contrast to *Housemates* (1917), Beresford's next novel, *God's Counterpoint* (1918), stands out in his canon, for several reasons.[1] According to Beresford himself, it was the first English novel that was thoroughly informed by Freudian psychoanalytic ideas ("Déclin," 259).[2] It was also the only one of his novels that he *acknowledged* to have been thoroughly influenced by psychoanalysis ("Déclin," 259). Finally, it suffers from clinical obtrusiveness more than any other of Beresford's novels. Nevertheless, as a pioneering work, its flaws are instructive. They raise the question of whether reliance on one psychological source primarily, and in particular the Freudian source, weakens the artistic merit of the novel, making it too much of a temptation to use the source overly systematically and blatantly.

As in earlier works, the novel operates from a developmental perspective, but explanations of the protagonist's adult behavior give incidents from childhood much greater weight. The father is viewed as more of a repressive force than in previous novels, and the consequences for the protagonist's psyche are explored more fully. Beresford's knowledge of psychosomatic illness and dreams also makes his characterization more vivid. In keeping with the close association in Beresford's mind between psychical research and psychology, he frames his protagonist's release from repression as a moment of illumination. Nevertheless, as Beresford himself acknowledged, the protagonist's transformation would not be as believable or perhaps even understandable without some knowledge of Freudian dynamics of repression. As in *Housemates,* the protagonist's "cure" involves talking, and literature is viewed as therapeutic.

As the narrator claims in the opening apology, *God's Counterpoint* traces the atypical conditions that lead to the enlightenment of Philip Maning, the protagonist (*God's,* 9). In this novel Beresford emphasizes more of the sexual and psychological aspects of enlightenment than the intellectual, which had been stressed in both *Jacob Stahl* and *Housemates*. Philip's particularly punitive father is shown to be the dominant influence in his early years. He internalizes his father's repressive "Don'ts" (*God's*, 13), and the unstated feelings of insecurity and incompetence presumably aroused by his father's characteristic attitude are crystallized during an episode when Philip is 14. On his way to the train station, anticipating a feeling of grandeur when he will observe leisurely the harried workers on the opposite platform, Philip passes through a tunnel: "And then without the least warning, he suffered a sensation that strongly reversed his anticipation of glory. He became suddenly aware of himself as of something small and negligible, a creature of ignoble thoughts and ambitions. And the self that watched had no relief of conscious superiority" (*God's*, 19–20). Though in itself a trivial incident, the event and the "beastly, mean feeling" that Philip associates with it develop into a complex through repetition.

The second incident highlighted by Beresford as illustrative of Philip's restrictive upbringing occurs when he is 17. He and a friend, Georgie Wood, hear feminine cries from a woods as they pass and on further investigation happen on a couple making love. The incident seems "beastly" to both of them (*God's*, 24). Georgie later throws off his shame and jokes about the scene; "[b]ut Philip thrust his horror from him, deep down into the unknown spaces of his subconsciousness; whither it sometimes emerged at night, in dreams that shook him with visions of some vague and awful threat; so that once he cried out in his sleep, and woke to hear his own voice repeating 'No; No. Please. *Please* don't.' He got out of bed, then, and prayed desperately. What terrified him was not the note of fear but the undertone of repressed longing" (*God's*, 24–25). Henceforth, beastliness and sexuality are closely associated in Philip's mind (*God's*, 33). These sensations are linked to literature, which has already been made an area of prohibition by Philip's father.[3] Mr. Maning's opinion about the Oscar Wilde scandal, that hanging is too good for Wilde, fills Philip's mind with the "horror of unimaginable evil" and gives him a feeling of being small and helpless, similar to that experienced when in the tunnel (*God's*, 34). Nevertheless, Philip determines to embark on a literary career by working for a publisher and must deceive his father by pretending indifference in order to do so. His choice implies his subconscious attraction to the forbidden area.

Philip's father exerts less overt control on his son from this point on and dies just after Philip, at 27, becomes engaged. However, Philip encounters several father figures, who clearly demonstrate that Philip's feelings of inferiority and fear of emotions relating to sexuality persist. Their actions also inadvertently exacerbate these feelings. Whenever Philip innocently displays these emotions, he is either misunderstood and chastised by these figures or there is the threat that he will be. One of the father figures, the romance novelist Edgar Norman, whom Philip idolizes, chastises him for what Norman considers to be Philip's attempt to pick up a woman by gazing at her. For Philip, though, this is a moment of heightened illumination (*God's,* 56). The woman, Evelyn, reappears five years later, hired on at the publishing firm where Philip works. Soon after Philip's feelings for her are aroused, he has what he refers to as an abasement experience on the way to work, similar to the one that occurred in the tunnel (*God's,* 70). Some days later, his employer, another father figure, makes advances toward Evelyn. Philip openly reprimands him at the risk of being fired and then succumbs to his own passion for her by kissing her. His natural response is marred, this time by the threat of punishment and being charged with hypocrisy by his employer (*God's,* 114). Beresford astutely observes that "in that instant of fear, all the mischief of Philip's life-long repression had been cruelly aggravated" (*God's,* 115). He responds consciously by attempting to keep Evelyn remote and ideal, but Beresford employs dreams to convey Philip's inner state of tormented desire. In one dream Evelyn transforms into a "great white ewe that wore a horrible aspect of lascivious humanity" (*God's,* 133). Another suggests that Philip associates sexuality with shame and public exposure (*God's,* 180).

Philip eventually marries Evelyn, though only after he obtains the assurance from her that they will abstain from carnal relations. Subsequently aroused by Evelyn's French cousin Hélène, whom he refers to as a "serpent" in a slip of the tongue (*God's,* 200), Philip relaxes his puritanical conviction briefly on his honeymoon. Evelyn becomes pregnant and bears a child. Thereafter, he is increasingly determined to preserve Evelyn as "an unattainable, intangible ideal" (*God's,* 236). Beresford intimates the psychic toll that this aim is taking on Philip through dreams and by suggesting that his illnesses are psychosomatic. He suffers neuralgia and insomnia and feels divided (*God's,* 273). His mental state is likened to a prison (*God's,* 258, 312). Evelyn, for her part, experiences hysteria until she sublimates her desires into creative writing (*God's,* 260). For several years their relationship remains blocked, until Hélène makes a visit.

About the time of Hélène's arrival, Philip finds a poetic correlative for his tunnel experience in Francis Thompson's "Hound of Heaven" (*God's,* 312), the first of subconscious changes in him. He then has what turns out to be a prophetic dream. Though outwardly Philip detests Hélène, her arrival provokes in him a "new kind of dream" in which he embraces her, before she transforms into Evelyn and then his mother (*God's,* 296).[4] Meanwhile, Evelyn finally decides to leave Philip, telling him that she is doing so because his mind is "poisoned and unhealthy" (*God's,* 304). Philip's long-felt fear of feeling abasement now finds its fulfillment in reality (*God's,* 312). The feeling leaves him open to seduction by Hélène, who readily takes the opportunity, and they leave the Maning home together (*God's,* 321). Part of Philip's attraction to her is that he is able to confess his tortured emotions to this collaborator in evil (*God's,* 317). She also educates him so that he begins to participate in the adventures of life (*God's,* 330).

As evidence of Beresford's idealism, he frames Philip's return to mental health as an integrating revelation. Following a break with Hélène, Philip experiences a moment of vision about humanity in which "[a]ll apparent discords and ugliness were, it seemed to him, but accentuations of the eternal rhythm; the necessary beat of an undertone, God's counterpoint" (*God's,* 331). Returning to Evelyn, he once again makes a confession, this time of his madness and moral suicide in departing with Hélène (*God's,* 376–77).

Several flaws weaken the effect of this novel. Philip's exposition of what he refers to as his pathology in his childhood perhaps resembles too closely a case study. Also, despite Beresford's cloaking of Philip's transfiguration as a moment of spiritual insight, the believability of this sudden change relies too heavily on knowledge of the Freudian principle of the cathartic release of repression. However, these flaws in themselves do not constitute the main problem of this novel. Nor does the problem arise, as Reinald Hoops claims, because the novel deals with an unusual individual of interest only to the psychologist (Hoops, 99). Rather, in his enthusiasm for applying Freudian insights and scientific objectivity, Beresford does not permit the reader to get close enough to the protagonist, to feel either his agony or his joy. This problem is compounded by the fact that the priggish, fastidious Philip is not a particularly likeable character to begin with.

Nevertheless, not all critics found it to resemble a case study too closely. Edward Shanks, for example, stated, "No doubt Mr. Beresford has chosen the scenes and episodes best fitted to his purpose: the book could not otherwise have been the deep, disturbing, and engrossing study of personality which in fact it is."[5] Perhaps equally important to Beresford was the fact that the novel sold better than any earlier one of his, though "only a modest 6,000 copies or so in the original edition," according to Beresford. These sales were particularly encouraging as the novel had been rejected by Beresford's publisher, Cassell's, on moral grounds and had been taken up by Gerald O'Donovan at Collins "with the warning that he did not expect it to sell" ("Memories," 204).

Though a courageous experiment in subject matter, Beresford, in my opinion, is much better off when he absorbs the Freudian material more fully, allowing psychological conflicts and resolution to arise naturally out of dramatic incident, and refraining from providing explanation of them. His work is more engaging when he draws eclectically and subtly on a variety of intellectual and psychological sources.

In *An Imperfect Mother* (1920), Beresford more nearly achieves integration of his Freudian materials into an aesthetic whole, though the total effect is marred by a "Retrospect" that unnecessarily underlines the psychogenesis of the protagonist's "slight departure from the normal" (*Imperfect,* 307).[6] The main focus of the novel is the resolution in adulthood of the conflict arising from an overly close bond between mother and son, which presumably originated in an oedipal complex (though this aspect of the relationship is left vague). Despite that bond, the son, Stephen, is not as fastidious as Philip Maning, and his sexual impulses receive more attention. Dreams and Freudian symbolism convey the nature of his desire and the dynamics of Stephen's relationships with women. Aside from this Freudian influence, Beresford's work also betrays the influence of Adler's inferiority complex in its portrayal of the father. The concepts and language of the "new" psychologies reinforce the intensity of characters' moods. Resolution of the conflict hinges on misinterpretation of a hysterical response.

The vicissitudes in the relationship between Stephen, the eldest son, and his mother, Cecilia, are, on the whole, traced convincingly. Unfulfilled in her marriage, the selfish, passionate Cecilia unfairly leans on Stephen for intimacy and love until she realizes that he has become self-sufficient, at which point she deserts the family. She embarks on a career as a London actress, taking her younger lover, a church organist, with her. Stephen's father is devastated by his wife's desertion; he regresses, goes insane, and dies of "sheer inanition" (*Imperfect,* 115). Stephen's response to her decision, however, is ambivalent. Though he has an "obsession" for his mother, and their arguments over her leaving are described as "lover's quarrels," he feels some freedom at the thought of losing his mother (*Imperfect,* 65, 67, 68). This feeling is heightened because Stephen has recently experienced his first infatuation with a girl, Margaret Weatherly, the 14-year-old daughter of the schoolmaster (*Imperfect,* 12). Both Margaret and his mother are subsequently unattainable, and Stephen's desires for them mingle in his dreams (*Imperfect,* 132).

Left to his own devices, Stephen pursues a career in building, under the guidance of his employer, Dickinson, another father figure (*Imperfect,* 129). Following several years of separation from his mother and two sexual adventures, aborted because of thoughts of her at critical moments (*Imperfect,* 138, 150, 185), Stephen, lonely and desirous of a wife, seeks out his mother. As he awaits her at a stage door, he catches his second glimpse of Margaret, the girl who had entranced him many years before. We are told that "she had appeared, leaping suddenly out of the even background of his life, at two critical moments of spiritual disturbance arising from his relations with his mother" (*Imperfect,* 198). Perhaps too conveniently, it turns out that Stephen has plenty of opportunity to meet Margaret, since she travels in the same social circles as his mother. However, Stephen realizes that if he falls in love with her, he will risk destruction, for several reasons: Margaret is far above him in social standing, and therefore unattainable; love for her would preclude faithfulness to his mother (*Imperfect,* 198); and, most fundamentally, he fears that his response to Margaret's ideal beauty will be obsessive. "The passion would grow until it dominated him; until his sanity, his regard for all the reasonable joys of life, was drowned in one overwhelming lust for possession" (*Imperfect,* 203).

The dynamics of the scene in which Margaret and Stephen are drawn together is subtly reinforced with Freudian imagery. At the request of his six-year-old half-brother, Chris, Stephen self-consciously displays his building prowess by erecting a tower out of blocks. In a bid to capture Chris, her defiant little son, Cecilia inadvertently knocks over the tower. Cecilia puts the boy to bed while Stephen reconstructs the tower. Margaret admires his talent, stating, "You really do it awfully well," and expresses curiosity about visiting his "real building" (*Imperfect,* 216). She eventually does so, and Stephen takes her up in the crane bucket, where she realizes that Stephen is different from the other men with whom she has been flirting (*Imperfect,* 233). The symbolism of the mother, faced with a rival, attempting to castrate the son before he succeeds in captivating his lover through phallic prowess, would not likely be lost on, and might even seem obvious to, modern readers inured to Freud. Consider-

ing, however, that not one of the 50 to 60 reviewers of Beresford's previous novel, *God's Counterpoint,* even recognized that the novel was psycho-
analytically influenced, it is probable that the imagery would have
appeared fresh to contemporary audiences ("Déclin," 261).

In spite of Stephen's initial success, Cecilia is not yet willing to sur-
render to her rival, especially when Stephen reveals to her that the day
she sensed he was no longer dependent on her was the exact day Margaret had smiled at him while at school (*Imperfect,* 242). At Stephen's
first setback with Margaret, he comes in despair to Cecilia. He confesses
that he has seen Margaret with another man and that she laughed cruelly at him, reminding him of his mother's laugh in response to
Stephen's begging her not to leave with the organist (*Imperfect,* 280–
81). His remark that he felt like banging his head against the wall trig-
gers Cecilia's memory of an incident from his childhood when she
laughed at him and he actually did bang his head. This revelation would
have been more convincing to the reader had incidents developing
Stephen's childhood relationship with his mother initially been portrayed by Beresford. Nevertheless, since Cecilia realizes that her hysterical laugh had been forced from her by her love for Stephen and that
Margaret's must have been as well, she has the balance of power in her
hands (*Imperfect,* 281). Instead of concealing this insight from Stephen
and attempting to keep him for herself, she decides to make him a present of his desire by revealing that both hers and Margaret's laughter
was hysterical and defended against feelings of dividedness (*Imperfect,*
287). Beresford's idealism surfaces briefly as he has Cecilia impute her
action to the "motive of self-renunciation" (*Imperfect,* 287). Stephen pursues Margaret with renewed vigor and marries her, despite opposition
from her father.

Apparently aiming at objectivity, Beresford claims that his "excres-
cent" retrospect "may be taken as a kind of appendix, or lengthy foot-
note, designed to give a detached historical summary of certain subsequent events" (*Imperfect,* 307). Unfortunately, in keeping with the
academic apparatus to which it is compared, the retrospect has the effect
of suggesting to the reader that the previous narrative should be viewed
as a scientific case study. Virginia Woolf may very well have taken her
cue from it when she claimed, in her review of the novel, that, "in the
ardours of discovery [of the new psychology], Mr. Beresford has unduly
stinted his people of flesh and blood. In becoming cases they have ceased
to be individuals."[7] Another perceptive critic, Katherine Mansfield, perhaps taking *her* cue from Woolf's review, commented on the "essential

emptiness" of the book, by which she meant its lack of real emotion (Mansfield, 172). Perhaps not surprisingly, the American critics did not find Beresford's psychoanalytic experiment as much of an impediment to its qualities as a novel. Ludwig Lewisohn in the *Nation* claimed that "the story is woven with great delicacy and with unobtrusive skill and is remarkably interesting. Yet it is doubtful whether really great fiction would thrive on so much scientific awareness."[8] W. H. C. at the *New Republic* went so far as to state that " 'An Imperfect Mother' is certainly one of the best of the recent English novels. The author is secure in the consciousness of a ripe and finely developed art."[9]

In *Love's Pilgrim* (1923) Beresford overcame his apparent enthusiasm for scientific objectivity and avoided the clinical retrospect.[10] Though he treats psychological themes similar to those in his earlier psychoanalytic novels, his varied sources are less obtrusive and the net result is a far more convincing study of an individual. The protagonist, Foster Innes, is similar to Stephen Kirkwood in that his bond with his unfulfilled mother is overly close; to Philip Maning in that he is repressed and fastidious about sexuality; to Wilfrid Hornby in that he narrates his own story; and to Jacob Stahl in that he is a self-conscious cripple. Though Beresford continues to explore Freudian insights about the mother fixation, he draws more centrally on the imaginative implications of the inferiority complex (as developed by Adler and Jung) and also brings his interest in psychical research, idealism, and mysticism more fully into play.

Having inherited his disability from his father, Foster Innes's defect has drawn him closer to his mother because of her overprotectiveness of him and since he believes that "[n]o woman, except my mother, could ever love me completely since I was incomplete" (*Love's,* 26). The physical basis of his feeling of incompleteness, inferiority, and fragmentation is compounded by his sense of divided loyalties following his mother's "sinister" response to his half-hearted attempts at love relationships (*Love's,* 36, 43, 58, 121). His subsequent effort to hide his disability warps him in some respects because he moves into a fantasy world as compensation (*Love's,* 58). This situation persists until he becomes angry at his mother after she tells him that his desire to have a relationship with a farmer's daughter, Claire, cannot be fulfilled. His anger prompts him to free himself from his mother's domination (*Love's,* 158). Foster's burgeoning relationship with Claire receives a setback, however, when she confesses that her father, Mr. Morton, has been tried for the murder of his wife (though she believes that her mother committed suicide).

Foster's loyalties remain split on a subconscious level until, during a drive, he views a panorama with Mr. Morton and experiences a moment of heightened illumination. This experience gives them "a mystical knowledge of one another" and removes any doubt in Foster's mind that Mr. Morton is indeed innocent (*Love's*, 244). As William James had argued in *Varieties of Religious Experience,* this supernatural moment of certainty begins the process of healing dividedness.[11] For Foster this process is completed when he fulfills a selfless quest as "love's pilgrim" to find Claire's sister, who has hysterically confessed to the murder of her mother and then run off into a storm. Though Claire has acted as a confessor and carried out a natural analysis on Foster, thus helping him on the road to individuation, his love for her is essentially selfless. It is, therefore, fulfilling, unlike his love for his mother. *Love's Pilgrim* confirms once again Beresford's ability to depict unusual aspects of character naturally, arising out of dramatic incident, and to convey the complexity of human relationships with sensitivity.

More Realism

During the years in which Beresford concentrated on the specifically psychoanalytic novel he also wrote *The Jervaise Comedy* (1919), a relatively slight novel and somewhat repetitive of *The Mountains of the Moon*.[12] Like the earlier novel it offers a socialist critique of an unproductive aristocratic life with its fixed rules of behavior and evinces an attraction to the vitality of an individual in the servant class. In this case the protagonist, Graham Melhuish, a wealthy playwright, falls in love with Anne Banks, the daughter of a tenant farmer, and comes under the influence of her socialist chauffeur brother, prompting his decision to join in a socialist farming scheme in Canada. Unlike the earlier novel, *The Jervaise Comedy* suffers from an overly didactic lecture on socialism at its close. Nevertheless, Beresford experimented with compression in the novel, unfolding the events in little more than 24 hours. Its real saving graces, though, are its refined tone and charming style, repeatedly praised by contemporary reviewers.

The Prisoners of Hartling (1922) continues the critique of the aristocracy but less directly and centrally.[13] More important, Beresford also returns to a study of the issue of inheritance and its impact on the family, this time one held in bondage by anticipation of wealth and power from a relative's will. Typical of postwar novels, the protagonist, Arthur Woodroffe, is a war veteran, in this case one who has returned to his

practice of medicine in a slum area; typical of a Beresford novel, the protagonist is restless and questions his ideals, in this case of self-sacrifice.
Believing that "[t]he world owed him five years of youth!" Woodroffe
leaves behind his "dirty job" to respond to an elderly and wealthy distant relative's request to visit him at Hartling. There he takes on the
position of personal medical adviser to old Kenyon, only gradually
becoming aware of the vulture-like characteristics of the family members, who were "crouched in a horrible group about this one aged man;
waiting gluttonously for his death in order to divide the spoil" (*Prisoners*,
74). Nevertheless, he is not immune to the power exerted by the old
man and realizes, "They were the slaves of a benevolent autocrat who
demanded no service from them except respect. Hartling was a Utopia,
a Thelema in which there was no necessity for work; and one soon for-
got that it was also a prison" (*Prisoners*, 98). If any of the family leaves to
embark on lives of their own, Kenyon gives them to understand that
they will be dispossessed. Though tempted by the old man's wealth,
Arthur is saved by his love for Eleanor, a granddaughter who serves as
secretary and who is different from the others.

This novel's most striking features are the stifling atmosphere of anxious anticipation and jealousy mingled with slackness in the Hartling
household; the vivid descriptions of the old man's power and the family's
predatory nature; and the novel's suspenseful ending, which thankfully
veers away from the excessively sentimental by avoiding having Arthur
and Eleanor inherit the money. Beresford cleverly considered a darker
side of "communistic life" by creating a miniature dystopia based on
landed wealth (*Prisoners*, 98). The numerous reviewers seem to have
missed this twist on Beresford's socialist critique, though Rebecca West
did refer to it as "an exceedingly ingenious book written round a quite
original idea" before lamenting the lack of pleasure to be found in it.[14]
Its inclusion in Collins' Pocket Novel series suggests, though, that it was
something of a popular success.

Novels of Mystical Awakening

From the beginning of his career Beresford showed sensitivity to mystical moments of illumination in his protagonists, based on his own similar experiences. The novels of this period (1924–1929) typically focus
more completely on characters' awakenings and development of their
mystic sensibilities and the principle of the open mind. Their differences
bring these characters into conflict with the herd mind and its fixed

habits. *Unity* (1924), *The Monkey Puzzle* (1925), *That Kind of Man* (1926), *The Tapestry* (1927), *All or Nothing* (1928), and *Real People* (1929) all fall into this category, with *The Monkey Puzzle* and *The Tapestry* being the most substantial and most carefully crafted.

Unity actually blends Beresford's interests in psychology and mysticism, though it presents them on a popular level embedded in a romance tale.[15] The novel features a female protagonist, Katherine Emily Louise Willoughby, a relatively rare occurrence in Beresford's canon. Early on the attractive girl recognizes her several selves and names herself Unity in an attempt to bring them all into line. However, she remains divided, reckless, and impulsive. Longing for novelty, she experiments with three arts—music, painting, and writing—and also with men. While on a train with one childlike worshiper, Brian Jessop, she meets the gaze of another man, whom she feels has a message for her, but she fails to make further contact. Beresford weaves into the story the imagery of marionettes and a puppeteer, conveying Unity's fear of being controlled by an unseen puppeteer that she names Fate. After acquiescing to Jessop's proposal of marriage, Unity moves with him to South Africa and Sydney, where he drowns while drunk. Unity takes up acting and returns to England where another worshiper, Michael (Lord Kettering), convinces her to marry him, though she intuits that Fate is tricking her again. At the wedding she locks gazes with the man that she had seen on the train, who turns out to be a mystic friend of Michael's called Adrian Gore. This incident is the crisis of the novel: she realizes that she should be marrying Adrian but feels helpless to stop the proceedings, again viewing herself as a marionette. Adrian mysteriously disappears and Unity settles into a rut until she feels the urge to escape into the country, where she and Michael encounter Adrian, who has been expecting them. Both she and Adrian have mystic sensibilities and Unity now becomes aware that she is "a pilgrim soul who had missed her destiny and blundered into a net of material adventures" (*Unity,* 257). Beresford focuses on her psychological responses to this painful situation. Though she desires freedom, she does not want the responsibility of controlling the destiny of three lives (*Unity,* 281). Again she acquiesces to Fate, returning home with Michael but now aware that, on encountering Adrian, "[f]or an hour she had been single, whole, a united personality" (*Unity,* 292).

The final chapter leads up to a melodramatic ending. Unity sinks back into indecision until an interview with Michael's concerned mother resigns Unity to self-sacrifice. She must wait to express this to Michael since he has gone off to minister to a dying friend. On his return he glances at Unity's open diary, which betrays her longing for Adrian and her irresolution. Michael, who was out of his depth during the encounter with Adrian, has since changed and realizes that he must take the road of self-sacrifice, which he does literally. During a storm he drives back to his friend's widow, and Unity has a prevision of his car driving into a chasm in the road. She now realizes that she has not been worthy of Michael.

One can see why this novel, first serialized in a woman's magazine, was a modest success at the potboiler level. It develops the fantasy of the beautiful heroine, with handsome men at her beck and call, who is spellbound by a mysterious potential love and desolated by the loss of her actual lover. However, *Unity* also contains some features characteristic of Beresford's more serious work. Beresford had first employed the imagery of marionette and puppeteer in his short story "The Lost Town" and, like a number of his stories, the idea of a controlling Fate plays a central role in this novel. Beresford would repeatedly return to the theme of the potential and temporary unification of divisive elements through mystical experience. He would also develop with more psychological depth and clarity the idea of a female protagonist with three selves in *Cleo* (1937). Class tensions shape the nature of relationships in *Unity* as in many other Beresford novels. Though it received unenthusiastic reviews, *Unity* is pivotal in Beresford's canon for a biographical reason: the £500 that Beresford received for it provided the impetus for him to quit his job at Collins and take his family to France, where his changed working conditions enabled him to write several more substantial novels ("Memories," 211).

One of these novels, *The Monkey Puzzle*, traces the spiritual and psychological growth of a country squire, Tristram Wing, and his intuitive wife, Brenda, and their clashes with the herd mind, in this case malicious, gossiping philistines in a west country village.[16] At the outset Tristram's defense of his wife to the local vicar against the charge of adulterous behavior starts him thinking independently, at the age of 35. He finds an image for the prickly dilemma in which he finds himself in the *Araucaria imbricata* or "monkey puzzle" tree with its defensive thorns that prohibit climbing. Beresford develops this image, and the words "puzzle" and "monkey" by themselves, as a motif with larger and larger implications throughout the book. As a teenager Brenda had already puzzled out a personal philosophy of selfless love and noninterference, realizing the futility of trying to alter the character and habits of other

people. "A lover of humanity" (*Monkey*, 8), she has now become the victim of gossip because she was seen allowing a scruffy young artist, Abby
Mattocks, to kiss her, but as she explains to her husband, they were both
in an exalted state of being and she felt that the kiss would help inspire
his work. Abby has since gone back to London, but when Tristram
determines to take on the village, to assail the monkey puzzle, standing
for habit and fixed opinion, the Wings invite Abby back. Abby has a
touch of the Blakean in him, as a visionary with a single passion "to portray what he believed to be the truth" (*Monkey*, 86), and he is perceived
by some to be mad. He is also possessed of a childlike simplicity and is
figured as a monkey in the sense that the monkey tree of prejudice presents a dilemma for him and that he is part of the puzzle for Tristram
(*Monkey*, 134). Like Brenda, Abby is an outsider and an intuitive type.
He intuits that this summer of drought will "mark the supreme crisis of
his life" (*Monkey*, 122), and it does. Infused with Brenda's spiritual
energy, he paints his masterpiece, a nonrepresentational work of a pool
that captures Brenda's (or, as he refers to her, Hildegarde's) essence. In
an ecstasy he claims to her, "I've drawn you as a wooded pool in half-
sunlight, Hildegarde, with all your lovely surface beauties, all of them,
and they're lovely, lovely, but simply nothing compared to the deeps of
the pool from which they spring" (*Monkey*, 189). Even a local doctor
passing Abby painting on the bridge senses Brenda's presence in the
painting (*Monkey*, 194). Shortly after, the artist is brutally attacked and
his painting destroyed. Brenda tries to deny that a crime has taken place
by rationalizing that Abby has destroyed his painting and fallen from
the bridge in a fit of passion, though she is overwhelmed by a vision of
the actual attack by village thugs (*Monkey*, 223). By this time her
instinct to inspire creation has been transformed into her own role as
"the instrument of creation," as she has become pregnant. Nevertheless,
she cannot remain in this tranquil world of comfort and must eventually
face the truth of what has happened, which shatters her philosophy of
detachment and makes her aware of the limits of her self-sacrifice. She
realizes that she has abdicated responsibility by "avoiding all the cutting
edges of the monkey puzzle that had so perplexed Tristram, simply by
letting people alone" (*Monkey*, 265) and, following Abby's death, she
knows that she must instead try and understand the gospel of others in
order to deal with their impingements. As the novel closes, the couple
contemplates the mystery of Abby's awakening through Brenda, his
creation of his masterpiece and the seemingly senseless destruction, yet
another kind of monkey puzzle. However, they resolve not to set their

opinions against one another's in defensiveness. This openness contrasts with the final image of the village gossips as voracious insects consuming the latest scrap of gossip, about the birth date of the Wings' son. The static nature of the villagers is neatly conveyed by the return to an image very similar to one which opened the novel, of them as blowflies completely engrossed by their defilement.

Beresford put more thought into the artistry of this novel than in some others. The motifs of monkey and monkey puzzle, the shadow of a poplar signifying the dark truths Brenda does not want to contemplate (*Monkey*, 251), and image of the gossips as blowflies help make the complex issues come alive to the reader. Through Abby Mattock, Beresford expresses some ideas about art and its relation to life. Art is "creating the symbol of a universal truth that wasn't recognized until the artist showed it," says Mattock on one occasion (*Monkey*, 134). After he is assaulted, Mattock brings up the disturbing idea that brute force offers the only real freedom and that it rules the world of sensibility (*Monkey*, 264, 266). Unlike Brenda, he has "chucked" all philosophical systems in favor of art, which cannot be explained. Given the type of nonrepresentational art that Mattock does and the opposition to him in this society, we might speculate that underlying this story is Beresford's anxiety about the dangers of leaving behind representation in art in favor of experimentation, an anxiety expressed more directly in *Writing Aloud*. Certainly Mattock, and to a lesser degree Brenda, represents the "other" who is scapegoated because he is feared for his unorthodoxy. Though several critics lamented the prominence of the expository element in this novel, they also frequently found it praiseworthy and absorbing. At least two numbered it among his best. It does have the power to move the reader, with its dramatic and genuinely passionate portrayal of the maliciousness of gossips and the destructiveness that arises out of ignorance and prejudice. In these features and especially in its portrayal of the misunderstood outsider it resembles *The Hampdenshire Wonder*. These strengths probably account for *The Monkey Puzzle* being reprinted several times and translated into French (though Beresford was accused of plagiarism on it).[17]

Another kind of awakening concerns Beresford in *That Kind of Man*.[18] As in *God's Counterpoint,* the protagonist, Henry Blackstone, becomes aware of his repressed self through the influence of a young woman, in this case a 1920s flapper who has borne the illegitimate child of his son. Blackstone, a writer, then finds himself developing an attraction for a fellow writer who had fallen in love with him 10 years ago, and the conflict heightens between his pagan and puritan selves. His writing is the main benefactor of the division within him since he begins to express himself more completely and, thus, more honestly. However, tension within his family (probably based on Beresford's own experience) also heightens, and in the end his temperament prevents him from leaving them. At the denouement, though, Blackstone is on a creative threshold with a new idea for a story based on a revision of the Dr. Jekyll and Mr. Hyde fable, in which the two warring elements would be united. The main significance of the novel is that it places front and center the theme of dealing with and overcoming dividedness, a theme that would continue to preoccupy Beresford.

The Tapestry also bears some resemblance to *God's Counterpoint,* dealing with the growth of the protagonist from childhood, but it focuses much more on the spiritual development of the protagonist than the earlier psychoanalytic novel.[19] With considerable craftsmanship, Beresford intricately weaves through the novel the protagonist's response to the central image of a tapestry depicting the fight of Joshua with the Amorites as a reflection of his progress on the quest to overcome a restrictive Victorian upbringing and attain the mystic's life. John Fortescue's religiously orthodox aunts are the ones creating the tapestry, and initially as a small child it is taboo for him to tamper with it. Work on it progresses almost invisibly (*Tapestry,* 6), and though John cannot as a boy see the work as a whole he knows the pattern and becomes fascinated by it. He experiences a sense of power as he fantasizes himself in the role of Joshua commanding the sun and moon to stop. Ironically it is this biblical scene that precipitates his "awakening to unknown possibilities in the world at large" after he questions the veracity of the event based on his lessons in science (*Tapestry,* 17). His discovery of the allegorical nature of the tapestry leads him to question all kinds of assumptions, and further revelations follow: his father has been unfaithful to his mother; his mother is not actually his mother; she has abandoned him; and John is in anything but the position of Joshua. Left to his own resources at 18, John falls abruptly into life, moves to Nice, and enters two years' hard labor as a bricklayer's laborer. An encounter with his degenerate alcoholic father in France along with his homesickness drives him back to England, where he finds out that his father has been intercepting money sent to him by his "mother." Reminiscent of the *Jacob Stahl* trilogy, John then apprentices with an architect. He also decides to finish the tapestry left by his aunts, out of a sense of duty, and it becomes a record of his acts and emotions. At a crisis in his life he once again feels like Joshua, after a love-interest, Viva, enlists him to destroy the portrait of her painted by her father. He fantasizes that if he carries out the crime he would be "high above the world with his head in the clouds that were so near to God, able in his magnificent isolation to disregard the opinions of the teeming struggling world down there in the valley of Ascalon" (*Tapestry,* 161–62). Afterward, in his shame and realization that he will be excluded from the world of her family, "he felt less like Joshua than the hare that crouched by his horse's feet, slinking from the notice of a world that completely overlooked its existence" (*Tapestry,* 165). In a sense John's existence is overlooked since the family of Viva immediately goes abroad. Not until seven years later does he again encounter and marry the passionate Viva, who continually wavers in her morality. As John becomes successful he forgets about the tapestry until his drunken father drowns, and John wonders, "Was the pattern of all these strange tapestries known to some Almighty Architect from the beginning . . . or had every man and woman the power to alter in some degree the design of his or her record?" (*Tapestry,* 257). Though he believes that only a filling in of the background remains in his tapestry, he is wrong since he catches his wife in adultery with another architect and strangles him. Viva then commits suicide, though she exonerates John. In the care of his sister-in-law, John returns to the tapestry as a penance, but it also becomes a talisman and a therapy since he is able to recover scenes from his past life never remembered before. On completing it he feels peace and serenity; he sees it, and his life, not as a diversity of subjects and events but as "a single and indivisible composition" (*Tapestry,* 309). The allegory of Joshua brings him the insight that regardless of the value we place on incidents as trivial or significant, they all ultimately have equal importance outside of ourselves. Believing in the "oneness of everything," John is poised to enter the life of the mystic, which he does as a brief postlude confirms.

Though the murder-suicide in this fiction comes close to melodrama, the novel avoids sentimentality at the denouement, since the loving sister-in-law realizes that she has lost John for good. Reviewers on the whole found this work charming, and critic Annie Russell Marble called it "an intriguing novel of excellent craftsmanship," but two of the more notable critics, Edwin Muir and L. P. Hartley, suggested that despite its virtues it lacks imaginative and emotional power.[20]

In both *All or Nothing* (1928) and *Real People* (1929) Beresford explores further his interest in the development of the mystic personality. These novels are also connected, as the protagonist of the former, James

Bledloe, reappears in the latter and influences its protagonist, Charles Moore, to accept the preeminence of spiritual reality, a theme increasingly stressed in Beresford's canon. At the outset of *All or Nothing,* James Bledloe feels conflicted about his inheritance, reminiscent of Arthur Grey in *The Mountains of the Moon,* and like Henry Blackstone in *That Kind of Man* he feels blocked by his dual personality. Only after he has developed faith in "unselfed" love does he become unified and dispose of his wealth. Eventually his antagonistic wife joins him on his quest, perhaps reflecting a wish-fulfillment on Beresford's part. In *Real People* Charles Moore resembles Beresford in that he has studied and found wanting various creeds and systems. He is vaguely dissatisfied until he discovers a power for "seeing" through matter, and he becomes a mystic. By the end of the novel he possesses the gift of prophecy, prompting his son-in-law to wonder about the limits of determinism and to suggest that certain "real" people, such as the mystic protagonists of these novels, might be able to exercise a small influence on destiny. Both novels are typical of Beresford's serious fiction, criticizing pursuit of wealth for its own sake, questioning restrictions based on class and conventional morality, and evincing Beresford's longstanding belief in the potential spiritual evolution of mankind.

Forays into Mystery and Detective Fiction

Along with mystical novels, Beresford also tried his hand at the more popular genres of mystery and detective fiction, with limited success. Postwar Britain had experienced a boom in these genres, and Beresford had played a small part in setting it off by signing for Collins publishers Freeman Wills Croft, who was, in Beresford's opinion, "a first-class writer of detective fiction" ("Memories," 210). Croft is now generally considered one of the founders, along with A. C. Bentley, Agatha Christie, and Dorothy Sayers, of that golden age of detective fiction in Britain between the wars. Beresford evidently enjoyed these types of fiction and reportedly read Agatha Christie aloud by the fireside. We can speculate that they appealed to his sense of reason and to his fascination with the probing of motivations. A passage from *Writing Aloud* suggests Beresford's none too surprising emphasis on characters' psychology in these genres:

> The author may be visualised as the unseen expert who manipulates his puzzle to the growing wonderment and interest of the reader. This is the

ideal method of the detective story, and any book written on these lines must hold some critical mystery that, when revealed, gives the clue to the whole tangle. The "mystery" need not, of course, have anything to do with crime. It may be nothing more than a queer eccentricity in the character of the chief person of the story; possibly even in that of a subsidiary person. (Writing, 140)

Beresford's first foray into the field, *The Decoy* (1927), is really more of an adventure or thriller story than a mystery, although Beresford does embed in the plot a mysterious disappearance that involves treachery; the protagonist is the victim and finds himself in the position of having to defend himself against the false charge of embezzlement.[21] Beresford termed the book "an unhappy accident" (*Writing,* 80), but this judgment is too harsh since *The Decoy* has some redeeming features despite an implausible premise and sentimental ending. Most notably it shares with Beresford's more substantial mystical novels the themes of awakening, in this case from gullibility, and of release, from the stifling life of an English banker. The protagonist, Phillip Legrand, is one of Beresford's conscientious young men with a tendency to idealize women. Feeling the first stir of spring, he incredibly agrees to act as the decoy for his cousin Henry, who admits to having swindled funds from the tradition-laden bank for which they both work. Phillip slips away to France temporarily to give Henry the time to escape to a country in South America where they will not extradite him for embezzling. In France Phillip takes on the role of a young landscape artist, Dubois, and feels nervous about being pursued. While painting he encounters a young American woman, Nita, whom he rescues from a rakish artist acquaintance, Galvain. The two become friendly, though Phillip continues to pretend that he is French, until during the crisis of a forest fire he switches to speaking English; she becomes wary of him, believing that he is probably in the secret service. Phillip travels to Paris to collect the expected letter from Henry, and en route he meets a French film magnate, Henri Beaufort, who is interested in Phillip's escape story. His offer of a position to Phillip strikes an unbelievable note in the plot, but this incident is developed against Phillip's rising awareness that the letter is not going to materialize. Hearing of Nita's renewed friendship with Galvain finally precipitates Phillip into action, and he returns to England to seek the truth about Henry by confronting his Uncle James, Henry's father, and the manager of Chetwynd's. Phillip's discovery that Henry has played the traitor comes as no surprise to the reader. The bank has hushed the matter up but has seized Phillip's inheritance as compensation.

Now free, but penniless, Phillip applies to Beaufort for a position but must first prove his innocence. Though intending to martyr himself, he confesses his dilemma to Nita in a moment of intimacy (*Decoy,* 222), and she enlists the financial support of her father, who sees in Phillip a kind of Don Quixote. The two lovers trace Henry to New York only to find that he has disappeared after embezzling again and that Uncle James has investigated the destination of the stolen notes and discovered the truth. The novel closes sentimentally with Phillip and Nita on the brink of their new relationship. It is an entertaining tale, plot-driven but, as is typical with Beresford, showing insight into the psychology of the idealist protagonist.

Beresford's next effort along this line, *The Instrument of Destiny: A Detective Story* (1928), corresponds more closely to the classic detective tale, in that a murder is committed by a single person, but it uses the relatively unusual device of having the murderer be an unwitting person, in this case a seven-year-old boy.[22] Beresford employs the classic country-house setting, with suspects limited to members of the family and servants of the victim, an aged patriarch with one source of manipulative power left to him, his considerable fortune. The scenario of the patriarch controlling those who stand to inherit recalls *The Prisoners of Hartling* and is one that Beresford would return to in *The Inheritor* and *The Benefactor*. In *The Instrument of Destiny* everyone at the house stands to gain by the old man's death, and thus all are potential suspects, including the protagonist, Bernard Fytton, a King's counsel who acts as amateur detective. Beresford sustains tension partly through his characterization of Bernard as he becomes aware that his wife may well be implicated in the murder and that he can no longer keep an open mind about the situation. Bernard brings in an astute Scotland Yard detective who resolves the mystery satisfactorily and it ends with a philosophical summing up, characteristic of Beresford: "Blame! Every one was to blame and no one. They were all creatures caught in the net of a destiny that was not perhaps so blind as it was commonly supposed to be. The victim himself had primarily been to blame in his avarice and lust for power. If he had been other than he was, he would have been still alive" (*Instrument,* 326–27). Reviews were typically lukewarm, though L. P. Hartley asserted that Beresford's first detective novel "might well arouse jealousy in more practised exponents of this particular art."[23]

Another mystery story, *An Innocent Criminal* (1931), also shows psychological insight, particularly as it develops Beresford's characteristic theme of the divided self. Though the plotting is rather clever, and Beresford does show restraint in dealing with the clues, the novel adds nothing new either to the genre or to Beresford's canon. Despite generally positive reviews, Beresford did not write another fiction of this type, the evidence from his subsequent novels suggesting that he was not content merely to entertain.

Chapter Six

Social, Family, and Mystical Novels of the 1930s and 1940s

Novels of the 1930s

In his realistic novels of the 1930s Beresford continued several of his preoccupations, initially harking back to novels of love and the family, reminiscent of the *Jacob Stahl* trilogy, and then returning to idealist and mystical protagonists who overcome their dividedness. Not surprisingly, some of these fictions are repetitive, offering nothing new, while in others he manifests a tendency toward sermonizing, as story, plot, and even character give way to theme and philosophy.

Love's Illusion (1930) is linked with *Real People* (1929) by its retrospective element, but in this case the protagonist, Geoffrey Philips, recalls an affair from 30 years ago that shattered his illusion of romantic love and the ideal woman.[1] The incident brings to mind the "Madeleine" section in *Jacob Stahl,* though the tone in the later work is much more regretful of lost illusions and ideals. The confirmed bachelor Geoffrey actually believes that his naïveté represents his true self, which he has covered over with his critical intelligence and mistrust, particularly of women. Though the plot is simple and commonplace (one reviewer went so far as to call it "hackneyed"), several reviewers found the sparse and economic prose poetic and dignified and the character of Geoffrey a success as a "limpid portrait of immature manhood."[2]

Beresford's next novel, *Seven, Bobsworth* (1930) also has its roots deep in the writer's past, but it is one of those novels that stands out in his large canon as a clever and successful experiment.[3] Beresford constructed the work as a kind of fictional "biography" cum social history of Bobsworth, an early Garden City suburb based on Letchworth.[4] In a preface he claims to have reluctantly taken on the role of literary executor for one Fiddler, an architect of the suburb in the sense that he was the press agent for the scheme, and owner of number seven, Bobsworth (hence the title) for almost 20 years, thus intimately acquainted with its development. Beresford's protest that he will not take any responsibility for the book immediately piques the reader's curiosity, along with the information that Beresford never really liked Fiddler, believing that he secretly sneered at Beresford and that he was the victim of an inferiority complex (*Seven*, 31). In establishing verisimilitude Beresford goes so far as to suggest that Fiddler's neighbor Mrs. Crosby, who has selected the papers and will bear responsibility for complaints, can be reached in care of the publisher.

The reason for Beresford's hesitation soon becomes clear. Fiddler's memoir is not the "official" history of Bobsworth from 1903 to the 1920s, since he has already published that, but rather the tale of its inner development. In reality it is a satirical exposé of the ulterior motives of the "philanthropists" behind the scheme, who are moguls of big business, which is the primary shaping, manipulative force on the city from beginning to end. The chapters following the preface present mock-biographies of these men. Sir James Cobbett is a "business organizer" and "creator of values" who turns around failing companies by repackaging their products. Through organizing Bobsworth he intends to procure for himself an inexpensive baronetcy. Lord Grout, a newspaper magnate, uses Bobsworth to self-advertise and to increase the circulation of his papers. These two assign Fiddler with the task of "smoking" out the first inhabitants, colorful cranks, and replacing them with respectable clerks: individuality gives way to sterile conformity. As Fiddler puts it, the first-developed neighborhood "had moved from crankdom to clerkdom, without touching that fortunate middle state in which a man may be the equal of his fellows" (*Seven*, 220). But the satire does not stop there since Beresford sends up the individualists, many of whom espouse ideas that interested Beresford himself at various stages in his development, including agnosticism, orthodox religion, spiritualism, Christian Science, and socialism. He gently mocks their dogmatic beliefs that they have cornered the market on the truth, and he questions their commitment to these beliefs in the face of economic and social pressure.

As the years roll by the nature of Bobsworth changes, which Beresford expresses by presenting the suburb as a developing character, with Fiddler in the role of doting father. On one of a number of similar occasions the narrator claims, "But to me Bobsworth is as a child whose development I have watched. I remember its early waywardness, its charming unconventional manners, before the heavy hand of Lord Grout descended upon it, as falls the hand of some worldly-minded schoolmaster, to crush out originality and mould the plastic mind and disposition into some approved type" (*Seven*, 168). Ironically, in this transformation into conformity it becomes a microcosm of middle-class English life. Bobsworth comes to serve as the vehicle for a satire on the sanitizing of English life under the pressure of advertising. In this we occasionally glimpse a Swiftian touch, as in Fiddler's claim that "we Midlanders represent in some way a kind of typical Englishness, and so have to take upon ourselves the responsibilities borne by the best-hated and most abused nation in the world. It certainly seems to me that so long as you are living in England, your chief pride should lie in being as little English as possible" (*Seven*, 238).

Aside from the targets of satire, the book employs several techniques, including irony and self-consciousness, that make it appear quite modern. The ironies multiply, and some are at Beresford's expense, beginning in the preface when we discover that Beresford has essentially been rejected as a potential tenant in the neighborhood by Fiddler in 1910 (*Seven*, 26). He also includes some self-mocking diary entries of Fiddler, for example Fiddler's observation that "[o]ur friend seems to be going in hot and strong for mysticism? A form of consolation" (*Seven*, 33). One of the central ironies is that Fiddler, sent to smoke out the eccentrics, befriends them and is forced into a double life. However, the greatest occurs at the close of the novel when a commercial interest tries to turn Fiddler out of his house by buying him and then by intimidating him. The digging of company workmen around his house causes the chimney to collapse, killing Fiddler. Thus he becomes the victim of the capitalist system that has employed him. Just as the big business concerns have exposed the soil around his house and its foundations, causing it to collapse, once Fiddler's memoir comes to light he exposes the moral bankruptcy of those responsible for the instant suburb. Throughout the work Beresford is self-conscious about the relationship between fiction and biography, for example claiming in the preface that "[m]uch of this stuff would make good quarrying for a professional novelist with a marked realist bias, but it would be no good, neat" (*Seven*, 13). Given these elements it is no wonder that T. S. Eliot at Faber and Faber signed this book.

Beresford had been interested in the housing problem as early as the 1890s ("Memories," 86), and his knowledge of the advertising world and the architecture and building trades obviously served him well here. Like Beresford, Fiddler had been trained as an architect (*Seven*, 57), and Beresford has Fiddler employ some technical architectural terms in describing Bobsworth before undercutting the description by stating that Bobsworth has "a general effect of squatness" (*Seven,* 70). Beresford had also been disparagingly termed a Garden-City novelist by Katherine Mansfield to convey the hygienic atmosphere and predetermined nature of his fiction (Mansfield, 170–71); it is tempting to imagine this humorous, episodic novel, revealing the caprice and colorful personality of the Garden City, as his response to his critic.

Following a detective fiction, Beresford returned to the more traditional form of the realistic family novel and embarked on his second trilogy, *Three Generations,* comprising *The Old People* (1931), *The Middle Generation* (1932), and *The Young People* (1933).[5] The work deals with the development from 1867 to 1932 of the Hillington family, members of the lesser squirearchy. In a very conventional manner, it traces the incompatible temperaments within the family before focusing on one of the sons, Owen Hillington's, slow growth into independence from the prejudices of his family background and toward ideals such as selfless love that he attempts to practice with his own wife and children. Characteristically of Beresford's protagonists, Owen remains fluid and develops tolerance, in contrast to his brother Bob, the inheritor of the estate. In the first two volumes Beresford uncharacteristically emphasizes the narrative line rather than ideas. These two novels were praised for their distinctive characterization and quiet humor but criticized for their lack of force. The third volume unobtrusively weaves in more of Beresford's fundamental philosophy and ideas than the first two and also provides glimpses into changes in the postwar world, some of them disturbing and others to be welcomed as refreshing. Beresford's insight into the "fast set" provides a good example: "These loose-living, irresponsible men and women were merely giving way to the common desires and lusts that the respectable middle-classes shared with them, but could not afford to indulge. And you do not respect those who give way to desires that you yourself have been forced to inhibit" (*Young,* 35). The *Times Literary Supplement* reviewer emphasized the bleakness of the portrait, calling it "a profoundly searching study of life in post-War England, with its deadness, its futilities and its disbelief in human values."[6] Novelist William Plomer's comments more aptly serve as a summary of the entire trilogy: "It is put together with patience and understanding by a fair-minded man who knows what he is about, and in the primary meaning of the word it is a respectable book, sober, sensible, decent, and thoroughly English in its theme, style and characters."[7]

Most of the remaining novels penned by Beresford in the 1930s focus on individuals who are divided and achieve harmony through a mystical approach to life or who know their mystic way from the outset of the novel. Though these novels continue to show considerable psychological insight, they become increasingly sermonlike, emphasizing philosophy over aesthetics.

The Next Generation (1932) is worthy of remark for two main reasons: it was the first of the publisher Benn's "Ninepenny Novels, Leaders of Modern Fiction," and it features a female protagonist, Susan Flaxman.[8] In this novel Beresford shows optimism about the younger generation, represented by Susan, her brother, and her mystical companion, Siegfried Alexander. Susan and Alexander discover the voice of "inner wisdom" and encourage Susan's parents to reform themselves.

The Inheritor (1933) is a similarly slim novel reminiscent of The Prisoners of Hartling in its analysis of human responses to the potential of inheritance.[9] In The Inheritor, though, the wealthy patriarch has already died at the outset and the focus is on the rightful heir Marcus Brent, one of Beresford's simple and truthful souls who calls himself a fool. Beresford contrasts his selflessness and unconventional behavior in giving up the estate with the greed and maliciousness of the other relatives, who eventually suffer unhappiness despite their wealth.

In The Camberwell Miracle (1933) Beresford presents a variation on the simple soul and potential visionary in that the protagonist, Dr. Martin Davies, is a mystical healer who is aware of his vocation but who cannot explain it. However, unlike the plot-driven Inheritor, this novel has a definite thesis, arising out of Beresford's longstanding interest in faith healing which he had conveyed in numerous articles in The Aryan Path and which he summarized in The Case for Faith-Healing (1934). Various perspectives on faith healing dominate the narrative, and thus to a certain degree one's interest in and openness to the idea of faith healing will affect one's evaluation of the novel. Nevertheless, Beresford does generate dramatic tension by showing how Davies's actions arouse the opposition of powerful elements in society such as the conservative press and the General Medical Council. He also develops a human interest by focusing on an individual's approach to and cure by Davies, and the subsequent blossoming of her life.

That individual is Rosemary Henderson, daughter of Sir Geoffrey Henderson, medical surgeon. Her story opens the narrative. Beresford has drawn on his own past in creating hers: she succumbed to infantile paralysis at the age of two owing to the neglect of her nurse. Now a teenager, she becomes interested in faith healing after reading a feature on Martin Davies's curing ability in the Morning News. Her father pronounces the phenomenon a form of hysteria but her love, Richard Stoner, a specialist in nervous diseases and a psychoanalyst, is more open to the idea of faith healing, on which he expounds at length in chapter 3. However, he proposes the psychological explanation that the cure occurs when all the selves of a person pull in the same direction and overcome habit, which sounds very close to the one advanced by William James in *Varieties of Religious Experience* (1902). By using a case study similar to Rosemary's, Richard actually conducts a kind of psychoanalysis on her, conveying to her that there may be an unconscious part of her that has a vested interest in remaining crippled. However, Beresford ironically shows that Richard may also have such an interest since he fears that if restored her beauty would attract a more handsome man than himself (*Camberwell*, 38). At the close of the chapter Richard becomes aware of the crudity of his explanation and senses that faith and love are linked.

This feeling provides an appropriate transition to the life and activity of Martin Davies, since as we discover he represents these qualities. The Camberwell miracle of the title occurs when Davies performs a mass healing at Camberwell on a unified group of the faithful while his friend, the Rev. J. Broughton, recites the opening verses of the Sermon on the Mount. To the bafflement of those around him Davies is not religious nor is he above average in intelligence, but it seems as though his mind has become the servant of his spirit (*Camberwell*, 126). He is also a sympathetic character partly because he is so misunderstood and maligned. Soon after the healing, Davies secretly leaves for Amherst to escape unwanted media attention, and his disappearance is taken as evidence of his falsehood by members of the Medical Council now investigating the case. Rosemary seeks him out there, Richard's proposal of marriage and her sexual awakening having given her the impetus to be cured. Though Davies tells her to stop despising her simple, childlike self and to distrust her intelligence, it is not his words but the influence of his personality on her receptive one, along with his love, that awakens the inner knowledge necessary for a cure to take place. This attitude anticipates a major shift in Beresford's perspective away from reliance on reason and intellect toward an appreciation of and finally a conviction about the mystical, intuitive approach to life. Within three days a cure happens to Rosemary, growing out of her discovery of love and faith with Davies, but her father discounts Davies's role since the faith healer was not present during her healing. Meanwhile, the Medical Council, of which her father is a member, strikes Davies off its register and Davies has to appear in court in a libel case between two newspapers over his faith healing. The spirit of truth enters the courtroom when Rosemary, now married, and then Davies testify, and the libel action is withdrawn. Though the validity of faith healing is not definitely established, Davies is reinstated and the novel closes on a hopeful note with the narrator suggesting that over the course of time the belief in the control of the body by the mind will spread. Critics of the novel would call it sentimental, but it does present an insightful view of how a modern Christ might be received among different elements of society. In this Beresford once again acts as satirist, attacking everything from the dogmatic attitudes of church and medical groups to social snobbery (Gerber, 133).

This novel obviously tapped a vein of interest in the culture of the time, and it achieved a succès d'estime according to Tristram Beresford. Numerous letters of inquiry and praise arrived, and Beresford made contact with a larger circle of like-minded individuals, including faith healer Maud Royden and pacifist writer and editor Max Plowman. The latter recommended it to his friends, claiming to one of them that "[a]s a novel it's not much. But as a reasonable explanation of the faith of one who looks forward to a new era in the art of healing, based, not on magic or mere credulity, but on love and faith and the deepest psychological understanding, it's a heartening and to my mind important book."[10] The reviewers commented more positively on the artistic merits of the novel. Mary Crosbie in *John O'London's Weekly* found it an absorbing, "well-marshalled story, perfectly balanced and not afraid to discuss seriously a far-reaching question."[11] The *Times* reviewer wrote that *"The Camberwell Miracle* is a thrilling novel certainly, but it is much more than a novel. It is a record of spiritual experience presented so convincingly and sympathetically that it is difficult to resist it."[12]

The enthusiasm that Beresford evidently felt in writing *The Camberwell Miracle* carries through into his next novel, *Peckover* (1934), though this novel is less thesis-driven and may have engaged him because of a strong autobiographical element that merges with a fantasy.[13] It returns to the theme that had haunted him in the 1920s, the divided self. The treatment is not clinical or heavy-handed, though Beresford, as conscientious as ever, states in a prefatory note that he had "drawn upon the abundant technical literature dealing with dual personality" as well as consulting a book called *I Lost My Memory* by an anonymous author. Rather, the tone of this unusual romance is lighthearted without being superficial. In three parts, the novel traces Gilbert A. Peckover's desertion of his family, loss of memory, romance with and marriage to a new woman, rise of professional success as a builder, arrest for bigamy, return of his old personality, acquittal, and treatment by a psychotherapist.

The novel opens on the evening of 7 March (interestingly Beresford's birthday) 1933 with a movingly rendered portrait of the conflicts (obviously well-rehearsed) in the middle-class, suburban Peckover family. Unlike in others of his novels, Beresford convincingly develops the themes of dual personality and identity from the perspective of an ordinary man. On several occasions Beresford implies that Peckover is not some isolated abnormality but that dividedness and lapses of consciousness occur commonly with varying degrees of severity. Overall *Peckover* is a readable and humorous psychological romance that provides a twist on the context of freer relationships between the sexes and changing divorce laws. Veteran reviewer L. M. Field wrote that " 'Peckover' is a well told, amusing, friendly sort of novel, the story of real people, most of whom we are glad to meet, but it is also an honest, and for those who have not read much along the lines of abnormal psychology possibly a rather startling, account of one of its most interesting phases."[14]

On a Huge Hill (1935) returns to the subject matter of faith healing treated in *The Camberwell Miracle*.[15] The title is taken from John Donne's lines "On a huge Hill, / Cragged and steep, Truth stands, and he that will / Reach her, about must, and about must go"; some of the mystical incidents are based on those experienced by Beresford's friend Max Plowman.[16] The novel focuses on the metaphorical ascent of an unorthodox lawyer, James Kingden, into his mystic vocation. At the outset, the 37-year-old rescues his secretary, Helena Thorne, from a repressive life and marries her. Seven years later Helena witnesses a more profound example of her husband James's "power to lose himself completely in compassionate sympathy for another human being" (*Huge,* 53) when he cures his dangerously ill son, Bobby, of cerebro-spinal meningitis. This is the central incident of the novel (*Huge,* 57). The family doctor describes the incident as a case of faith healing, but the attendant nurse and Helena are more skeptical, and Helena henceforth becomes the main force of opposition to James's power. When James decides to give up his law practice after living for 44 years as an automaton, Helena resists and causes James to feel divided. James's law partner, Anthony Spincks, tells James of a coincidence, that Arthur Malleson, a novelist who has written a book on faith healing, has just become a client of the firm. James interviews Malleson and they achieve a temporary communion of spirits. In James's absence Bobby relapses and James realizes that he cannot draw on his reason to heal. James persists in embarking on his new way of life. To his surprise, when he tells his law partner, Spincks, of his intentions, Spincks confesses that he has the powers of a spiritualistic medium and that he has relied on James's presence all these years to keep his poltergeists at bay. From the time of an accident at 15, when Spincks was castrated and developed a cast in his eye, he has been emotionless. He now wishes to retire as well and to come and live near James with the hope of exorcising his demons. However, Spincks is repulsive to Helena, and her resistance increases as James gathers other disciples around him. She finally explodes when James visits a needy married woman, Mrs. Gordon, with the aim of curing her of arthritis. At the height of the tensions between the couple, James turns to Spincks, who advises him to go away and meditate. James acts literally on his comment that he needs to go up onto a mountain to pray (*Huge,* 263) and climbs a hill in the North Downs. At the crest he falls into a trance and has a vision of finding a revelation, perhaps of "the reign of spirit upon earth" (*Huge,* 268) and of meeting a fellow-watcher. Meanwhile Helena frantically tries to discover James's whereabouts, but Bobby has had a dream that Jesus has fetched his daddy. At James and Helena's reunion, James tells her that she must come first with him and she realizes his overwhelming love. Following another cure of warts on Bobby's hands, Helena is converted and expresses her desire that James should go on and cure Mrs. Gordon.

This ending is altogether too sentimental, and the novel throughout suffers from unbelievable plot twists and characterizations. In particular the details of Spincks's past and especially the effects of the loss of his interstitial glands are unconvincing and gratuitous, more a reflection of some favorite esoteric ideas of Beresford's about glands than anything else.

The Faithful Lovers (1936), dedicated "To my wife," is the most sentimental of Beresford's novels.[17] While dallying with a farm girl, the hero, Bryan Davys, spots another girl in a motorcar with her family and falls under her spell. She is Shirley Veheyne, the 12-year-old daughter of the local aristocrat, Colonel Edward Veheyne. In a typical Beresford scenario, Bryan resolves to make himself the social equal of the Veheynes in order to win Shirley. Unfortunately for him, Bryan's name becomes known to this family since the girl Bryan had been seen with becomes pregnant. Colonel Veheyne assumes that Bryan is the culprit. Bryan meanwhile announces his desire to make money and gain power. His unsuccessful pacifist writer father, Henry, introduces him to an influential businessman, Looe Spencer, who is impressed by Bryan's self-confidence.

When World War I breaks out, Spencer offers Bryan a large salary to run a munitions factory. In this way Bryan, who has unthinkingly accepted his father's pacifist principles, manages to avoid active service until 1917, when he is called before the Military Tribunal. In a second piece of bad luck, Colonel Veheyne, who remembers him, leads the tribunal. However, with better luck, Bryan meets Shirley afterwards and discovers that she abhors war and does not want him to fight. Though they have not met since their first sight of one another, they know that they are "destined lovers" (*Faithful*, 93). Nevertheless they do not have the opportunity to meet again for some time because Bryan is imprisoned for his conscientious objection before being sent to do farm work. Following the armistice, Bryan returns to the employ of Spencer and determines to clear his name about the rumor that he is the father of the Cornish farm girl's child. While in Cornwall, Bryan encounters Shirley's sympathetic mother and obtains an interview with the Colonel, now a harassed and lonely man, having lost one son in the war and with another son, Ned, who has been shell-shocked. Though Bryan admires Colonel Edward Veheyne as the ideal of the English gentleman, the Colonel views Bryan as a sample of a despised type, and refuses to alter his fixed opinion even after Bryan discovers the identity of the father of the illegitimate child.

In a determined effort to find Shirley an appropriate suitor, the Colonel takes the family to London for the season, where she is presented at court and courted by an eligible bachelor whom Shirley manages to keep at bay. On their return to Cornwall, Ned snaps and kills both himself and his mother in a car crash. This incident represents yet another deferral of the fulfillment of Bryan and Shirley's desire for one another since Shirley is left to care for her father. Meanwhile Bryan has been made a partner of the wealthy Spencer. Bryan's love for Shirley motivates him to imitate the kind of relation between a sympathetic landowner and his tenants in his factory. Finally, with the intervention of Edward's only surviving son, Miles, a pacifist and a doctor, Edward finally admits his error about Bryan, and the faithful lovers can join together. In his maturity and the vision of life that he has adopted Bryan has become the equal of the Colonel.

The sentimentality of this romance and the unbelievable strength of the bond between the two lovers based only on a moment of communion when Shirley was 12 mar this novel. As well it lacks the structure of ideas that typically provides Beresford's novels with some depth. Nevertheless, it conveys most strongly Beresford's feelings about the effect of the war, as, for example, in this comment about Ned: "He was no good to anyone now, not even to himself, a man spoilt and wasted like a hundred thousand others who had come out of the war broken for life" (*Faithful,* 196).

Despite its flaws, *The Faithful Lovers* was one of his most popular novels, judging by advertisements suggesting that 35,000 copies had been printed. Critical opinion on it divided quite sharply, American reviewers typically finding it "pedestrian," "tedious," and "colorless" whereas the British praised its avoidance of a too familiar unpleasantness and the glimpse it provided into a serene and pleasant way of living.

Cleo (1937) is a more notable addition to the Beresford canon since it features a female protagonist and rejects the ascetic's way to the mystic's sensibility, instead advocating a full engagement in life and love.[18] This novel most closely resembles one of Beresford's attempts at popular success, *Unity,* in that both feature female protagonists split into three selves, but *Cleo* is a more inspired, thoughtful, carefully crafted, and less blatantly psychological novel. Part of the inspiration derived from Beresford's first visit to the Lake District, which delighted him and which he described poetically in the third section of the novel. He made the motoring trip with Tristram, one reason he dedicated the novel to his son. *Cleo* essentially illustrates the lines from Blake used as the epigraph and as the final lines of the novel: "Who binds unto himself a joy / Doth the winged life destroy; / But he who catches the joy as it flies / Lives in eternity's sunrise."

The tripartite work traces the birth and development into maturity of Jane Ursula Flytche-Fitton, nicknamed Cleopatra in her cradle because of the "infinite variety" perceived in her by her clergyman father. In each of the three books Cleo, as she is called, comes under the influence of a different man, and different personalities within her come to the fore. In book 1 her cousin Tony becomes devoted to the precocious child, and she explains to him about her naughty self, Jane, and her "sister" self, Ursula, who is moral and religious. Most often she is the mediating Cleo. When she learns of the facts of life from the daughter in a Belgian refugee family, her Jane self dominates. Tony is horrified, and with refreshing directness she tells him that she does not want to marry until she is 25. Ursula, scholar and saint, takes charge following her religious conversion that coincides with puberty. Another cousin, Martin, catches a glimpse of the Jane in her and becomes detrimentally fascinated by "that rare combination of an exquisitely desirable body and an almost masculine intelligence" (*Cleo,* 104). Cleo gives way to Jane briefly and experimentally when she allows Martin to kiss her passionately but she has no feelings for him. When Tony proposes to her she refuses but allows him to kiss the Ursula in her.

In book 2 Cleo's "jade," Jane, is attracted to Latimer Tracey, and she agrees to marry him as long as he promises not to treat her as an inspiration and a saint. However, Latimer's prudishness proves his undoing, and Cleo separates from him, having learned the futility of trying to alter another person's character and having realized her overdependence on reason. By this point she has achieved independent wisdom, as revealed in the following passage on prayer: "Oh, how useless it was to pray that this, that, or the other thing might happen! The only thing to pray for was what the Church called a 'change of heart,' which meant that the devil in oneself, the only devil there was, should change his character and cease to tempt one any more. But how tasteless life would become if one's prayers were miraculously answered" (*Cleo,* 217).

In book 3 Cleo finds passion and learns how to live spontaneously after she encounters journalist Hilary Maitland, who has been inspired by the Romantic poets. Cleo takes to heart Maitland's speech, reflecting, "Yes, that queer young man was right, if you wanted to *be,* to forget your idea of yourself, forget all this ultimately foolish and useless business of dramatizing yourself as Cleo, Ursula, Jane and the rest of it, you had to act on impulse, trust to some vital, spiritual principle that has the power of welding all your separate selves into one. Integration by faith. Faith, whatever one might mean by it, was the great integrating power" (*Cleo,* 252). The two spontaneously drive to the Lake District and along the way discover their vital selves. Beresford reinforces the awakening with poetic descriptions of the landscape, as in the following: "With the coming of the sun, a thin drift of air had begun to stir, as if the wind itself had lain asleep on the moor and was now uneasily rising at the urgent call of a new day—the remote ghost of a wind that smelt of the cold earth, the primitive flux of growth in which it had lain all night. From somewhere, far away, came the tremulous bleating of invisible sheep, weakly patterning the immense stillness of the dawn" (*Cleo,* 255). Maitland catches the joy within Cleo, who now realizes that her "marriage was a piece of harlotry of the Cleopatra type" (*Cleo,* 278). Her personal revolution provoked by Maitland comes to a crisis when she lets go of her intellectual reserve, weeps, and feels a sense of wholeness. The couple is then free to express their passion physically as the novel closes. Beresford manages to avoid sentimentality perhaps because these two are among the most attractive of Beresford's characters, and the struggles within them and passion between them seem genuine.

The Unfinished Road (1937) centers on a character of a quite different nature to Cleo, one who knows his spiritual path without thinking about it.[19] He is John Bastable, a simple man who has a natural inclination to goodness and comes as a young man to believe absolutely in Christ (*Unfinished*, 62). The epigraph "And Jesus called a little child and set him in the midst of them" suggests this protagonist's childlike innocence and also reflects the premise of the novel, which speculates about the consequences of placing such a person in the midst of the modern world.

The novel begins by describing the setting into which John is born. As is typical in his novels, Beresford emphasizes physical place. John's father, novelist Merton Bastable, has a house built in the northwest of London in a new housing development, but the development collapses and the house is encroached upon by a lower class of houses. Bastable, who requires peace of mind in order to write, engages in a war with neighboring children in the years leading up to World War I, and the two conflicts are subtly parallelled. Young John first demonstrates his true nature when he makes overtures of peace to these children. At the outbreak of war John feels horror, unlike his brothers. After his brother Sidney goes missing and his mother, Violet, is killed in an air raid, John is left to break the news to his father. When his father is incapacitated by a disease of the spinal cord, John delays going to college so that he may look after him in an act of "spontaneous unselfishness" (*Unfinished*, 66). Merton is one of Beresford's intellects who is prey to opposing forces: though he briefly wills himself to be well again and walk, the shadow of fear crosses his mind and he falls and eventually dies.

Book 2 introduces us to two key characters, the Reverend James Compton Ridgwell and his daughter, Caroline. Ridgwell is searching for a curate and decides to hire John, who has by now graduated from Oxford. Ridgwell's wife describes John as an "original" (*Unfinished*, 121) and it soon becomes clear that he is naturally attracted to the poor. Subsequent scenes portray reactions in the parish to John, who follows the essence of Christ's teaching without any cant or intellectual pretensions. The wealthy in the parish dislike him and want to drive him out because they see him disrupting the social order. In effect he forces the town council's hand by persuading the poor to move to new council houses. With complete disregard for propriety he also associates with prostitutes and is falsely accused of using their services, though he actually treats them as human beings. Reverend Ridgwell very nearly succumbs to the gossip, but with the help of his daughter, Caroline, who is more perceptive about John, he stands up for his unusual curate against the monied forces. Nevertheless, John's unconventional behavior leads the bishop in a final climactic interview to insist that John be transferred. John, however, decides to resign his orders because he has felt fettered from carrying out his work by the assumptions associated with his role and the necessary circumspection. Sensing Christ's presence in the form of light as John speaks, Ridgwell experiences a conversion and also resigns. On leaving the cathedral they take note of this "monument to the living faith of an earlier century," and John comments that "[w]e have to go on from where they left off" (*Unfinished*, 255). Ridgwell is inspired with the aim of turning the abbey into a convalescent home and using the park for an enlightened housing scheme similar to Bourneville or Port Sunlight. Nevertheless, he is clear-sighted about the potential difficulties that lie ahead.

Housing schemes and the responses to them provide a unifying device in *The Unfinished Road*. The failure of the secularly motivated housing scheme described at the beginning leads to conflict as, ironically, does the success of the council housing scheme aided by John and Ridgwell. Beresford seems to suggest at the close, however, that when people with pure motives and faith undertake such a project a better result is possible. Ridgwell and John's housing plan will potentially reflect the "living faith" of the present age as the cathedral has done for an earlier age. The novel also has a biographical interest, as John's father, Merton Bastable the writer, bears considerable resemblance to Beresford; both, for example, have three sons, and Merton's thoughts on his career very likely reflect something of Beresford's own attitude: "But although Mr. Bastable believed with one side of his mind that he too could, given the time, do very much better if he tried, he never contemplated the possibility of living on his small capital while he produced a masterpiece. For the other, and more practical side of his mind—a side he rather disliked—was inclined to advise him that he had not the gifts or the patience to produce a masterpiece, however long he took over it" (*Unfinished*, 39–40).

Novels of the Collaborative Years

Similar to *The Unfinished Road, Strange Rival* (1938) also has a significant autobiographical element.[20] It is the first full collaboration between

Beresford and Esmé Wynne-Tyson, though published only under Beresford's name in order to fulfill his contract with Hutchinson's, and it conveys the nature of their attraction and developing relationship, though altering the circumstances of their meeting. The novel begins with the story of Trevor Lovelace, a wealthy landowner and essayist who is disillusioned with his life as he reflects back on it. None of his relationships with women, including his wife, have been fulfilling, and now that she has been dead for two years he has no interest in developing another relationship. However, he is introduced to Mrs. Amanda Westley and, after initial suspicion that she will impose her religion on him, he becomes her worshiping pupil; unfortunately, his encomiums on her graces are a little overdone. Beresford manages to generate some conflict: Amanda's unfaithful husband is still alive, and Trevor also realizes that he has a "strange rival" in what Amanda refers to as the Divine Mind. Trevor's test comes when he must let Amanda go to help her repentant husband in Malaya. The novel closes on a sentimental note, however, with a telegram from Amanda announcing that her husband has died and that she is returning. In fact, the sentimentality throughout this novel and particularly the worshipful stance of the protagonist toward the heroine weaken this work considerably.

Snell's Folly (1939), with its detached ironic tone and satirical impulse, is a much stronger novel.[21] It was a solo effort, though Beresford noted in his diary that Wynne-Tyson insisted that he add another 450 words to the draft.[22] The title underwent several changes: apparently originally titled "Beggar's Hotel,"[23] it was listed in a publisher's catalogue as *The Philanthropist* before being assigned the final title.

Snell's Folly tells of Mark Snell's, the third richest man in England, fascination with discovering how the other half lives and shows the result of his philanthropy. Snell encounters some street musicians and endows them financially. He then visits a rooming house in disguise, where he listens to the endlessly varied stories (*Snell's,* 59). Snell has a closer brush with the reality of street life when he is robbed of his last five pence and knocked down, an incident that lands him in Charing Cross Hospital. The first of two books ends with Snell articulating his new view that there is no such thing as money and enlisting his loyal manager, Benson, in his investigations of street people.

Book 2 opens with the story of a down-and-out journalist, Albert Wickens, who becomes interested in the source of a new building, a "super doss-house" where an accident has taken place. His initial suspicion that the hotel-like operation is a front for some kind of criminal activity gives way to resignation that philanthropy is involved, and he attempts to discover the identity of "Matthew Smith," the pseudonym used by Mark Snell. Meanwhile, Snell has taken a trip around the globe to examine labor conditions. The self-confident and self-controlled Snell returns and accesses his building in the guise of a rent-collector in order to gain the opportunity of listening to the residents. As his cover begins to deteriorate, Snell once again runs into trouble, this time being mistakenly accused of betting on the street. He is once again rescued by the faithful Benson. Snell plans a luncheon-party at the "mystery building, later called the 'Beggars' Hotel' and finally known as Snell's Folly" (*Snell's*, 238). The invited dignitaries are treated to a carte blanche meal but are blocked in and forced to view the hundreds of lodgers that Snell has paid to walk in front of them, in this "last supper." The guests are offended by this stinking exhibition, but after it is over the comment that closes the chapter, "Pretty filthy all that, of course; but after all not our affair," suggests that Snell's gesture has been futile. Nevertheless, in the closing chapter we return to the street person who opened the novel, one Willie Baker, an adroit match-seller disabled in a car accident, who is now worth nearly £10,000. A wealthy Lady "client" moved by Snell's exhibition offers Willie an allowance of 30 shillings a week and suggests that he can now go and live in the country. For Willie this represents a disaster since he lives for his role, "able to give something so much more precious than he took, the gift of making people feel pleased with themselves" (*Snell's*, 255). Though he will now have to retire and will be condemned "to rot in idleness," he exercises his gift one more time and makes the Lady feel as though she had done something splendid (*Snell's*, 255).

The satire in the novel is well balanced. On the one hand, "Snell's folly" has been to meddle in the affairs of the underclass, since no one becomes any happier through their financial elevation. Beresford targets the misguided rich whose philanthropy is motivated by the wrong reasons, notably for self-gratification. At the beginning of the novel Snell looks to relieving others as a means of escaping boredom (*Snell's*, 31). He condescendingly thinks about the people he is helping as specimens and his housing project as an experiment "constructed for his amusement" (*Snell's*, 173). On the other hand, Beresford does not idealize the poor but shows them as quite willing to take advantage of philanthropy, even under false pretenses, as in the case of the match-seller who is in reality quite wealthy. Some of these people reflect the corruptness of the system that perpetuates their poverty. Though Beresford does indict the "credit-capitalist system" (*Snell's,* 174), he suggests that the source of the problem lies deeper, in the chains that bind individuals. Mark Snell starts to listen to humanity, and listening is an important motif running through the novel. He develops the capacity for introspection and realizes that he has just as much been the slave of his moneymaking gift as other men have been the slave of less socially acceptable masters such as alcohol. Only by becoming aware of these chains and opening oneself to inspired knowing will humanity progress. Until that begins to happen, philanthropy will only serve as a patch on a crumbling system. Beresford suggests that Snell has achieved some insight when, even though he has been abused and cheated by his beneficiaries, he carries through his educational lesson of having the unemployed process past the gluttonous dignitaries. In his semiautobiographical novel *The Prisoner,* Beresford described the novel and his hopes for its success:

> if there was an implicit criticism of social conditions under capitalism, there was nothing that could be called propaganda, nothing more than a cynical, detached commentary on the contrast between the extremes of wealth and poverty—a point entirely overlooked by his reviewers. It had been one of his better books, with some clear-cut characterization, and lightened by a dry humour. And on the whole it had been very favourably noticed. Indeed, soon after publication he was hopeful that it might be a real success. There had been one or two "bites" from the English film studios. But nothing came of that, and the book did not sell beyond his usual figure of between five and six thousand. (*Prisoner,* 251)[24]

More accurately than the reviewers, Gerber summarizes the novel's strengths, stating that "*Snell's Folly* brings to light a rare aspect of Beresford's imagination, a fine ability to draw a whole gallery of Dickensian characters. The total effect is a nice balance of irony, humour, philosophy, and serious social comment, a *Comedie Humaine* in miniature" (Gerber, 148).

Following this novel, Beresford turned his attention for the next two years to speculative fiction on which he collaborated with Esmé Wynne-Tyson. He returned to social realism with *The Benefactor* (1943), which recalls *The Unfinished Road,* in that the main conflict arises over decisions regarding a slum tenement, and resembles *Snell's Folly* in its theme of the uses and abuses of wealth and its focus on personal responsibility.[25] The novel centers on Olaf Henderson, one of Beresford's well-meaning, truthful young protagonists, whose contact with a mysterious patron,

Maning, launches his career as an architect and nets him a wife, Maning's granddaughter. However, Maning, the benefactor, is eventually exposed as fundamentally unethical, one of Beresford's morally weak father-figures, though he inadvertently becomes the benefactor of Henderson's spiritual growth.

Beresford's next novel, *If This Were True* (1943), returns to the theme of faith healing, recombining elements encountered before in Beresford's novels and adding nothing new.[26] The protagonist, Lewis Arkwright, resembles Olaf Henderson in that both possess a strong ethical sense. This quality leads him to seek out spiritual truth from a number of father-figures and to discover faith healing, despite being raised in complete ignorance of religion because of his own father's fear of prejudicing him. The climax occurs when Lewis, in a typical scenario, cures his skeptical father of a spinal cord disease. Unfortunately, the ideas overwhelm incident in this novel and it reads like a tract, though the conclusion with its rising dramatic tension does draw one in.

In contrast, *The Long View,* published in the same year as *If This Were True,* focuses more on straight storytelling, and this probably helps account for its near best-seller status (at least 48,000 copies were sold).[27] Nevertheless, a strong antimaterialist, pacifist stance does emerge. Esmé Wynne-Tyson claims to have given Beresford the idea for this novel: "the two ways of life, outward success or inward integration."[28] The novel counterpoints the stories of the twins Robert (Bob) and Stephen Bolsover, who are as similar as chalk and cheese. Armed with a practical bent and lots of bluster, Bob succeeds in business and prospers from World War I. Stephen is a more passive character who takes up teaching. His experience as a soldier, however, convinces him of the "disgusting insanity of war" (*Long,* 118), and he determines to set up an independent school that promotes pacifism after the war is over. The impetus to put the plan into action comes from the woman he loves and marries, Constance, a divorcée. Beresford contrasts the experience of several of Stephen's boarders with Bob's son Bill's traumatic school experience in the "public" (i.e., private) school system. Nevertheless, both Stephen's favorite pupil, Phil Gordon, and Bill are sacrificed in World War II. On visiting Stephen, Bob provides the key to making sense of the characters in this novel when he reads and comments on Shaw's *Back to Methuselah* (1921). Bob dismisses Shaw's idea that people with a zest for life might be able to extend their longevity given a skip in evolution, and that "short livers" might die of discouragement when they came into contact with these "long livers." However, this is essentially what happens to Bob. Lacking purpose and filled with regrets, he dies shortly thereafter, presumably of inanition. Stephen and Constance are to be seen as "long-livers," happy and fulfilled. They express and teach the long view, that the betterment of society is possible, a view that only incidentally involves socialism: "When there are enough people who are willing to sacrifice their personal ambitions and desires in the effort to—to bring peace and good-will, the social and economic conditions will find themselves" (*Long,* 189). Their belief that Bob the capitalist "outlived his success by living on into a period that is ceasing to have any use for his particular kind of brain" ends the novel on an unduly optimistic note (*Long,* 191–92).

The cleverness of *The Long View* lies in the way that it presents a balanced view of both lifestyles and the justifications for each. In Bob Bolsover Beresford conveys a rather convincing portrait of the materially successful businessman. He is not simply a villain, even sending Stephen £1,000 in aid of his school, but the sorts of doubts that such a man might have after having made all his conquests seem insightful.

Beresford continued to collaborate with Wynne-Tyson on several more novels, two of a metaphysical and speculative bent, and one of a more realistic nature, *The Gift* (1947), before he decided to write another solo effort, *The Prisoner,*[29] that was published before *The Gift,* in 1946. Esmé Wynne-Tyson claimed that Beresford began to write an autobiographical novel but became frustrated with it because he realized that he could not tell the whole truth and did not want to give a false impression. He then laboriously produced *The Prisoner,* which she claimed veers away in its characterization from the real people in Beresford's life, though "it retained the actual events and some of the conflicts of his own life."[30] Beresford seems to have characterized both himself and his wife harshly, but this novel is probably the closest of any of his to being an autobiography of Beresford's psychological and emotional life. In this sense it provides a counterpart to his rather unemotional autobiography. Wynne-Tyson asserted that the unfortunate effect of this novel was never corrected, but she also speculated that the novel prompted a psychological catharsis for J. D.[31]

The novel traces the growth and development of Paul Barnet from unthinking, conservative provincial lad to highly self-aware, reasoning, and yet disillusioned novelist and quester after spiritual knowledge. Like Beresford, Paul is crippled and suffers from bullying and feelings of abasement, but unlike Beresford he achieves a precocious success as a singer. His singing ability garners him the attention of his social superiors, notably Canon Merton and his 16-year-old daughter, Caroline, the latter whom Paul worships, a typical response of Beresford's male protagonists. It does not seem, though, as if he has much of a chance to attain Caroline because of his class standing—he is the son of a Congregational minister and works as a junior clerk in a law office. His chances decrease after a mentor introduces the 21-year-old Paul to socialism; he declares his independence and moves to London. Now a materialist, under the guidance of another mentor he experiences a kind of secular conversion "like being born again" into the profession of letters (*Prisoner,* 87). He reviews for the *Westminster Gazette* while continuing to work as a lawyer until the modest success of his first novel, a fantasy called *The Prodigy* (closely based on *The Hampdenshire Wonder*), prompts him to take up writing full-time. Meanwhile, Caroline, with whom he has continued to correspond, has broken off an engagement. Paul returns to his hometown of Medboro, explains his convictions of socialism and agnosticism to Caroline, and proposes to the rather conventional girl, whom he aims to educate further. They honeymoon in Cornwall.

Subsequent events continue to correspond roughly with Beresford's own life, though he apparently rearranged some elements for artistic purposes. The major exception to autobiographical accuracy would appear to be when, during World War I, Caroline discovers the man she ought to have married, a distant aristocratic relative who dies in a prison camp. After this point the novel increasingly focuses on the deteriorating relationship between Paul and Caroline, exacerbated by religious differences. Gemma Carrington, the fictionalized version of Esmé Wynne-Tyson, frees him from the bondage that his marriage has become. Attracted by "the poised, understanding mentality of hers" (*Prisoner,* 269), he separates from his wife and embarks on a platonic relationship and literary collaboration with Carrington. As the novel closes, Paul hopes that the seeds of spiritual knowledge they will sow might find fertile soil, but this is balanced with his awareness of "the state of Europe in this summer of 1945" (*Prisoner,* 271).

One of the strengths of this novel is its development of the motif of prisons and the necessity for escaping them in order to achieve integration. The novel is about learning not to follow traditions unthinkingly, whether they are religious, political, or literary; at one point a character applies to the iconoclast Barnet the words of Tennyson: "Nothing is sacred, all must go." Paul follows a pattern of becoming aware of prisons and then seeking release from them. These prisons take various forms. Initially Paul is confined by the dogmas of conventional religion and conservative thinking. Later the prisons are materialism, marriage, and middle-class family life. Reflecting back on his life he realizes that he has created his own prison by falsely conceiving "his own importance in relation to a world that was, at the last analysis, only an illusion of the senses, a transitory, mental concept" (*Prisoner,* 268). Closely related to the prison theme is a minor theme of overcoming duality. Beresford provides the insight that novel writing enables Paul to attain resolution of inner conflicts (*Prisoner,* 96).

The Prisoner is also remarkable for its autobiographical aspects. Parts of the novel are quite passionate, suggesting full engagement with its subject matter, and it convincingly expresses the protagonist's feelings of anger, frustration, and suffering in his marriage. If the portrait of Caroline as conventional, weak, and cowardly is harsh, Beresford balanced it with characteristic honesty by portraying Paul's weaknesses of vanity, of failing to understand his wife's viewpoint, and of his tendency to avoid conflict. Beresford also provides insights into the psychology of the young aspiring author and has Paul make apparently candid assessments of himself as a writer that might tentatively be associated with Beresford himself. Though Paul aspires to make a lasting contribution to the world's literature, he does not believe that he has done so. His popularity has been hampered by the lack of sex in his novels, his seriousness, and his versatility. Altogether, though *The Prisoner* repeats many of the details of Beresford's other autobiographical novels, it is probably more complete and candid than any other.

Beresford's final published novel, *The Gift,* is much more idealistic than *The Prisoner.*[32] Jane Forman, a housemaid, has always desired to be the mother of a really good son. The title refers to the answer to her prayers in the form of her boy Luke, yet another one of Beresford's innately good characters. Though Luke never proselytises, he alienates some, puzzles others, and converts a few by his example to pacifism and the gospel of universal love. Like David Shillingford in *What Dreams May Come,* Luke runs into serious trouble when he is indicted for inciting a soldier to desert the military. A reluctant judge commits him to a mental institution, where he cures the mental distress of a number of patients and even converts the medical supervisor to his principles as the novel closes.

The collaborators of *The Gift* faced the difficulty of making an incredibly good person compelling, and they did not completely succeed. However, some dramatic tension is sustained through the repeated rejections of Luke and the labeling of him as an abnormality (reminiscent of the fate of another of Beresford's characters, the Wonder, with his extraordinary mental powers). The novel raises a fundamental question of the nature of truth, as in the judge's interior monologue:

> What is Truth? Truth absolute; not the truth of fact and observation—neither of them unchallengeable even in a Court of Law—but the comprehensive Truth about the origin, meaning and final purpose of life. All religious bodies claimed to have found it, but their accounts differed one from another, and there was no particular reason, unless it were the desire to shirk further inquiry, why you should choose one answer rather than the next. If it were a fact that "truth is great and will prevail," then we had not found it yet. Certainly the truth of Christianity could not be said to have prevailed if we were compelled to incarcerate a man who practised it in its original purity. (*Gift,* 203)

The novel also suggests why society cannot accept the truth. As Dr. Morgan asserts, "We can't speak the truth, not as I said *tout court,* because it's generally bad business in commercial circles, and an undiplomatic and often a dangerous thing for any Government to do. And above and beyond all that, because we don't recognize the truth when we see it, and can't even be honest with ourselves" (*Gift,* 221).

Beresford's preoccupation with the quest for the truth in this final novel provides a striking parallel with his first novels, the *Jacob Stahl* trilogy, and suggests something of the remarkable continuity in Beresford's canon.

Summary of Realistic Fiction

The quest for truth is certainly the underlying unifying principle in Beresford's fiction. Out of this arises his predominant theme of psychic and spiritual enlightenment, typically prompted by the surmounting of divisiveness, by a mystical conversion experience, or by both. His protagonists are typically outsiders because they reject the dominant value system of society based on materialism. They learn to keep an open mind and reject herd thinking. These concerns help explain Beresford's lack of popular success and his weaknesses from a critical viewpoint, as well as suggest his strengths.

A reviewer of Beresford's *Jacob Stahl* books made the prescient remark that "it is doubtful that his trilogy will ever achieve a popular success. It will, however, appeal to those who take their fiction with a dash of thought."[33] Despite his early reputation as a thinking person's novelist, Beresford soon acted on his impulse to write a best-seller by producing *The Mountains of the Moon,* but he did not succeed, as he admits in his memoirs ("Memories," 163). Financial necessity as well as his role as reader for Collins continued to attract him to the best-seller:

> [T]here was a period in which I made an intensive study of such best-sellers as, among others, Edgar Rice Burroughs, Florence Barclay and Ethel M. Dell, in the endeavour to trace the particular qualities that had led to their excessive popularity. I was by no means the first publisher's reader to make that essay, and I had no greater success than my predecessors. Only one qualification seemed fairly certain, which was that the author must have an enthusiastic belief in the virtue of his or her own writing. Best-sellers are not produced by intellectual condescensions to the assumed taste of the library subscriber. ("Memories," 209–10)

Ironically it was partly because Beresford met this qualification of believing enthusiastically in his writing that he did not achieve popular success. He refused to compromise his principles, never succumbing to sensationalism. Though his psychological realism was labeled unpleasant, he never exploited sexuality in it and avoided sensational excesses even in his genre fiction. The attitude of characters in *The Benefactor* sheds light on Beresford's stance: "It made Olaf and Hedda sick to read of that kind of life in one of the increasingly frequent novels that were being written to the glory of fornication, drunkenness and the hectic pursuit of continual excitement. They both sampled one or two out of curiosity, and after that were careful to avoid them" (*Benefactor,* 147).

Beresford's weaknesses as a writer also partly derive from his enthusiasm for his subject matter. Like two of his models, Shaw and Wells, Beresford's concern with exposing and attacking habits of thought caused him to neglect the emotional nature of his characters ("Memories," 330). A number of Beresford's novels are overly didactic. Frank Swinnerton interestingly links Beresford's training in architecture and his pursuit of philosophy with the type of novel he wrote:

> I had learned that he [Beresford] had had an architectural training, and that although exercising his skill only as a pastime he was an expert cabinet-maker. Both facts seem to me to have interest in relation to his work, which to a technician has invariably the attractiveness of form and plan, measure and sincerity, if not of richness or exuberance. But I

learned further, and with just as much instruction, that his favourite reading was in philosophy, which explained why, apart from the little masterpiece, "The Hampdenshire Wonder", and the Jacob Stahl trilogy, so many of his novels are written as if in illustration of theory. (Swinnerton, *Autobiography,* 291)

Beresford's restrained and meditative personality also helps account for the emotional reticence in his fiction, as he was early on made aware by his superior on the *Westminster Gazette,* Hulda Friedricks: "The chief fault she found in me was that 'I didn't let myself go,' by which she meant that I was inclined to be too intellectual and lacked 'passion,'—a fault that my temperament prevented me from rectifying" ("Memories," 180).

Beresford's strengths arise from his questing nature and his mental integrity. He excelled at candidly portraying conscious as well as unconscious psychological conflict in his protagonists as they struggle toward individuation. His rapid assimilation of the ideas of psychical research and the "new" psychologies placed him at the forefront of psychological novelists, but he did not remain there, partly because his innovations were thematic rather than stylistic. As an empiricist he argued that stream-of-consciousness technique and even first-person narration artificially limited the presentation of reality. The necessity to earn his living from writing also made him reluctant to make stylistic experiments. His thematic innovations, including his probing of the mother fixation and the inferiority complex as well as his objective "case-study" approach to other "abnormalities" of character frequently earned him the disapproval of critics who believed that these "unpleasant" and "atypical" subjects were outside the proper sphere of fiction. This type of criticism was biased, and Beresford's forays into "abnormal" psychology can be seen retrospectively as ahead of their time, given the more positive attitude toward the assimilation of other fields of discourse, including the psychological and psychiatric, into the novel in the late twentieth century.

Beresford's integrity also made him an astute critic of society. In novel after novel he chronicles the breaking up of the old rigid social order in England; frequently his novels deal with figures who cross social barriers in their love relationships, though not always successfully. He also repeatedly depicts sons' struggles to break out of the fixed patterns of thinking of their Victorian fathers, in this regard following the models of Butler, Wells, and others. As a satirist Beresford's method is typically to present characters who discover values and ways of life, including belief in the spiritual nature of reality, pacifism, and vegetarianism, that contrast with the mainstream of society. In choosing these alternatives they achieve an uncommon degree of integration, harmony, and sometimes happiness. In Beresford's later novels his satire frequently takes the form of presenting the ideal in the form of a single Christlike character and then demonstrating the gap between him and the mass of humanity. The vision is not despairing, however, since Beresford typically shows the ideal character having an influence on one or even a few other characters. At the close of these novels Beresford indicates the potential for change, deriving from his faith in the spiritual evolution of mankind.

Beresford's strongest novels are those in which he avoids overly didactic commentary; the ideas arise naturally from dramatic conflict, and he expresses them artistically through the skillful weaving of motifs. Among those of his realistic novels worth reviving are the *Jacob Stahl* trilogy, *God's Counterpoint* (as an early example of the English psychoanalytical novel), *Love's Pilgrim, The Monkey Puzzle, The Tapestry, Seven, Bobsworth, The Camberwell Miracle, Cleo, Snell's Folly,* and *The Long View*. These novels will appeal to audiences curious about the psychological and social forces that shaped the first half of the twentieth century, to those disturbed by fixed patterns of thinking and not satisfied with the status quo, and to those with a questing nature who are open to exploring the spiritual aspects of human existence.

Chapter Seven

Scientific Romances and Speculative Fiction

Though Beresford's psychological realism provides the greatest claim for his historical recognition, his scientific romances and speculative fiction have a contemporary relevance that gives them the strongest potential of drawing a new, if selective, audience to Beresford's work. The eight novels that Beresford wrote in this vein also demonstrate an imaginative power that is wanting in some of the later, repetitive, psychologically realistic novels. That power suggests something of the deep-rooted pleasure that he found in fantasizing about the future, as well as his commitment to the ideas and principles motivating his writing of these works. Through his scientific romances and speculative novels Beresford found the greatest scope for his dominant theme of the reeducation of human beings, a satirical impulse that unfortunately resulted occasionally in didacticism.

As with Beresford's work as a whole, it is difficult to characterize his scientific romances and speculative fiction, a factor that probably contributed to their lapse into obscurity despite fairly favorable original reviews (when the books were reviewed at all). In *Scientific Romance in Britain 1890–1950*, Brian Stableford has identified Beresford as one of six major writers of pre–World War I scientific romance and one of four who also made major contributions in the interwar and World War II periods. Stableford defines a scientific romance as "a story which is built around something glimpsed through a window of possibility from which scientific discovery has drawn back the curtain."[1] Scientific romances give the impression of being grounded in scientific possibilities by using scientific jargon but frequently involve "plausible impossibilities" (Stableford, *Scientific,* 8). One of the genre's central themes is "the impact of evolutionary theory on traditional views of man's place in nature, and on moral and metaphysical philosophies" (Stableford, *Scientific,* 6). This description applies reasonably well to five of Beresford's fictions: *The Hampdenshire Wonder* (1911), *Goslings* (1913), *What Dreams May Come* (1941), *A Common Enemy* (1942), and *The Riddle of the Tower* (1944). The first is grounded in the theories of skips in evolution put forward by Bergson, Shaw, and others; in the last three novels (written in collaboration with Esmé Wynne-Tyson) Beresford is more or less warily optimistic about the evolution of mankind onto a higher plane of existence. However, unlike his mentor H. G. Wells, Beresford is less interested in physical evolution and scientific advances or the horror of alien invasion than in the possibility of spiritual transformation precipitated by trauma and in the social implications of consequent reorganization. He also wrote three novels that are more accurately labeled speculative, one futuristic political and social novel, *Revolution* (1921), and two metaphysical allegories (again, written in collaboration with Wynne-Tyson), *Quiet Corner* (1940) and *Men in the Same Boat* (1943).

All eight of these novels are visionary and iconoclastic. Although the descriptions and character motivations tend to be realistic in these novels, they share with the closely related genre of fantasy a subversive element. As Rosemary Jackson argues about fantasy novels, Beresford's novels compensate for deficits in society resulting from cultural constraints, open up onto that which is outside dominant value systems, and trace "the unreal and the unseen of culture: that which had been silenced, made invisible, covered over and made absent."[2] After expressing alternative desires these novels tend to retreat from unsettling implications as order is restored. The degree to which they fulfill these roles offers a basis on which to evaluate them. Though several of these novels are personal compensation fantasies, through them Beresford variously offered a critique of western assumptions and knowledge, or capitalist, materialist culture and typically proposed a cooperative socialist alternative based on individual selflessness and responsibility. Since Beresford had a strong faith that humanity was progressing toward an increased spirituality, his satire does not tend to be despairing or nihilistic. It is certainly not as harsh as Swift's nor is it ever directed against the human condition itself. The recurring targets of his satire might be described variously as habit, convention, entrenched thinking or unthinking behavior, or mindless adherence to respectability and the status quo.

Prewar Scientific Romances

Beresford's first essay into the realm of scientific romance, *The Hampden-shire Wonder* (1911), is both personal compensation fantasy and satire. It presents a striking contrast to his first novel, the autobiographical *Jacob*

Stahl, both in subject matter and in style, and yet it shares with the realistic novel a strong autobiographical root, as Beresford's description of its conception reveals:

> For many years I had amused myself with the fantasy of a child who, from his earliest years, displayed the gifts, the scholarship and the authority that were noticeably lacking in my own make-up. It was the form of compensation-fantasy that is responsible for most day-dreams, the effort to attain in the imagination the rewards that by reason of our lack of gifts we are unable to attain in fact. I had never attempted to express this idea in writing, but as soon as I had finished the first volume of the "Jacob Stahl" trilogy, I found the beginnings of this new story clamouring for expression, started it at once and, despite one check in the middle, finished it within four months. ("Memories," 341–42)

The child is named Victor Stott in the novel, which explores the development and treatment by society of this "abnormal" child genius. His stupendous intellect enables him to make sense of the phenomena of life from his own observation before he devours the accumulated knowledge of civilization, most of which he rejects. More directly autobiographical is the unnamed narrator, a journalist who is approximately the age of Beresford when he wrote the novel. The narrator has experienced "a long period of sorrow" (*Wonder,* 68) that ends abruptly at about the time he turns 40, which appears to correspond with Beresford's period of distress during the breakup of his first marriage. More significantly, he has an open and questing mind, as did Beresford.

The novel opens with a chance encounter in a train compartment between the studious narrator and the child, who is under two years old, with his mother. Initially the narrator is repelled by the freakish appearance of the child with his abnormally large and completely bald head, but he is entranced by the child's intellectual gaze. Beresford cleverly plants the seed of his satire in the fellow passengers' contemptuous attitudes belying their anxiety, which they express after the child has departed. The remainder of part 1, the shortest of the novel's three parts, is taken up by the narrator's first-person account of his associations with the child's rather remarkable father, Ginger Stott, a phenomenal cricketer. Following an accident that finishes his career, Ginger entertains marriage, with the aim of teaching a son to play. This description is presented as the notes toward a biography, a technique used to increase the assumed veracity of the report.

Part 2 shifts to third person because, as the narrator explains, he was out of touch with the child for six years, though he does occasionally offer his interpretation of events in first person. It chronicles the meeting and marriage of Ginger and Ellen Mary Jakes, the birth of Victor, and Ginger's desertion two years later. Following Victor's birth, attention gradually shifts to the horrified response of the villagers, particularly to that of the rector, Crashaw, who believes Victor is possessed after the child denies the existence of God. The exceptions to this response come from the local magnate and anthropologist, Challis, and his psychologist assistant, Lewes. Recognizing that this "Wonder" child might be a sign of the future evolution of man, the idealist Challis provides a haven for Victor and puts his entire library at the child's disposal. Challis acts as a sounding board for the astonishing theory of life articulated by the Wonder once he has assimilated all of the knowledge available in books. Though Challis does not fully comprehend the theory, he describes it as an "appalling synthesis" (*Wonder*, 176) that would mean the end of philosophy. Dramatic tension increases as Challis is confronted by the rector, who is determined to submit the boy to Church and State education. At this point the Wonder takes on a symbolic role, as by persecuting him the rector seeks to crush "an elusive spirit of swiftness which has no name, but may be figured as the genius of modernity" (*Wonder*, 212).

As part 3 opens, the narrator is returning to the Wonder's neighborhood in Hampdenshire to work on a book on the progress of the philosophical method. He obtains the Wonder's confidence for a brief period and attempts to report the rare statements made by the Wonder, for example on our erroneous conceptions of space and time (*Wonder*, 268–69), but he fails because of his inability to comprehend them. Eventually the Wonder's precocity and the narrator's realization of his own intellectual limitations bring the narrator to the brink of despair. Shortly after this, the Wonder goes missing. Through a dream-vision the narrator is able to locate the boy, who has drowned in a shallow pond, his body pressed into the mud. A verdict of accidental death is returned, but the narrator suspects that the Wonder has been murdered either by the village idiot, who may have felt rebuffed by the Wonder, or more likely by the fanatical and vindictive rector.

Such a summary does not do justice to Beresford's imaginative expression of philosophical ideas in the novel or to the ironic humor and gentle satire found within its pages. Most significantly, Beresford considered some of the implications of Henri Bergson's thought, particularly on evolution. The narrator quotes from Bergson's *Time and Free Will* and during his self-education the Wonder hesitates longer over *Creative Evolution* than the works of other philosophers.[3] In reaction to the determinism implicit in Darwin's evolutionary theory, Bergson had postulated that the overcoming of inert matter by the life force could produce genuine novelty; evolution in this sense is creative. Beresford suggests that Victor Stott is the consequence of a such a creative "skip." His father, Ginger, is "exceptional," but in the physical realm (*Wonder,* 27). His mother possesses a reasoning, "open and mobile intelligence" and is unfettered by academic study (*Wonder,* 69, 67). The suggestion is that Ginger's physical prowess was transformed into intellectual capacity and that the overwhelming desire of both parents to have a child without inherited habits or tendencies had an influence, but ultimately Victor's genius cannot be entirely explained. The Bergsonian influence does account for Beresford's inclusion of Ginger Stott's history in part 1, which is criticized by Stableford as "appear[ing] to have so little connection with the main theme as to be almost bizarre."[4]

In establishing the believability of the Wonder's extraordinary powers, Beresford drew on Galton's study of genius (*Wonder,* 68), on Schoneich's account of a seventeenth-century child wonder, Christian Heinrich Heinecken that Beresford had read in Frederic Myers's *Human Personality* ("Unchangeable," xvii), and on Myers's claims about genius: "There is no real departure from normality; no abnormality at least in the sense of degeneration; but rather a fulfilment of the true norm of man, with suggestions, it may be, of something *Supernormal*—of something which transcends existing normality as an advanced stage of evolutionary progress transcends an earlier stage" (Myers, 74). In the novel the narrator concludes that "[t]he child was supernormal, a cause of fear to the normal man, as all truly supernormal things are to our primitive, animal instincts" (*Wonder,* 61).

Much of the satire in the novel arises from the exposure of the limitations of human understanding as undermined by fear, habit, and prejudice. After the first edition, Beresford replaced the passage from Bergson's *Time and Free Will* with one from Hegel's *The Phenomenology of Mind* (1807, trans. 1910) on the truth-bearing role of knowledge (*Wonder,* 1917, 12). This alteration is appropriate since the novel suggests that people cannot handle the truth revealed through the Wonder's extraordinary knowledge. In fact, most of them cannot overcome their prejudice against him because of his appearance. It is ironic that the Wonder's gaze is feared and he is labeled "mad" and an "imbecile," since he emerges as consummately sane, especially in comparison with those around him. Nevertheless, he does have limitations. As Challis recognizes, "He has the imagination of a mathematician and a logician developed beyond all conception, he has not one spark of the imagination of a poet. And so he cannot deal with men" (*Wonder,* 193). Significantly, Beresford gives Challis the final speech in the novel, on "the uses of mystery." Through Challis, Beresford seems to suggest that, at the other end of the scale from ignorance and prejudice, total knowledge would be unbearable, that we will always have need of the mystic. Mystery is essential since "when all is known, the stimulus for action ceases; when all is known there is quiescence, nothingness. Perfect knowledge implies the state of being one—our pleasures are derived from action, from differences, from heterogeneity" (*Wonder,* 291).

In his memoir, Beresford recalled that he "found joy in the writing" of *The Hampdenshire Wonder,* and his enthusiasm comes across in its lively tone and in the easy manner with which he engages the reader with his speculations ("Memories," 342). Its originality lies in its imaginative reversal of the degeneration plots then common in novels influenced by naturalism. G. B. Shaw praised it when it first came out, and H. G. Wells found it "a great lark" ("Memories," 279). That it maintained its appeal is suggested by Graham Greene's determination to include it in the Century Library series in 1945.[5] In his 1971 autobiography Greene claimed that "*The Hampdenshire Wonder* remains one of the finest and most neglected novels of this period between the great wars."[6] Brian Stableford has most recently rediscovered the merits of *The Hampdenshire Wonder,* setting it in its context as "one of the great scientific romances. It is the first important story based on serious speculation about the intellectual nature of a human who has reached a higher evolutionary stage" (Stableford, *Scientific,* 103).

Beresford enlarged the scope of his next scientific romance, *Goslings* (1913), published in the United States as *A World of Women.*[7] It traces a variety of adaptations to the advent of a plague that decimates the male population of Asia and Europe and leaves only 1,500 men living in Britain, where the action of the novel takes place. Plague novels had been written before Beresford's, as had a number of novels exploring the implications of a world run or entirely populated by women, including Walter Besant's *The Revolt of Man* (1882), Elizabeth Corbett's *New Amazonia: a Foretaste of the Future* (1889), and F. E. M. Young's *The War of the Sexes* (1905).[8] Beresford's novel differs from most of the other plague novels by presenting the plague as an opportunity for the renewal of society along more just lines; it differs from most of the novels in which women rule the world by not depicting women's assumption of power either as a failure or as a utopia but instead by dealing realistically with the types of problems women of the prewar era would potentially face, from lack of skills in industrial production, to conflict within the groups that emerge, to depression in the wake of such a trauma. Nevertheless, Beresford shows the experiment born out of necessity as a partial success, largely dependent on the degree of successful adaptation to the new circumstances by differing types of women as well as by individual women.

The novel at the outset counterpoints the lives of the respectable, suburban, and materialistic Gosling family with the attitudes of their former boarder, Jasper Thrale, one of Beresford's ascetic, idealist protagonists. He warns of the plague, which has originated in China, but is ignored by the self-interested British press until the threat moves nearer to home. Aside from the attitude of the press, Beresford satirizes the Evangelical explanation of the plague and the inability of political leaders to deal with the calamity that unfolds. He is careful to establish the general scientific plausibility of the plague by having Thrale speculate that a bacillus may have changed its life habit and become harmful to man; however, Beresford cleverly suggests that neither the theory nor its particular effects on men are able to be tested because the investigators succumb to the deadly virus with its primary symptom of rapid paralysis. As the deaths mount, services cease, and panic and looting break out, the focus shifts from the stoic Thrale to the bewildered Goslings. Initially they refuse to accept the alteration to their routine until necessity forces them. Gradually they begin "to fulfill long-thwarted tendencies and desires" (*Goslings,* 83). The daughters begin to ransack shops, while Mr. Gosling deserts his family altogether for an attractive farm woman (*Goslings,* 115).

Book 2 covers the female Goslings' attempts to cope as the law of self-preservation comes into effect. Driven by their search for food, the two daughters, Blanche and Millie, journey with their mother into the countryside. Along the way they encounter those ready to defend their territory and possessions by force as well as those who take them in and offer advice. One of the latter, a former novelist who has started a farming commune, underlines an important theme of the novel, "Women are of all sorts," and suggests that they head toward a village off the track of exodus called Marlow (*Goslings,* 180). There they witness a degenerate male (formerly a butcher) with his bare-breasted harem before encountering Thrale as the book closes. By this time Blanche Gosling has emerged as the leader of the three women because she is more able to adapt to change than the others; Mrs. Gosling, "a suburban house-insect" (*Goslings*, 152) with specialized habits, cannot adapt and loses her interest in life.

In book 3 Thrale's explorations of the new world are briefly summarized. He has run across a fiesty former aristocrat named Eileen who has helped form a cooperative under the direction of a 19-year-old farm girl. The group hesitatingly offers Thrale the job of chief mechanic, subordinate to the girl, since, as Eileen puts it, "Men are so jolly good at machinery. We shouldn't miss them much if it weren't for that" (*Goslings*, 225). As the necessity for harvesting food has arisen, a new unstated law has come into being, "that every woman had a right to her share in the bounty of Nature, and the corollary was that she earned her right by labour" (*Goslings*, 217). The Gosling girls join the laborers, but after the harvest is done, Millie, whose advances have been rebuffed by Thrale, leaves to seek out the Dionysian butcher. Meanwhile, Eileen's intimacy with Thrale has increased, but he fears his feelings. The narrator insightfully suggests that once the basic need for food has been met, "women began to express themselves in their various ways. Aspirations and emotions that had been crushed by the fatigues of physical labour began to revive: personal inclinations, jealousies and resentments became manifest in the detail of intercourse; old prejudices, religious and social, once more assumed an aspect of importance in the interactions of individuals" (Goslings, 237–38).

A woman called Jenkyn revives religious fervor and the Jenkynites nearly succeed in casting out the prodigal Millie. However, one among their member is caught stealing and they are expelled. A new threat of flooding arises and Eileen and Thrale set out on a launch to open weir dams below the community. En route Thrale and Eileen openly acknowledge their love and return only to find growing despair in the community at the bleak future prospects. They set out again on bicycle to ascertain the situation in other parts of England and find even worse conditions. At Southampton they discover that a ship they had seen carries American men who come as friends rather than conquerors. The bacillus has lost its force in America, opening the possibility of regenerating society. The two idealists discuss the changes necessary, including the end of marriage and a more collective approach to child-rearing that will enable women to continue working (*Goslings*, 304–5). The potential is for a more just society based on equality, though Eileen recognizes "how unequal we all are from one point of view, and there must come a sort of aristocracy of intellect and efficiency. But underneath there will be a true equality for all that, and we shall see to it that no man or woman can abuse their powers by making slaves again. What a world of slaves it used to be, and we weren't even slaves to intellect and efficiency, only to wealth and to money, and to some foolish idea of position and power" (*Goslings*, 305 – 6).

The novel thus closes on perhaps an unrealistically optimistic note. However, in Jackson's terms, the novel is subversive in that it demonstrates the effects of removing cultural constraints, arguing that morality based on a certain set of circumstances would change with the development of a new set (*Goslings*, 264). It also suggests that the dominant value system based on money would be rendered useless and replaced by a barter system. Women, the invisible and silenced of society, move to the fore and are given voices. However, the novel stops short of placing a woman in the role of protagonist, perhaps its main weakness. Beresford may have felt uncomfortable narrating the novel from a woman's perspective or may have felt it necessary to have an "outsider" report on developments in the world of women. Some of the attitudes expressed toward women seem dated as well. Another concession to tradition is Beresford's embedding of a romance plot in the narrative, though in developing this Beresford replaces romantic conventions with a relationship based on practical friendship. The denouement, with the rescue by American males, may be disappointing and even distasteful to some, but Beresford subverts the traditional ending of romance in marriage through Eileen's talk of abolishing the institution altogether. The vision of a new society includes some very modern elements, reinforcing the potential recognized early on by Abel Chevalley that "another age will re-read" this "highly imaginative book" (Chevalley, 229). Finally, the novel eerily foreshadows the less extreme gender imbalance resulting from the decimation of the young European male population in World War I.

Postwar Dystopia

Beresford's postwar socio-political novel *Revolution: A Story of the Near Future in England* (1921) is more bleakly realistic in its prognosis and more pessimistic in its conclusion about the potential for the regeneration of English society than *Goslings*.[9] The novel deals with a socialist revolution that is touched off by the British government's failure to deal in

good faith with the demands of labor, and it closes as a regressive coun-
terrevolution occurs and the possibility of a manufactured war threatens.
Beresford's impulse to write the novel may owe something to the success
of Edward Shanks's *The People of the Ruins* (1920), which is mentioned by
Beresford's protagonist (*Revolution,* 239), but Beresford's vision is completely distinct. Whereas Shanks envisions another war during which his
protagonist becomes chemically preserved only to emerge 150 years later
to witness the return of civilization to barbarism, Beresford's novel, with
its focus on the practicalities of an immanent revolution, contains none of
the plausible impossibilities of scientific romance.[10] A letter written by
Beresford to Sir Edward Howard Marsh about *Revolution* suggests that
the topic of revolution had long preoccupied Beresford: "Did you let
some preconceptions of my attitude mislead you, because there is no one
more anxious to avert a revolution than myself? I have few deep-seated
convictions, but one of them is that a revolution never does any good,
and that, incidentally, was meant to be the moral of the book! . . . Winston was a perversion of Winslow, our nearest town in Buckinghamshire;
and I liked the association because in my mind I have pitched the scene
in Claydon, where we live—in theory."[11]

Though Beresford intended the novel to be a prophecy,[12] he avoided
turning it into a tract by placing in the foreground the experiences of a
family and its relations with others in the small village of Fynemore near
Winston as the national catastrophe unfolds. In the first few chapters of
the 10-chapter novel the conflict between conservative merchant Mr.
Leaming and his shell-shocked and visionary son Paul, the protagonist,
causes the dramatic tension to rise rapidly. The conflict vividly captures
the postwar antagonism between young male combatants and older
noncombatant males. Paul has recently emerged from four years (1918–
1922) of shell-shocked withdrawal, having shed the habit-bound thinking and prejudice of his class. He now possesses a "gift of sensibility"
marked by occasional mystical experiences. Nevertheless, he takes on
the pragmatic task of attempting to understand the issues on both sides
of the labor dispute and quickly realizes the seriousness of the situation,
in contrast to his father, who spouts the cliché that "revolution isn't in
the British temper" (*Revolution,* 33). He also reenters the business world,
working for his father's firm in London. While there he witnesses the
inspired union leader Isaac Perry disperse a potentially violent mob after
a general strike has been declared. Moved by Perry's sincerity and pacifism, Paul temporarily becomes partisan but returns to a neutral position, on the one hand volunteering with his father to bring in the har-

vest but on the other hand refusing to join the government military force. Even after the local squire, Lord Fynemore, brings news that Perry has been assassinated, Paul maintains his stance and proposes a town meeting to the reasonable aristocrat. Paul's impassioned speech has been inspired by Fynemore's daughter Angela's moving rendition of Chopin, and she becomes his first convert.

Beresford astutely keeps this potential relationship at the margin as he moves into the climactic scene in the novel—the meeting at which the local rebel leader, Jem Oliver, shockingly shoots the hotheaded Mr. Leaming, who has resorted to verbal abuse of Oliver. Overwhelmed with the unifying desire to save these people from further violence, Paul takes the stage and preaches a message of love and the necessity of working for the common good at this time of crisis. Moved by his selfless spirit, the crowd unifies and nominates him along with Lord Fynemore and Oliver to serve on a committee to manage the town's resources. As Paul stands with the other two he is seen as Christ between the two thieves (*Revolution,* 196).

The wave of spiritual emotion does not last, however, and deep-seated animosities revive, leading to further bloodshed. The final three chapters of the novel detail the reaction against the collectivist experiment after the death of Perry. Paul is arrested by Lord Fynemore's son Lord Winston for his visionary talk of a new power coming from outside the world. Lord Fynemore reports an incident vaguely resembling an episode of trench warfare, and Paul infers that Fynemore's son has been killed. Beresford then swiftly widens his scope to comment on the worsened conditions in England, concluding that "[t]he régime, in short, had most of the disadvantages of the Bolshevik oligarchy, with the difference that in England the owners still held the control; a state of affairs that was essentially unhealthy and inherently unstable" (*Revolution,* 239). This pessimistic view is ameliorated to some degree by Paul's personal vision of promise with which the novel closes. Paul has gained one convert in Lady Angela, whom he encounters on her estate. She remarks on the resurgence of decadence in London and implores him to return there with her to preach his gospel of spiritual transfiguration. He agrees, she plays Chopin by candlelight again, and his words bring her the awareness "that all human life was but a little candle burning in the great dark house of the world, a trembling light of aspiration and endeavour that would presently be quenched by the coming of the dawn" (*Revolution,* 252). Though the novel closes on a rhapsodic note, Beresford does not sentimentalize the work by any suggestion of personal romance between the two idealists.

The main innovation of this novel is its treatment of a shell-shocked protagonist. To my knowledge it is the first English novel to suggest that a shell-shocked victim has emerged from the trauma of war saner and with greater insight than those around him, who remain mired in rigid tradition and habit-bound ways of thinking. The depiction succeeds because Beresford humanizes Paul, showing him constantly struggling with his tendency to retreat from the conflicts that erupt around him. As Frederick Watson in the *Bookman* recognized, "The character of Paul—or rather the deft skill by which Mr. Beresford establishes him as an observer freed by his period of isolation and acute sensibility from the normal and natural prejudices of his class—is beyond praise."[13] In another review of *Revolution,* Virginia Woolf criticized Beresford for being too methodical and precise in his psychology; ironically she may have adapted the idea of the visionary shell-shocked victim, to a very different end, in her portrait of Septimus Smith in *Mrs. Dalloway.* Woolf also admonished Beresford for devoting so much energy to calculating how such a revolution would unfold, but one can infer from the review that she felt the novel was too political and felt uncomfortable because it dealt with an English revolution in the near future. She did admire the novel's "intellectual efficiency," great interest, and "highly exciting" and convincing scenes.[14]

Revolution does offer an especially dramatic expression of the need for self-renunciation and to work for the common good, by this point typical themes in Beresford's work. It also graphically depicts the dangers of self-interested political behavior and the difficulties of maintaining a pacifist stance amidst violence. As in earlier novels, *Revolution* briefly critiques both habit-bound conventional religion and religious hysteria (since Paul is championed as a great teacher of a new religion by a hysterical woman) (*Revolution,* 208). As an alternative, Beresford once again suggests that inspired idealists and mystics are the most likely to lead humanity forward, but the novel is not optimistic about the willingness of people to listen to such marginalized individuals. At the close, order is restored, but its imposition by force leaves the distinct and unsettling impression that the regime will not last.

Collaborations

Beresford did not return to speculative fiction and scientific romances in the novel form until the outbreak of World War II. In all of the remaining works of these types he collaborated with Esmé Wynne-Tyson, though she shared stated authorship on only two. She later claimed about their motivation that "we both believe that the work we did together during that period must contribute to the well-being of all who are receptive to it."[15] The emphasis must be placed on the phrase "all who are receptive to it" since these novels require open-mindedness in their readers, as they challenge the dominant value system based on materialism and attest to the spiritual nature of reality not restricted by the concepts of space and time. Wynne-Tyson referred to them as parables in fictional form,[16] and they have a strong educative aim.

Quiet Corner (1940) is a sentimental fantasy centering on 28-year-old Timothy Gadshill's escape from his false life and the development of his real conscience and vocation.[17] As the novel opens, he leaves stockbrokering in his father's firm to pursue his talent as an artist. In his wandering he comes upon an unusual square of Georgian houses and there encounters a little man, John Maximillian, who encourages Timothy to draw. Once John realizes Timothy's genius he persuades him to come to live in the square, called Halycon Place, a mecca for those who want to be themselves. Timothy meets John's family, including three daughters, Faith, Hope, and Charity, and John instructs Timothy on the few rules of the place: thou shalt not compel one another and "Do as thou wilt, so long as you don't upset anyone else by doing it" (*Quiet*, 57). He advises Timothy to try and speak the truth.

The rest of the novel is structured around a series of episodes in which Timothy encounters the other residents, all people who want to escape from the world. Initially he falls in love with 21-year-old Charity, or Cherry as she calls herself, who is quite aware that he has done so. The portraits of Anna and Stephen, two other residents who mother Timothy, bear some resemblance to Beresford's relationship with Esmé Wynne-Tyson. Both were martyrs who discovered that they were of one mind (*Quiet*, 72).

In order to attract Cherry, Timothy earns a living by portrait and theater drawing. Meanwhile, Cherry has a chance to become première danseuse in a ballet promoted by the nefarious Pop Cohen, who will expect favors from her. Cherry's father, John, advises the distraught Timothy to keep "loving and trusting her" regardless (*Quiet*, 233). This magic begins to work as Cherry permits him to take her to dinner. Eventually and predictably Timothy proposes and is accepted by Cherry. She has realized that Cohen is loathsome, changes her name back to Charity, and admits that she had been in love with Timothy from the first.

Though the denouement is rather abrupt and sentimental, *Quiet Corner* imaginatively explores the idea of a safe haven where people can live out their real consciences. However, the plot is driven forward by the complications involving Timothy and his relationship with Cherry. The novel is more whimsical and escapist than *Revolution* and other novels of Beresford's middle period that feature engaged and pragmatic mystics. Despite its rather limited appeal, it did not deserve to be completely passed over by reviewers as it seems to have been.

In *What Dreams May Come* (1941) Beresford returned to scientific romance, though this novel resembles *Revolution* to the extent that it features a protagonist whose shell-shock (this time on the home front in World War II) precipitates a visionary experience that he attempts to convey to his contemporaries with very limited success.[18] As with *Quiet Corner,* Wynne-Tyson contributed about half the ideas and characters, but with this one she also wrote the first draft of the section describing the utopian world of Oion that the protagonist visits.

Part 1 of the tripartite work describes with moving realism the unhappy childhood and youth of David Shillingford, a self-effacing and compliant boy. David's father, Ambrose, is a failed poet and a drunk, and the tensions that he causes in the family echo a by now familiar scenario in the Beresford canon. The novel also echoes *An Imperfect Mother* in that David's mother deserts the family, for her employer as we later discover. However, as first intimated by the epigraph from Blake's *The Land of Dreams,* part 1 focuses on David's response to various crises in several escapist dreams to his land of desire. Initially these are figured as compensations for his spiritual loneliness and as an illusion of the mind. However, the narrator suggests that these assessments are superficial and that David has actually pierced the veil into another tangible world that functions simultaneously to his own. During an out-of-body experience, David returns to the verdant land a third time after seven years' exile. He is now fully conscious and finds himself able to direct his movements through his thoughts. David enters a building in a city on a hill and encounters children at a lesson. He is able to communicate with them and instinctively knows the names of two, Noscol and Gourlaye, before awaking in his regular life. After World War II erupts, David, an ardent pacifist, is assigned to the Auxiliary Fire Service. Part 1 closes dramatically with David presumably being hit by a bomb while on duty.

In part 2 David is fully immersed in this other world of Oion, a harmonious utopia. Through his discussions with the girl Gourlaye we gradually learn of its features. Inhabitants communicate telepathically and progress occurs through perpetual enlargement of thought, making automatism impossible (*Dreams,* 147). The common divisions of time have become irrelevant. Each person's level of understanding is indicated by the color of his or her tunic: David begins with a child's dark blue though he quickly advances to the light blue of an inquirer. The body is in complete harmony with the mind and has been functionally and structurally simplified. Less food is consumed and none is cooked. Weight has decreased to 40 to 50 pounds, gender is less marked, sex is a negligible factor, and shame has disappeared. Language is no longer used to conceal but to convey the truth and to unify people. Reading is considered a tedious way of learning and, interestingly, 30 books housed in the House of Oion contain all that is worth reading. Through personal experience individuals learn a variety of tasks, from weaving to carving, to perfection. Education represents a process that must be continued throughout life. Individual achievement has been subsumed to the common goal of "all-knowledge" (*Dreams,* 156). Anticipating the postmodern questioning of originality, in Oion "[n]othing of intrinsic value, great literature and art, the discoveries of science, all that was best in philosophy and religion had *originated* in the mind of an individual. . . . All such discoveries were individual rediscoveries of ideas that had always existed in the universal content of Mind" (*Dreams,* 156). Counterpointed with these revelations are David's graphic descriptions of earthly conditions, which bear some resemblance to Gulliver's in Swift's masterpiece. David, however, futilely attempts to conceal the worst: "He had said nothing of the horrors of war and extreme poverty, or of the stunted, undeveloped lives lived by the great mass of the population. Life was one long battle not only between competitive nations and classes but between individuals" (*Dreams,* 134).

"All is well" (the greeting and farewell used by the Oions) for David until he experiences a dream of horror about the explosion in his old life, which causes conflict within him. Eventually he comes to a realization of his responsibility to return to "that hell of primitive man" (*Dreams,* 170) in order to help earthlings discover their potential immortality by conveying his vision to them.

Part 3, titled "The Pilgrim" and with the epigraph from Shakespeare, "What dreams may come / When we have shuffled off this mortal coil," tells of David's pilgrimage to convince various suspicious and prejudiced people of his message that universal happiness is possible under the direction of One Mind. David fails with both his mother and the village vicar, especially when he advocates to the latter attempting to understand Hitler rather than imitating his methods (*Dreams,* 200–1). Ironically, he finds a more receptive audience in the alienist treating him, Dr. Hood. David has brought his Oion body back with him, and the physical changes—including his drastically reduced weight and pulse rate and his transparency under X ray—convince Hood that David possesses the body of future man. As a scientist, though, Hood stops short of becoming David's disciple. His Aunt Laura more willingly believes and encourages David to write out his experience, which he does as a journal called *The City on the Hill.* However, her understanding is limited by "old thought-habits" (*Dreams,* 229) and, in the end, David acquires only one other convert, a young soldier named Greaves. Unfortunately, David's message leads Greaves to desert the military, and David is incarcerated. In prison his body begins to return to its original form and he passes through a dark night of the soul before his desire for Gourlaye brings her to him. Leaving an account of his talk with her, he finally abandons his body. At the close, the narrator sentimentally suggests that Greaves might become a new St. Paul, but the novel as a whole leaves one only too aware of the gap between this utopia and the "real" world.

What Dreams May Come is one of the broadest in scope as well as the most imaginative, idealistic, and lyrical of Beresford's scientific or, more accurately, metaphysical romances. The view of the evolved beings of Oion in their natural setting provides a striking contrast to the feared and alienated child Wonder with his complete spiritual blindness in *The Hampdenshire Wonder.* At one point in *What Dreams May Come* David explicitly denies that his vision is along Wellsian lines (*Dreams,* 212), and the book probably owes more to Blake, with its vision of a land of increased spiritual awareness and of the flame of immortality within human beings. One can also perceive the influence of J. W. Dunne's ideas on time and the fourth dimension, the latter idea referred to directly in the novel.[19] As well, Walter de la Mare provided both inspiration for and advice on this novel, which anticipates such visionary "psychotic-episode" novels as Doris Lessing's *Briefing for a Descent into Hell.*

Beresford's next novel resembles *What Dreams May Come* only in that the protagonists are nearly hit by a bomb during World War II. *A Common Enemy* (1942) hinges on a much more Wellsian incident, a cosmic near catastrophe, than his previous one, and like many of Wells's novels is journalistic in tone.[20] This socialist scientific romance opens with the Campion family's response to an alert signal and the subsequent bombing of their home. The father, Walter Campion's, comments on reading

The Long View, a book of scientific essays, sets the premise: "A cosmic cat-astrophe would do us good, teach us humility and at the same time help us to take the long view. This filthy war only puts us in blinkers by forc-ing us to look upon the very worst side of human nature. It provides no escape for the imagination" (*Common,* 10). That escape comes when a "dark stranger" (*Common,* 62) moves through the gravitational field of the solar system and causes Pluto to disappear from the system. On the earth the result is electrical discharges, tremendous volcanic eruptions, massive earthquakes, and red rain. The threat of German invasion dissipates in the wake of this global disaster, which changes the coastlines of the world and reduces the population by half. Campion, possessed by a queer strain of mysticism, intuitively decides to move his family to Halton, near Peterborough, where his brother has a farm. His best friend, Clive Spen-low, the voice of science, accompanies them although the move does not make sense rationally. The two, along with Campion's daughter Eleanor, who marries Spenlow, decide to start practical politics in an attempt to lay the foundations of the New World. Campion advocates cooperation, the barter system thrives, and money becomes valueless, characteristics that recall the emerging society in *Goslings.* A nephew, Edward, pilots them to various locations in Britain where they are able to observe the various organizational structures people have developed in order to cope with the catastrophe. These range from authoritarian rule to an egali-tarian system. As a provisional government strives to create a stable, peaceful society, the main opposition comes from a former industrialist, Mallock, who advocates a return to private ownership and a revival of industry. Campion realizes the necessity for reestablishing industry to build farm implements but successfully persuades the government that companies should be state-owned. Mallock, who has posed the only real threat, then emigrates to America. A benevolent oligarchy eventually emerges, with the motto "All for each and each for all" (*Common,* 197). At the close Campion meets with Russian, French, and German leaders in order to work on European unity. He realizes that out of the fight against "the common enemies of want and disease" "had come the beginnings of another victory, the victory of man over his own lower nature, all that tended to self-seeking at the expense of others, to an exaggerated indi-vidualism, to separation" (*Common,* 208).

Events occur within a 15-year period, although Beresford is realistic enough to have Campion voice as a hope that in the course of the next 1,000 years this new society might become more like a utopia, a per-spective that his family recognizes as the long view (*Common,* 207, 194).

Nevertheless, this essay-like novel is quite idealistic. The ideas are interesting, though the vision of the future seems incomplete since, for example, there is nothing about the fate of the monarchy and no real attempt to present and address any opposition to the direction taken. Wynne-Tyson, who contributed the basic premise, was disappointed in Beresford's treatment of the tale, as was reviewer Kate O'Brien, who called it "hopeful" but "dull."[21]

The didactic element of *A Common Enemy* reappears in *Men in the Same Boat* (1943), though this novella more closely resembles *Quiet Corner* with its element of spiritual allegory.[22] Wynne-Tyson stated about this full collaboration that the basic idea was hers: "a boatload of men torpedoed at sea, their lives before and after 'passing on', and one 'translating' (the passenger). J.D. caught fire and thought of three of the characters,—then we talked over their lives before and after, each contributing a bit, subject to the other's approval."[23] The book is premised on the idea of karma, rendered in colloquial terms by one of the characters: "The way he worked it out, you had to catch it in your next incarnation for all the bad things you'd done in this one" (*Men,* 23). The first of two books reveals through their actions and memories the stage of spiritual development reached by the seven men, who are initially identified by their roles (Old Man, Refugee, wireless Operator, Seaman, Padre, and Passenger), or race in the case of the Jew. One by one they die or commit suicide. The first to succumb is the Old Man, who has remained child-like because of an overdependence on women throughout his life. He is comforted by another character, the Passenger, and dies believing that he is traveling to his protective mother. Eventually only the Passenger, Justin, who has touched the lives of all the others either through word or action, remains, and he now feels a "devastating solitude." The most spiritually evolved of the group, he has rejected religious orders but has continually quested and renewed himself, often in opposition to popular opinion. He is a pacifist and has been working in the slums of New York. In his last hours he finds himself able to access his previous lives and realizes that he has been released from various bondages, including wealth and sexual love. Moving out of his physical form and into his spiritual essence, he steps out onto "what had once been the sea but was now only ever brightening, widening, sustaining Light that filled him with an intense, ineffable joy" (*Men,* 58). A brief objective report in the following chapter states that the clothes of a passenger have been found in the lifeboat, which has washed ashore; by the end of the novella, we are to infer that the Passenger has needed no further reincarnation.

Part 2 confirms the Passenger's idea that the wishes of individuals shape the nature of their next incarnation. It also demonstrates the subtle influence of the Passenger's words in the next lives of the characters, who occasionally have glimpses of their past lives. In his next life the Old Man, Andrew, is forced into independence from women when his mother dies and he cannot find a replacement. Instead he sublimates his desire into the study of philosophy and lectures on independence. Ironically, he dies while mountain climbing without a guide. The next lives of the Jew and the Operator receive the most attention, and their karmas become locked together. The former asserts his individuality in the socialist North American Federation in which he finds himself by escaping with stolen gold to a South American Republic. Self-consciously adopting the name of Antonio Cortez, he becomes a wealthy dictator. Ramon Ilario (the incarnation of the Operator) is a scientist who invents "the Annihilator," an electrical ray gun with disintegrating power. He offers his services to Cortez, and the two attempt to take over North America, only to discover that their opponents have developed a more powerful version of the weapon. Cortez calls Ilario's weapon a "boomerang," a word that brings back a vague remembrance of the Passenger's voice in Ilario's mind. The memory causes him to stop developing the weapon. Ilario is moved to protect his family and is forced to shoot the unrelenting Cortez. Ilario then writes out a statement explaining the need to end the war, before shooting himself, now aware that he has fulfilled his destiny of doing the right thing. He has discovered real power, "the power to put out of action that senseless series of reprisals he had set in motion" and he has the feeling of being called on as the novel closes (*Men,* 104).

The novella is allegorical to the extent that the characters stand for types whose lives are ruled by one sin or another, as with the Jew who is consumed by avarice and the lust for power, or by a virtue, as in the case of the long-suffering endurance of the Seaman. In the Passenger, Beresford presents another modern-day Christ-figure who emphasizes taking personal responsibility for one's actions and whose own actions demonstrate compassion. Beresford avoids a pat formula by depicting imaginative and unforeseen consequences for the characters in their next lives. The tale of Cortez and Ilario even has an eerie prophetic quality about it, capturing the basic scenario—an escalating arms race—of the Cold War. Reviewing the book in the *Spectator,* novelist John Hampson noted the similarity of situation to James Hanley's *The Ocean* but drew attention to the originality of *Men in the Same Boat* in following the characters beyond the point of death; he found the novella "thoughtful, stimulating and provocative."[24]

Beresford's final speculative fiction, *The Riddle of the Tower* (1944), rivals *What Dreams May Come* in its imaginative power and is the most critically acclaimed of Beresford's late scientific romances.[25] The plot recalls *What Dreams May Come*: the protagonist, Arthur Begbie, is knocked unconscious by a bomb blast during a World War II air raid and experiences a panoramic vision of the future of mankind; on his return to consciousness after 48 hours he conveys his vision to a sympathetic and understanding listener. *The Riddle of the Tower*, however, differs from the earlier work as Begbie's vision covers a condensed history of the world from its creation to its extinction, a scenario that Beresford had first experimented with in the brief prologue to *Signs and Wonders* (1921), called "The Disappearance of Man." Begbie's vision offers a stark contrast to the utopia presented in *What Dreams May Come* in that he foresees the complete triumph of conformity as humans devolve into subterranean automatons resembling insects in their collective and instinct-driven behavior. Beresford drew on a variety of sources, some of which are directly acknowledged, in shaping this vision, including E. M. Forster's "The Machine Stops," Huxley's *Brave New World,* Wells's *The Time Machine, Outline of History,* and *Phoenix,* Plato's *Republic,* C. P. Haskins's *Of Ants and Men* and *Societies and Men,* and E. N. Marais's *The Soul of the White Ant.* It anticipates Orwell's *1984* among other totalitarian dystopias.

The first part of the seven-part novel establishes Arthur Begbie's character and quandary. A middle-aged liberal and publisher of left-leaning books, Begbie has become disillusioned with democracy, which he sees as an excuse for capitalism. To a fellow war-committee member he observes, "The old methods of the capitalist, individualist society have landed us in a second major war within twenty-five years. And it doesn't need a wise man to realize that if we continue to practise them, we'll soon be heading for a third" (*Riddle,* 11). His thinking on independent lines has been stimulated by his reading of a book called *Automatism* submitted to his firm by one Paul Detmold. Detmold, who visits Begbie, argues that the determining factor in the rise and fall of the dominant nation-states throughout history is mankind's fundamental automatism. People tend to decline into habits of thought and the mass mind tends toward inertia (*Riddle,* 16). A society that tends toward likeness will be unable to deal with unfamiliar situations and will be self-destructive. Detmold interprets the "Tower of Babel" parable as suggesting "that we can't get to heaven by purely physical means. If we try to and if we just conceivably could succeed in attaining the condition in which all the people were one and spoke the same language—metaphorically of course—we should be heading straight for the kind of civilization we find in the hive and the termitary; become, in fact, one hundred per cent automatons" (*Riddle*, 23). Though Begbie does not agree that some measure of automatism is not right and necessary, he finds Detmold compelling, and his arguments continue to affect Begbie in a discussion of postwar reconstruction at his club when the bomb strikes.

Detmold's theory serves as the premise of the novel and conditions Begbie's vision that begins in part 2 with a pinpoint of light. As in *Men in the Same Boat,* a wish or desire for something causes it to occur in this visionary realm out of time and space. Begbie wishes for greater illumination and witnesses a vast spinning wheel of light come into being. He then desires form and views a primeval forest and the evolution of man. At the speed of thought he enters again into a particular world in time. He is now Aakisti in the utopian land of the Island People. They become divided and are then invaded by the warfaring Marodians. Begbie returns to what is now termed the center of the universe and decides to take advantage of his "godlike ability to stand aloof and watch" various civilizations as they rise and decline. The pattern of wars prompts a strong antiwar sentiment in Begbie, who believes that the solution can only be in "the unification of all the nations of mankind" (*Riddle*, 67). The only redeeming feature in all the misery of the war-torn world of 1944 that Begbie observes from his new perspective is that Christ's message has not been killed.

Part 4 moves into the future world of mankind, initially viewed as a comparative utopia by Begbie. There is order, efficiency, and consistency, even in nature since extensive enclosures have eliminated the threats of inclement weather. With prescience Beresford shows that this society has developed what we would now call virtual reality. By touching a switch a professor (with whom Begbie telepathically communicates) summons on a screen "with a complete effect of depth and solidity, the sight of a small string orchestra," which then plays (*Riddle*, 81). Nevertheless, this is a strange, and not a brave, new world (*Riddle*, 82), a supertotalitarian state that has come into being after a third world war. There is no happiness, sympathy, or compassion, and individual action is the cause for laughter since conformity prevails. The arts have been eliminated along with individual genius and infectious diseases. The State practices selective breeding and training, and mothers have no contact with their children after they are born. Most citizens live in enclosures or beneath the ground, but surface workers chosen by their low mental ability must face the unconditioned air outside of the enclosures in order to grow food. Underlying this "perfected social organism" (*Riddle*, 86) is fear of external enemies, as Begbie discovers. Fear is the great cohesive force that has caused this race to develop a common purpose. Begbie nearly yields to the mass mind of this society before wishing himself out of it only to witness the destruction of the surface area of this land by robot planes.

Begbie's curiosity about the fate of these creatures causes him to skip forward in time. The creatures are now more ant-like in appearance and more like automatons. Begbie ponders what it is that keeps this machine running and toward what end, "that major riddle of the universe" (*Riddle*, 123). This desire frees him once again and he moves on to witness the autumn of the universe and the "Great Calamity." In a nearly waterless subterranean world the creatures are now fully insects that exist to support the "great Mother," the queen of the hive. Begbie witnesses a horrific "wedding procession" as the future queens move to the surface of the rusting earth and await their prince consorts. Chaos erupts in the old termitary as the old queen dies, and Begbie frees himself once again, thus not quite witnessing the final suicide of the earth.

Part 7 deals with Begbie's responses to his odyssey after he returns to consciousness in a London hospital bed two days after the explosion. Unlike David in *What Dreams May Come*, Begbie does not seek converts to his horrific preview but feels alienated until Detmold helps him make sense of his experience. One of Beresford's highly evolved mystics, Detmold explains that Begbie accessed "the cosmic mind" but was attracted only to subjects of personal interest (*Riddle*, 143). Shaped by his concern with sociology (and his fascination with Detmold's book), Begbie's vision thus represents only one of many logically possible independent potentialities; it is a relative truth expressed through an individual allegory. Detmold points out that fear becomes an increasingly dominant force in binding the civilizations together in a common purpose. But the vision has shown how useless and destructive a method fear is. Courage would not have been any more positive a force, speculates Detmold, and the suggestion is that spiritual love might be a more perfect cohesive force. Detmold reminds Begbie that totalitarian states based on material premises always fail, though they exert a powerful hold over man because they are based on the "eternal Truth," that man must eventually submit "to That which is greater than himself" (*Riddle*, 151). An ideal

State, Detmold argues, would be founded instead on disciplining one's own mind and ridding it of hatred, greed, and fear. The truth of this begins to sink into Begbie's consciouness as he realizes that "[o]ur aim should be a sort of divine anarchy, in which every man should, as it were, tune into the Divine Will and be both God-governed and self-governed" (*Riddle,* 151). Their conversation ends as the dawn breaks, symbolically suggesting some hope for the future.

Though this last section is overly didactic, the ideas are compelling enough to hold the reader's attention. The novel as a whole is certainly strongly tied to its historical context and can be read as a frustrated response to nearly five exhausting and disillusioning years of warfare with the Nazi totalitarian regime, but it is not limited by that context. The themes of conformity versus individual expression or safe, habit-bound thinking versus independent thought are still relevant. The strong antiwar message, encapsulated in the phrase that "war begets war—inevitably and increasingly" (*Riddle,* 68) will continue to appeal to a modern audience. The visionary sequences make the ideas come alive and are among the most vividly and imaginatively drawn scenes in Beresford's scientific romances. In a relatively long review of *The Riddle of the Tower,* John Betjeman urged people to "read this awful warning. It is a great feat of the imagination."[26] Helmut Gerber called it "the most inspired and effective novel of Beresford's last phase" and placed it in the league of Orwell's *1984* (1949) (Gerber, 167).

In his scientific romance and speculative fiction Beresford expresses similar aims and ideals as in the rest of his canon, notably the reeducation of human beings, but the speculative work is frequently more effective in conveying satire vividly because it allows greater scope to his imagination. All of Beresford's work in this vein presents psychological or more frequently spiritual awakenings, typically in the protagonist. Though the circumstances of the awakenings are often painful, the characters gain new insights into their condition and those of their fellows. Often protagonists' experiences lead them to realize the spiritual nature of reality and the limitations of the concepts of space and time. All of these protagonists are iconoclasts in one way or another, and most are outsiders and observers. A few are more spiritually evolved, practical mystics. Alternatively, the protagonists encounter such mystics. All of the novels dramatically depict the futility of violence, revolution, and war. Most of them suggest the potential of love, and of the essence of Christ's teaching, particularly as contained in the Sermon on the Mount. Once the protagonists learn of an alternative way of progressing peacefully they typically feel compelled to convey their insights, but with decreasing success in the later novels. None of these novels are blindly or sentimentally optimistic. Even when Beresford does present a utopia, as in *What Dreams May Come,* it is contrasted with the present world of the protagonist. Also, with characteristic balance, Beresford explores the darker side of the collectivist vision of Oion in *The Riddle of the Universe.* These novels illustrate Beresford's tenet that one cannot compel adherence to any creed, but they also suggest that he did believe in universal truth. In the words of Detmold in *The Riddle of the Tower,* "The ultimate truth is one and indivisible, but for us it has a thousand different facets whose illumination depends upon our angle of reflection" (*Riddle,* 142).

Chapter Eight
Summation

Dreamer, idealist, iconoclast, humanitarian, pacifist, socialist sympathizer, philosophical thinker, conscientious reviewer, courageous literary critic, thwarted literary experimenter, writer of both speculative and conventional short stories, psychological and mystical novelist, scientific romancer, quester after Truth: all of these terms describe facets of Beresford's life and work; none of them does full justice to this extraordinarily productive and versatile thinker and writer.

Considering his achievement, Beresford's beginnings seem inauspicious. His repressive, evangelical, Victorian upbringing in the provinces did not provide him with a sense of his vocation. He suffered from a physical disability, though it may have conditioned him to strive in order to overcome obstacles. It certainly prevented Beresford from receiving a conventional and conforming education that he in retrospect considered a blessing. Once Beresford had been prompted by several mentors to articulate his feelings of imprisonment that arose from his narrow upbringing, he was well on his way to becoming an independent thinker, questioning all traditions and accepted dogma. Nevertheless, he came into his real vocation relatively late, after a frustrating career in architecture, though this experience ultimately provided both subject matter for and a sense of form in his writing.

Despite being an outsider, Beresford's persistence, talent, and humane qualities of honesty, conscientiousness, and humor helped establish him in the literary world just prior to World War I. His early psychologically realistic, autobiographical novels were considered quite daring and gained him the reputation of being a writer with considerable promise. In his late semiautobiographical novel *The Prisoner,* Beresford, in the guise of his protagonist, Paul, provided an assessment of this phase of his career. He placed himself in the group of neo-Georgians, including Rupert Brooke, D. H. Lawrence, Gilbert Cannan, Hugh Walpole, Frank Swinnerton, Middleton Murry, and Katherine Mansfield,

> the writers in various modes who were presently going to usurp the thrones of Wells, Arnold Bennett, or even Meredith and Hardy. And in

that company, Paul did not feel himself out of place. He was accepted by such impresarios of literature as Eddie Marsh and Edward Garnett as being among those who counted for something now and might very well count for more in the future, an intellectual and a realist, but gifted with imagination and a taste for fantasy that still found occasional expression in his sketches for the *Westminster Gazette* and, unpaid, contributions to Middleton Murry's *Rhythm,* that afterwards became *The Blue Review.* (*Prisoner,* 183)

Beresford, however, never achieved the outward signs of success anticipated by his early promise, as did a colleague like Hugh Walpole, since Beresford's novel sales rarely reached more than 6,000 copies per volume. Later in *The Prisoner* Beresford gives insight into the post-1920s phase of his career: "His writing never became perfunctory. He always began and generally finished his books with zest and confidence. He got some excellent reviews but they very rarely expressed a whole-hearted enthusiasm, and those that did praise him were invariably in the less influential papers" (*Prisoner,* 214). By this stage he believed that he had "no potentiality of ever getting into the same class of accomplishment as an Aldous Huxley or a Charles Morgan" (*Prisoner,* 214). In his attempt to account for his frustrating situation, perhaps the most revealing comment that Beresford makes in *The Prisoner* is that "[t]here must be some quality in his [protagonist Paul's] intelligence and writing that made no appeal to a larger public. He was not good enough to be counted among the best writers, and, in one sense, too good to be popular" (*Prisoner,* 251).

Certainly, as has been mentioned at various points in this book, the quality of Beresford's work was recognized by a number of contemporaries who praised him highly, including Gerald Gould, Abel Chevalley, Edward Shanks, John Galsworthy, and Frank Swinnerton. Swinnerton made one of the most insightful comments in considering Beresford the "intellectual" and one of the "reflective lights of this younger generation" along with E. M. Forster (Swinnerton, *Autobiography,* 281, 290). These attributes do not, however, guarantee for the novelist either the highest critical acclaim or popularity. Beresford was not treated as favorably by the younger generation of experimental writers eventually known as the modernists, that is, by those who paid him any attention at all, including Virginia Woolf and Katherine Mansfield. As the modernist aesthetic gained momentum, Beresford was left in the rather awkward position of being a nonmodernist Georgian, along with a number of other worthy but formally traditional writers who have until recently been relatively neglected.

Though Beresford felt that he could not take the financial risk in experimenting, his motivation for writing also helps explain his avoidance of modernist obfuscation. Because he felt compelled to articulate the truth as he discovered it, he valued subject matter over manner, claiming that "I had always been inclined to put Life before Art; and if Art cannot, however cryptically, tell me something about being by becoming a magic casement opening onto fiery realms of the imagination, I count it only as a diversion of the academic mind" ("Memories," 322). Beresford's whimsical short stories and the stream-of-consciousness style of *Writing Aloud* (1928), with its revelations about the creative process, offer just a glimpse of his potential as an experimenter.

By choosing to illustrate in fiction his fundamental principles, such as that this is a spiritual and not a material universe, he practically guaranteed, too, that he would never be a popular writer, although he could write competently in popular forms such as the detective novel and could turn out stories acceptable to the American magazines. In the earlier part of his career, his compunction to draw on some of the rather startling insights of the "new" psychologies in order to present his characters more fully and realistically, however unpleasant that might be, garnered him neither a popular following nor critical approval. Later on, his treatment of various unorthodox beliefs in his fiction, from Theosophy and faith healing to pacifism and vegetarianism, and his avoidance of sensationalising sexuality, alcoholism, and other popular topics helped prevent him from reaching the level of best-seller.

Beresford deserves serious reconsideration because at his best he addressed serious topics in his fiction, with commitment, perception, and sensitivity. Most often he did this through dramatic incident and avoided proselytizing or propagandizing to the extent of his far better-known mentor, H. G. Wells. Typically and most passionately he wrote about individuals who awaken from the slumber of "normality" and become outsiders, whether ignored or persecuted by society. Through his fiction Beresford taught the folly of following traditions unthinkingly. With gentle satire he critiqued the dominant values of modern materialist culture, though he was not averse to turning his satire to values and ways of seeing that he held dear, including mysticism, as in *Seven, Bobsworth*. As an idealist, Beresford believed in the spiritual evolution of mankind, and he advocated the value of faith. He realized that no belief system could be imposed on others, which made him skeptical of socialism in practice and caused him to emphasize personal responsibility as a starting point from which to build a more equitable society. In a moving and yet discriminating tribute to Beresford, R. H. Ward captured the essence of his contribution: "His achievement as a writer was the holding up of a mirror for men following his own path of development, a path familiar to many in the years through which he lived. He wrote the spiritual history of an age struggling to free itself from a spurious and materialistic Christianity, of its revolt into unbelief and of its rediscovery of the meaning of the life and words of Jesus. If more had been willing to accompany him on this pilgrimage, and to submit to his guidance, the world he has just left might well have been a decenter one."[1]

Beresford's pilgrimage, in particular his evolving concern with the spiritual in the modern world and role as social critic, was shared by writers who followed him, notably Graham Greene, Aldous Huxley, C. S. Lewis, George Orwell, Evelyn Waugh, and Charles Williams. At least one of these, Graham Greene, has indicated his admiration of Beresford, claiming that at the beginning of his career Beresford was his idol;[2] the possibility of Beresford's influence on Greene and on the other writers needs to be investigated further.

Many of the values and life choices that Beresford advocated through his fiction were ahead of his time and have since become more influential and acceptable, including pacifism, vegetarianism, and cooperative models of living. Thus, not only does Beresford deserve a place in literary history for his early and perceptive novels of psychological and psychoanalytic realism and for his innovative early short stories, but he could also claim a new, if selective, audience. It might be his prescient fantasies, which occasionally open into those "fiery realms of the imagination," that most readily gain him this. With their blend of warning and vision of mankind's potential they seem even more relevant today than when published, in light of current interest in cooperative models of society and a sustainable economy as illustrated in the classic *Small is Beautiful* (1973), *The Chalice and the Blade* (1988) and *For the Common Good* (1989). To the end of reintroducing Beresford, the following works should be reissued: *What Dreams May Come* and *The Riddle of the Tower*, along with *The Hampdenshire Wonder, The Jacob Stahl* trilogy, *Nineteen Impressions, The Monkey Puzzle, The Camberwell Miracle, Cleo,* and *Seven, Bobsworth*.

Aside from his accomplishments as a writer, Beresford made an even rarer achievement as a humane, beloved, and integrated person. This was not without struggle. His life was often unsettled and even chaotic.

At various points he felt divided, suffered from depression, and felt conflicted and frustrated by aspects of his family life. Frequently he was harried by financial anxiety. Nevertheless, those who knew Beresford comment most frequently on his gentleness, tolerance, kindness, and compassion, qualities buoyed by a vigorous sense of humor. In the words of R. H. Ward, "His achievement as a person excelled by a good deal, I think, his achievement as an artist, which is only to say that he was an artist of the most important kind, an artist in living. What he did and said so honestly and compassionately he did and said out of a warm and amused understanding of persons, whom he saw as they were, creatures both good and bad, yet capable of being translated into a spiritual condition which is beyond these antitheses" (Ward, 214).

Notes and References

Preface

1. *New York Times,* 11 June 1911, 369.
2. W. L. George, *A Novelist on Novels* (1918; reprint, Port Washington, N.Y.: Kennikat Press, 1970), 65; hereafter cited in text.
3. Abel Chevalley, "J. D. Beresford," in *The Modern English Novel* (1924; reprint, New York: Haskell, 1973), 228; hereafter cited in text.
4. Gerald Gould, *The English Novel of To-Day* (1924; reprint, New York: Books for Libraries Press, 1971), 50–51; hereafter cited in text.
5. J. D. Beresford, *Writing Aloud* (London: Collins, 1928), 53; hereafter cited in text as *Writing.*
6. J. D. Beresford, *The Invisible Event,* vol. 3 of *Jacob Stahl* trilogy (London: Sidgwick and Jackson, 1915), 388; hereafter cited in text as *Invisible.*
7. J. D. Beresford, "Memories and Reflections" (Jon Wynne-Tyson private collection, 1946), 347; hereafter cited in text as "Memories."
8. Helmut E. Gerber, "J. D. Beresford: A Study of His Works and Philosophy" (Ph.D. diss., University of Pennsylvania, 1952); hereafter cited in text.

Chapter One

1. J. D. Beresford, *The Early History of Jacob Stahl,* vol. 1 of *Jacob Stahl* trilogy (London: Sidgwick and Jackson; Boston: Little, Brown; New York: G. H. Doran, 1911); hereafter cited in text as *Jacob.*
2. Adelaide was born in 1837.
3. Tristram Beresford, "J. D. Beresford: A Portrait from Memory" (unpublished typescript, 1984), 2–3; hereafter cited in text as "Portrait."
4. J. D. Beresford, *The Case for Faith-Healing* (London: George Allen & Unwin, 1934), 29; hereafter cited in text as *Case.*
5. Stanley J. Kunitz and Howard Haycraft, eds., "J. D. Beresford," in *Twentieth Century Authors: A Biographical Dictionary of Modern Literature* (New York: H. W. Wilson, 1942), 130.
6. William G. Niederland, "Clinical Aspects of Creativity," *American Imago* 24 (1967): 7; hereafter cited in text.
7. J. D. Beresford, *What I Believe,* I Believe: A Series of Personal Statements, no. 1, ed. R. Ellis Roberts (London: W. Heinemann, 1938); hereafter cited in text as *What.*

8. J. D. Beresford, *The Hampdenshire Wonder* (London: Sidgwick and Jackson, 1911; New York: G. H. Doran, 1917 [as *The Wonder*]); hereafter cited in text as *Wonder*.

9. Karl Beckson, *London in the 1890's: A Cultural History* (New York: Norton, 1992), 115.

10. J. D. Beresford, "The Discovery of the Self: An Essay in Religious Experience," *Aryan Path* 2 (March 1931): 133; hereafter cited in text as "Discovery."

11. J. D. Beresford, *A Candidate for Truth*, vol. 2 of *Jacob Stahl* trilogy (London: Sidgwick and Jackson, 1912); hereafter cited in text as *Candidate*.

12. *Morning Post,* as cited in advertising endpiece to *Invisible,* 389.

13. Dorothy Richardson, "Foreword," *Pilgrimage* (1938; reprint, London: Virago, 1982), 10.

14. J. D. Beresford, Introduction to *Pointed Roofs* by Dorothy Richardson (London: Duckworth, 1915), v–viii.

15. Frank Swinnerton, *Swinnerton: An Autobiography* (Garden City, N.Y.: Doubleday, 1936), 291; hereafter cited in text.

16. Frank Swinnerton, *The Bookman's London* (London: Allan Wingate, 1951), 140.

17. See also David Keir, *The House of Collins* (London: Collins, 1952), 236–37.

18. J. D. Beresford, *The Camberwell Miracle* (London: W. Heinemann, 1933); hereafter cited in text as *Camberwell*.

19. J. D. Beresford, unpublished letter to John Cowper Powys, 22 April 1937, National Library of Wales, Aberystwyth.

20. Ibid., 26 April 1937.

21. Max Plowman, *Bridge into the Future: The Letters of Max Plowman,* ed. D. L. P. (London: Dakers, 1944), 610–11.

22. Esmé Wynne-Tyson, unpublished letter to Helmut Gerber, 11 January 1951. Jon Wynne-Tyson private collection.

23. Ibid.

24. Ibid.

25. Ibid.

26. J. D. Beresford, unpublished diary. Jon Wynne-Tyson private collection.

27. Ibid., 25 February 1939.

28. Ibid.

29. J. D. Beresford, unpublished letter to John Cowper Powys, 26 April 1937, National Library of Wales, Aberystwyth.

30. Frank Swinnerton, *The Georgian Literary Scene 1910–1935* (1935; reprint, London: Hutchinson, 1969), 241; hereafter cited in text.

31. Mary Agnes Hamilton, *Remembering My Good Friends* (London: Jonathan Cape, 1944), 141–42; hereafter cited in text.

32. Esmé Wynne-Tyson, unpublished letter to Helmut Gerber, 11 January 1951.

Chapter Two

1. J. D. Beresford, "Psychoanalysis and the Novel," *London Mercury* 2 (1919–1920): 434; hereafter cited in text as "Psychoanalysis."

2. Samuel Laing, *Modern Science and Modern Thought* (London: Chapman and Hall, 1885); *Human Origins* (London: Chapman and Hall, 1892).

3. J. D. Beresford and Kenneth Richmond, *W. E. Ford: A Biography* (London: Collins, 1917); hereafter cited in text as *Ford.*

4. F. W. H. Myers, *Human Personality and Its Survival of Bodily Death* (London: Longmans, Green, 1903).

5. Ernst Haeckel, *The Riddle of the Universe at the Close of the Nineteenth Century,* trans. Joseph McCabe (London: Watts, 1900).

6. J. D. Beresford, unpublished typescript of the introduction to "The Unchangeable Priesthood," xv; hereafter cited in text as "Unchangeable." A similar point is made in Beresford's autobiographical novel *The Prisoner* (as quoted in Gerber, "J. D. Beresford," 169).

7. Henri Bergson, *Time and Free Will: An Essay on the Immediate Data of Consciousness,* trans. F. L. Pogson (London: George Allen, 1910); and *Matter and Memory,* trans. Nancy Margaret Paul and W. Scott Palmer (London: George Allen, 1911).

8. J. W. Dunne, *An Experiment with Time* (London: A. and C. Black, 1927).

9. 25 November 1931, as quoted in Reinald Hoops, *Der Einflus der Psychoanalyse auf die Englische Literatur* (Heidelburg: Carl Winters Universitatsbuchhandlung, 1934), 104-5; hereafter cited in text. Similar points are made in *What,* 34; and J. D. Beresford, "Le déclin de l'influence de la psycho-analyses sur le roman anglais," trans. M. Vernon, *Mercure de France* 190 (1 September 1926): 259; hereafter cited in text as "Déclin."

10. J. D. Beresford, "A New Form of Matter," *Harper's* 138 (May 1919): 803–10; "The Crux of Psychical Research," parts 1 and 2, *Westminster Gazette,* 6 March 1920, 8; 13 March 1920, 8; "More New Facts in Psychical Research," *Harper's* 144 (March 1922): 475–82; hereafter cited in text as "More."

11. Gerber, "J. D. Beresford," 28. Beresford attributed a psychical influence involving reincarnation to his lifelong friendship with Arthur Harvey James, who was killed at war in 1917 ("Memories," 163).

12. J. D. Beresford, *H. G. Wells,* Writers of the Day Series (London: Nisbet, 1915).

13. J. D. Beresford, "The Successors of Charles Dickens," *Nation and Athenaeum* 34 (29 December 1923): 487–88; hereafter cited in text as "Successors."

14.   Beresford shared an interest in the Society For Psychical Research with Richmond, who wrote on education, including *The Permanent Values of Education* (1917) (Gerber, "J. D. Beresford," 29).

15.   As cited in Norman Sherry, *The Life of Graham Greene,* vol. 1 (London: Cape, 1989), 98.

16.   Beresford mentions having discussed Freud and Jung with Ford in the winter of 1912–1913 (*Ford,* 288).

17.   E. Pugh, "Four," *The Bookman* (London) 53 (November 1917): 62.

18.   J. D. Beresford, with E. O. Hoppé, *Taken from Life* (London: Collins, 1922), 217; hereafter cited in text as *Taken.*

19.   Kunitz and Haycraft, *Twentieth Century Authors,* 131.

Chapter Three

1.   J. D. Beresford, "The Paper-Seller," *Academy,* 25 January 1902, 99; "A 'Things Seen,' " *Academy,* 31 May 1902, 563.

2.   J. D. Beresford, "A Test of Friendship," *Westminster Gazette,* 10 June 1908, 2; "Miranda. VI. On Idealism," *Westminster Gazette,* 11 July 1908, 2.

3.   J. D. Beresford, *Nineteen Impressions* (London: Sidgwick and Jackson, 1918); hereafter cited in the text as *Nineteen.*

4.   J. D. Beresford, unpublished letter to Sir Howard Edward Marsh, 14 February 1918.

5.   *Times Literary Supplement,* 31 January 1918, 56.

6.   J. D. Beresford, *Signs and Wonders* (Waltham Saint Lawrence: Golden Cockerel Press; New York: G. P. Putnam's Sons, 1921); hereafter cited in text as *Signs.*

7.   *Saturday Review* 132 (2 July 1921): 19; Edward Shanks, "Fiction," *London Mercury* 4 (1921): 434.

8.   *Saturday Review* 132 (2 July 1921): 19.

9.   Brian Stableford, "J. D. Beresford 1873–1947," in *Supernatural Fiction Writers: Fantasy and Horror,* ed. E. F. Bleifer (New York: Scribner's, 1985), 1:459; hereafter cited in text as *Supernatural.*

10.   J. D. Beresford, *The Imperturbable Duchess and Other Stories* (London: Collins, 1923), vii; hereafter cited in text as *Imperturbable.*

11.   *Times Literary Supplement,* 6 December 1923, 850.

12.   J. D. Beresford, *The Meeting Place and Other Stories* (London: Faber and Faber, 1929), 299; hereafter cited in text as *Meeting.*

13.   *Punch, or the London Charivari* 177 (25 September 1929): 364.

14.   Ibid.

15.   J. D. Beresford, *Blackthorn Winter and Other Stories* (London: Hutchinson, 1936), v; hereafter cited in text as *Blackthorn.*

16.   *Times Literary Supplement,* 7 March 1936, 201.

Chapter Four

1. A. St. John Adcock, "John Davys Beresford," in *Gods of Modern Grub Street* (London: Sampson Low, Marston, 1923), 39; hereafter cited in text.

2. J. D. Beresford, "The Tendency of Recent Fiction," *Bookman* (London) 78 (May 1930): 107.

3. See also Katherine Mansfield, *Novelists and Novels* (London: Constable, 1930), 172; hereafter cited in text.

4. Gerber makes a similar point about Beresford's changing technique, although he does not link it to a Freudian influence (Gerber, "J. D. Beresford," 197).

5. Beresford of course had literary precedents in Thomas Hardy's *Jude the Obscure* (1897), among others.

6. William James, *The Principles of Psychology,* 2 vols. (1890; New York: Dover, 1950), 1:104-27.

7. J. D. Beresford, *The House in Demetrius Road* (London: W. Heinemann, 1914; New York: G. H. Doran, 1914); hereafter cited in text as *House.*

8. J. D. Beresford, *The Mountains of the Moon* (London and New York: Cassell, 1915); hereafter cited in text as *Mountains.*

9. J. D. Beresford, *These Lynnekers* (London and New York: Cassell; New York: G. H. Doran, 1916); hereafter cited in text as *Lynnekers.*

10. Annie Russell Marble, *A Study of the Modern Novel, British and American Since 1900* (New York: Appleton, 1930), 166.

11. Gerber claims that Beresford portrays Wells as A. B. Ellis in *The Invisible Event,* a character that is consistent with the A. B. Ellis drawn in *These Lynnekers* (Gerber, "J. D. Beresford," 30).

12. J. D. Beresford, *Housemates* (London and New York: Cassell; New York: G. H. Doran, 1917); hereafter cited in text as *Housemates.*

Chapter Five

1. J. D. Beresford, *God's Counterpoint* (London: Collins; New York: G. H. Doran, 1918); hereafter cited in text as *God's.*

2. Given Beresford's strict definition of the psychoanalytic novel, his assertion would appear to be accurate.

3. Philip's father chastises him for reading Shakespeare at a very early age (*God's,* 14–15).

4. The dream suggests, among other things, that Philip unconsciously realizes that both Evelyn and his mother have a sexual aspect and are not embodiments of the lofty ideals that he has made them out to be.

5. Edward Shanks, "Reflections on the Recent History of the English Novel," in *First Essays on Literature* (1923; reprint, Freeport, N.Y.: Books for Libraries Press, 1968), 183.

6. J. D. Beresford, *An Imperfect Mother* (London: Collins; New York: Macmillan, 1920); hereafter cited in text as *Imperfect*.

7. Virginia Woolf, "Freudian Fiction," in *The Essays of Virginia Woolf 1919–1924*, ed. Andrew McNeillie (London: Hogarth, 1988), 3:195–98.

8. *Nation* 111 (17 July 1920): 74.

9. *New Republic* 24 (8 September 1920): 52.

10. J. D. Beresford, *Love's Pilgrim* (London: Collins; Indianapolis: Bobbs-Merrill, 1923); hereafter cited in text as *Love's*.

11. William James, *Varieties of Religious Experience: A Study in Human Nature* (1902; reprint, London: Longmans, Green, 1912).

12. J. D. Beresford, *The Jervaise Comedy* (London: Collins, 1919).

13. J. D. Beresford, *The Prisoners of Hartling* (London: Collins; New York: Macmillan, 1922); hereafter cited in text as *Prisoners*.

14. Rebecca West, *New Statesman* 18 (18 March 1922): 678.

15. J. D. Beresford, *Unity* (London: Collins; Indianapolis: Bobbs-Merrill, 1924); hereafter cited in text as *Unity*.

16. J. D. Beresford, *The Monkey Puzzle* (London: Collins; Indianapolis: Bobbs-Merrill, 1925); hereafter cited in text as *Monkey*.

17. See Gerber, "J. D. Beresford," 106; "Memories," 233.

18. J. D. Beresford, *That Kind of Man* (London: Collins, 1926; Indianapolis: Bobbs-Merrill, 1926 [as *Almost Pagan*]).

19. J. D. Beresford, *The Tapestry* (London: Collins; Indianapolis: Bobbs-Merrill, 1927); hereafter cited in text as *Tapestry*.

20. Marble, *Study of the Modern Novel*, 166. Edwin Muir, *Nation and Athenaeum* 40 (26 March 1927): 898; L. P. Hartley, *Saturday Review* 143 (26 February 1927): 317.

21. J. D. Beresford, *The Decoy* (London: Collins, 1927); hereafter cited in text as *Decoy*.

22. J. D. Beresford, *The Instrument of Destiny: A Detective Story* (London: Collins, 1928; Indianapolis: Bobbs-Merrill, 1928); hereafter cited in text as *Instrument*.

23. L. P. Hartley, *Saturday Review* 145 (30 June 1928): 844.

Chapter Six

1. *Love's Illusion* (London: Collins; New York: E. P. Dutton; New York: Viking Press, 1930).

2. *Times Literary Supplement*, 13 February 1930, 120.

3. J. D. Beresford, *Seven, Bobsworth* (London: Faber and Faber, 1930); hereafter cited in text as *Seven*.

4. Esmé Wynne-Tyson, unpublished letter to Helmut Gerber, 16 January 1951.

5. J. D. Beresford, *The Old People*, vol. 1 of *Three Generations* trilogy (London: Collins, 1931); hereafter cited in text as *Old*. *The Middle Generation*,

vol. 2 of *Three Generations* trilogy (London: Collin., 1931); hereafter cited ill uoyt as *Middle. The Young People,* vol. 3 of *Three Generations* trilogy (London: Collins, 1933; New York: E. P. Dutton, 1934); hereafter cited in text as *Young.*

  6. *Times Literary Supplement,* 25 May 1933, 362.

  7. William Plomer, *Spectator* 150 (9 June 1933): 844.

  8. J. D. Beresford, *The Next Generation* (London: E. Benn, 1932).

  9. J. D. Beresford, *The Inheritor* (London: E. Benn, 1933); hereafter cited in text as *Inheritor.*

  10. Plowman, *Bridge into the Future,* 484–85. Graham Greene judged *The Camberwell Miracle* "a dramatized essay on faith-healing" (Sherry, *Life of Graham Greene,* 412).

  11. Mary Crosbie, *John O'London's Weekly,* as cited in advertising end-piece to *Peckover* 299.

  12. *Times Literary Supplement,* 9 November 1933, 770.

  13. J. D. Beresford, *Peckover* (London: W. Heinemann, 1934; New York: E. P. Dutton, 1935); hereafter cited in text as *Peckover.*

  14. L. M. Field, *New York Times,* 27 January 1935, 7.

  15. J. D. Beresford, *On a Huge Hill* (London: W. Heinemann, 1935); hereafter cited in text as *Huge.*

  16. R. H. Ward, "J. D. Beresford: Artist in Living," *Aryan Path* 18 (May 1947): 213; hereafter cited in text.

  17. J. D. Beresford, *The Faithful Lovers* (London: Hutchinson, 1936; New York: L. Furman, 1937); hereafter cited in text as *Faithful.*

  18. J. D. Beresford, *Cleo* (London: Hutchinson, 1937); hereafter cited in text as *Cleo.*

  19. J. D. Beresford, *The Unfinished Road* (London: Hutchinson, 1937); hereafter cited in text as *Unfinished.*

  20. J. D. Beresford, *Strange Rival* (London: Hutchinson, 1938).

  21. J. D. Beresford, *Snell's Folly* (London: Hutchinson, 1939); hereafter cited in text as *Snell's.*

  22. J. D. Beresford, unpublished diary, 10 February 1939.

  23. J. D. Beresford, unpublished diary, 22 January 1939.

  24. Beresford notes negotiations about making a film of *Snell's Folly* in his diary, 31 May 1939.

  25. J. D. Beresford, *The Benefactor* (London: Hutchinson, 1943); here-after cited in text as *Benefactor.*

  26. J. D. Beresford, *If This Were True* (London: Hutchinson, 1943); here-after cited in text as *If.*

  27. J. D. Beresford, *The Long View* (London: Hutchinson, 1943); here-after cited in text as *Long.*

  28. Esmé Wynne-Tyson, letter to Helmut Gerber, late August 1950.

  29. J. D. Beresford, *The Prisoner* (London: Hutchinson, 1946); hereafter cited in text as *Prisoner.*

  30. Esmé Wynne-Tyson, letter to Helmut Gerber, late August 1950.

31. Esmé Wynne-Tyson, letter to Helmut Gerber, late August 1950.

32. J. D. Beresford, with Esmé Wynne-Tyson, *The Gift* (London: Hutchinson, 1947); hereafter cited in text as *Gift*.

33. *New York Times,* 26 May 1912, 324.

Chapter Seven

1. Brian Stableford, *Scientific Romance in Britain 1890–1950* (London: Fourth Estate, 1985), 8; hereafter cited in text.

2. Rosemary Jackson, *Fantasy: The Literature of Subversion* (London: Methuen, 1981), 3, 4; hereafter cited in text.

3. Henri Bergson, *Creative Evolution,* trans. Arthur Mitchell (London: Macmillan, 1911).

4. Brian Stableford, *"The Hampdenshire Wonder,"* in *Survey of Science Fiction,* ed. Frank W. Magill (Englewood Cliffs, N.J.: Salem Press, 1979), 2:948.

5. J. D. Beresford, unpublished diary, 26 April 1945.

6. Graham Greene, *A Sort of Life* (London: The Bodley Head, 1971), 97; hereafter cited in text.

7. J. D. Beresford, *Goslings* (London: W. Heinemann; New York: Macaulay, 1913 [as *A World of Women*]); hereafter cited in text as *Goslings*.

8. These works are mentioned in Stableford, *Scientific,* 106.

9. J. D. Beresford, *Revolution: A Story of the Near Future in England* (London: Collins Sons; New York and London: G. P. Putnam's Sons, 1921); hereafter cited in text as *Revolution*.

10. Stableford criticizes the novel for its lack of "hypothetical innovations" (Stableford, *Scientific,* 179), but this misses the point, that Beresford is attempting to come as close to the present reality in England as possible.

11. Unpublished letter to Sir Edward Howard Marsh, 25 January 1921. New York Public Library, New York. See also *Writing,* 120.

12. Beresford mentions this in the foreword to the American edition.

13. Frederick Watson, "Four at a Venture," *Bookman* 59 (March 1921): 232.

14. Woolf, *Essays,* 3:280.

15. Esmé Wynne-Tyson, unpublished letter to Helmut Gerber, August 1950.

16. Esmé Wynne-Tyson, unpublished letter to Marcus Beresford, 8 March 1947.

17. J. D. Beresford, *Quiet Corner* (London: Hutchinson, 1940); hereafter cited in text as *Quiet*.

18. J. D. Beresford, *What Dreams May Come* (London: Hutchinson, 1941); hereafter cited in text as *Dreams*.

19. Beresford was clearly influenced by Dunne's ideas; see *What,* 57.

20. J. D. Beresford, *A Common Enemy* (London: Hutchinson, 1942); hereafter cited in text as *Common*.

21. Kate O'Brien, "Fiction," *Spectator* 168 (23 January 1942), 90.

22. J. D. Beresford, with Esmé Wynne-Tyson, *Men in the Same Boat* (London: Hutchinson, 1943); hereafter cited in text as *Men*.

23. Esmé Wynne-Tyson, unpublished letter to Jon Wynne-Tyson, 5 August 1943.

24. John Hampson, "Fiction," *Spectator* 171 (13 August 1943), 156.

25. J. D. Beresford, with Esmé Wynne-Tyson, *The Riddle of the Tower* (London: Hutchinson, 1944); hereafter cited in text as *Riddle*.

26. John Betjeman, "Awful Warning from Mr. Beresford," *Daily Herald,* 25 October 1944, 2.

Chapter Eight

1. R. H. Ward, "J. D. Beresford," 214.

2. Graham Greene, interview, 1976, broadcast on B.B.C. television, 9 January 1993; information provided by Jon Wynne-Tyson.

Selected Bibliography

PRIMARY SOURCES

Novels

The Early History of Jacob Stahl. Vol. 1 of *Jacob Stahl* trilogy. London: Sidgwick and Jackson; Boston: Little, Brown; New York: G. H. Doran, 1911.

The Hampdenshire Wonder. London: Sidgwick and Jackson, 1911; New York: G. H. Doran [published as *The Wonder*], 1917.

A Candidate for Truth. Vol. 2 of *Jacob Stahl* trilogy. London: Sidgwick and Jackson, 1912.

Goslings. London: W. Heinemann; New York: Macaulay [published as *A World of Women*], 1913.

The House in Demetrius Road. London: W. Heinemann, 1914.

The Invisible Event. Vol. 3 of *Jacob Stahl* trilogy. London: Sidgwick and Jackson, 1915.

The Mountains of the Moon. London and New York: Cassell, 1915.

These Lynnekers. London and New York: Cassell, 1916.

Housemates. London and New York: Cassell; New York: G. H. Doran, 1917.

God's Counterpoint. London: Collins; New York: G. H. Doran, 1918.

The Jervaise Comedy. London: Collins, 1919.

An Imperfect Mother. London: Collins; New York: Macmillan, 1920.

Revolution: A Story of the Near Future in England. London: Collins; New York and London: G. P. Putnam's Sons, 1921.

The Prisoners of Hartling. London: Collins; New York: Macmillan, 1922.

Love's Pilgrim. London: Collins; Indianapolis: Bobbs-Merrill, 1923.

Unity. London: Collins; Indianapolis: Bobbs-Merrill, 1924.

The Monkey Puzzle. London: Collins; Indianapolis: Bobbs-Merrill, 1925.

That Kind of Man. London: Collins; Indianapolis: Bobbs-Merrill [published as *Almost Pagan*], 1926.

The Decoy. London: Collins, 1927.

The Tapestry. London: Collins; Indianapolis: Bobbs-Merrill, 1927.

All or Nothing. London: Collins, 1928.

The Instrument of Destiny: A Detective Story. London: Collins; Indianapolis: Bobbs-Merrill, 1928.

Real People. London: Collins, 1929.

Love's Illusion. London: Collins; New York: E. P. Dutton; New York: Viking Press, 1930.

Seven, Bobsworth. London: Faber and Faber, 1930.
An Innocent Criminal. London: Collins, 1931.
The Old People. Vol. 1 of *Three Generations* trilogy. London: Collins, 1931.
The Middle Generation. Vol. 2 of *Three Generations* trilogy. London: Collins, 1931.
The Next Generation. London: E. Benn, 1932.
The Inheritor. London: E. Benn, 1933.
The Young People. Vol. 3 of *Three Generations* trilogy. London: Collins, 1933; New York: E. P. Dutton, 1934.
The Camberwell Miracle. London: W. Heinemann, 1933.
Peckover. London: W. Heinemann, 1934; New York: E. P. Dutton, 1935.
On a Huge Hill. London: W. Heinemann, 1935.
The Faithful Lovers. London: Hutchinson, 1936; New York: L. Furman, 1937.
Cleo. London: Hutchinson, 1937.
The Unfinished Road. London: Hutchinson, 1937.
Strange Rival. London: Hutchinson, 1938.
Snell's Folly. London: Hutchinson, 1939.
Quiet Corner. London: Hutchinson, 1940.
What Dreams May Come. London: Hutchinson, 1941.
A Common Enemy. London: Hutchinson, 1942.
The Benefactor. London: Hutchinson, 1943.
If This Were True. London: Hutchinson, 1943.
The Long View. London: Hutchinson, 1943.
Men in the Same Boat. With Esmé Wynne-Tyson. London: Hutchinson, 1943.
The Riddle of the Tower. With Esmé Wynne-Tyson. London: Hutchinson, 1944.
The Prisoner. London: Hutchinson, 1946.
The Gift. With Esmé Wynne-Tyson. London: Hutchinson, 1947.

Collections of Short Stories

Nineteen Impressions. London: Sidgwick and Jackson, 1918.
Signs and Wonders. Waltham Saint Lawrence: Golden Cockerel Press; New York: G. P. Putnam's Sons, 1921.
The Imperturbable Duchess and Other Stories. London: Collins, 1923.
The Meeting Place and Other Stories. London: Faber and Faber, 1929.
Blackthorn Winter and Other Stories. London: Hutchinson, 1936.

Uncollected Short Stories

"The Paper-Seller." *Academy,* 25 January 1902, 99.
"A 'Things Seen.' " *Academy,* 31 May 1902, 563.
"A Test of Friendship." *Westminster Gazette,* 10 June 1908, 2.
"Miranda. VI. On Idealism." *Westminster Gazette,* 11 July 1908, 2.
"Vision." *Westminster Gazette,* 15 June 1912, 2.
"Management." *Westminster Gazette,* 10 May 1913, 2.

"Pipes: A Study in British Endurance." *Westminster Gazette*, 16 February 1918, 1–2.
"The Old Champion." *Manchester Guardian*, 2 October 1927, 20.
"The Expert." *Manchester Guardian*, 3 November 1927, 18.
"The Hairdresser." *Manchester Guardian*, 15 November 1927, 22.
"An American in Paradise." *Manchester Guardian*, 22 November 1927, 20.
"Master and Servant." *Manchester Guardian*, 29 November 1927, 20.
"Undesirable Knowledge." *Manchester Guardian*, 12 December 1927, 16.
"The Peasant." *Manchester Guardian*, 27 January 1928, 20.
"The Pricked Balloon." *Manchester Guardian*, 26 March 1928, 16.
"J's Education." *Manchester Guardian*, 12 April 1928, 16.
"The Parasite." *Manchester Guardian*, 25 June 1928, 18.
"Artificial Sunlight." *Manchester Guardian*, 4 July 1928, 30.
"Betterment." *Manchester Guardian*, 12 March 1930, 22.
"High Time." *Manchester Guardian*, 7 March 1934, 18.
"The Way Home." *Manchester Guardian*, 11 August 1936, 18.
"Washing-Up." *Manchester Guardian*, 9 November 1936, 16.
"Parachutist." With Esmé Wynne-Tyson. *Manchester Guardian*, 23 July 1940, 10.
"The Parting." With Esmé Wynne-Tyson. *Manchester Guardian*, 20 December 1940, 10.
"The Maginot Line." *Christian Science Monitor*, 8 May 1941, 22.
"The Worrit." With Esmé Wynne-Tyson. *Manchester Guardian*, 11 June 1941, 4.
"Here and There." With Esmé Wynne-Tyson. *Manchester Guardian*, 13 October 1941, 4.
"From a Height." *Christian Science Monitor*, 25 February 1942, 20.
"The Swollen-Headed Ghost." With Esmé Wynne-Tyson. *Manchester Guardian*, 27 November 1942, 4.
"Waters of Lethe." With Esmé Wynne-Tyson. *Manchester Guardian*, 4 March 1943, 4.
"Top of the Hill." With Esmé Wynne-Tyson. *Manchester Guardian*, 11 June 1943, 4.
"This Desirable Property." With Esmé Wynne-Tyson. *Manchester Guardian*, 8 March 1944, 4.
"Other Corners." With Esmé Wynne-Tyson. *Woman's Magazine*, September 1945, 17–19.

Nonfiction Books

H. G. Wells. Writers of the Day Series. London: Nisbet, 1915.
Taken from Life. With E. O. Hoppé. London: Collins, 1922.
The Case for Faith-Healing. With a preface by H. R. L. Sheppard. London: G. Allen and Unwin, 1934.

What I Believe. I Believe: A Series of Personal Statements, no. 1. Edited by
R. Ellis Roberts. London: W. Heinemann, 1938.

The Idea of God. New Foundations, no. 1. Edited by R. H. Ward. London:
James Clarke, 1940.

Essays, Reviews

"The Reading Competition." *Punch,* 4 March 1908, 1171.

"On Ghosts." Letter to the [London] *Times,* 2 January 1914, 3b.

"Mr. Maartens and the Realists." *Westminster Gazette,* 30 May 1914, 2.

Introduction to *Pointed Roofs.* Vol. 1 of *Pilgrimage,* by Dorothy Richardson. London: Duckworth, 1915, v-viii.

"The 'Maltruist'." *Westminster Gazette,* 6 January 1917, 1–2.

"Average Man." *Westminster Gazette,* 26 July 1918, 1–2.

"Moments of Inspiration." *Athenaeum* (1919): 340–41.

"A New Form of Matter." *Harper's* 138 (May 1919): 803–10.

"Psychoanalysis and the Novel." *London Mercury* 2 (1919–1920): 426–34.

"The Crux of Psychical Research." Part 1 and 2. *Westminster Gazette,* 6 March
1920, 8; 13 March 1920, 8.

"More New Facts in Psychical Research." *Harper's* 144 (March 1922): 475–82.

"The Successors of Charles Dickens." *Nation and Athenaeum* 34 (29 December
1923): 487–88.

"Common-Sense of the Book Trade." *Nation and Athenaeum* 35 (27 September
1924): 775–76.

"Unpleasant Fiction." *Bookman* (London) 68 (April 1925): 11.

"What Literary Men Believe in Religion." *Literary Digest* 87 (31 October 1925):
24–25.

"Le déclin de l'influence de la psycho-analyses sur le roman anglais." Translated
by M. Vernon. *Mercure de France* 190 (1 September 1926): 257–66.

"My Religion." In *My Religion: Essays by Arnold Bennett, Hugh Walpole, R. West,
J. D. Beresford, and Others.* London: Hutchinson, 1925; New York: Appleton, 1926, 55–61.

"Experience." *Manchester Guardian,* 30 December 1927, 16.

"The Work of Henry Williamson." *Bookman* (London) 73 (January 1928):
207–8.

"The Plane Trees." *Nation and Athenaeum* 42 (4 February 1928): 682.

"New Books That Ought to Be Better Known." *Bookman* (London) 75 (December 1928): 166.

"Experiment in the Novel." In *Tradition and Experiment in Present-Day Literature:
Addresses Delivered to the City Literary Institute by R. H. Mottram, J. D.
Beresford, and others.* London: Oxford University Press, 1929, 25–53.

"The Mysterious in Real Life." *Bookman* (London) 77 (December 1929): 177.
Read over B.B.C., 14 October 1937, as "Things I Can't Explain: News
from Nowhere."

"From London," *Aryan Path* 1 (January 1930): 46–50.

"The Tendency of National Policy." *Aryan Path* 1 (February 1930): 111–14.

"Towards a Universal Religion." *Aryan Path* 1 (March 1930): 148–52.

"Art and Religion." *Aryan Path* 1 (April 1930): 254–57.

"From London." *Aryan Path* 1 (May 1930): 331–34.

"The Tendency of Recent Fiction." *Bookman* (London) 78 (May 1930): 107–8.

"On Exorcising Evil." *Aryan Path* 1 (June 1930): 389–92.

"Science and Religion." *Aryan Path* 1 (July 1930): 460–63.

"Looking towards 1975." *Aryan Path* 1 (August 1930): 495–99.

"The Colour Line." *Aryan Path* 1 (September 1930): 566–69.

"Personal and Impersonal Methods." *Aryan Path* 1 (October 1930): 652–56.

"The Soul's Dark Cottage." *Nation and Athenaeum* 48 (4 October 1930): 13–15.

"Personal and Impersonal Methods." *Aryan Path* 1 (November 1930): 741–44.

"The Road to Knowledge." *Saturday Review* 150 (8 November 1930): 586–87.

"Utopias." *Aryan Path* 1 (December 1930): 800–803.

"Stones for Bread." *Aryan Path* 2 (January 1931): 47–51.

"Synthesis." *Aryan Path* 2 (February 1931): 115–19.

"God and His Shadow." *Aryan Path* 2 (March 1931): 207–11.

"The Discovery of the Self: An Essay in Religious Experience." *Aryan Path* 2 (March 1931): 131–36; (April 1931): 237–43; (May 1931): 309–14.

"The Chaos of Modern Psychology." *Aryan Path* 2 (June 1931): 399–403.

"The Gift of Love." *Aryan Path* 2 (June 1931): 375–79.

"The Phenomena of Spiritualism." *Aryan Path* 2 (July 1931): 460–65.

"Indian Art: Exhibition in London." *Aryan Path* 2 (August 1931): 560–64.

"The Appearance of Dogma." *Aryan Path* 2 (September 1931): 595–600.

"The Moral Aspect of Reincarnation." *Aryan Path* 2 (October 1931): 679–83.

"Automatism—I. Natural Impulse and Free Will." *Aryan Path* 2 (November 1931): 766–70.

"Automatism—II. Two Ways to Realization." *Aryan Path* 2 (December 1931): 836–41.

"Unemployment: Past Karma and Future Hope." *Aryan Path* 3 (January 1932): 37–40.

"God and His Shadow." *Aryan Path* 3 (March 1932): 107–11.

"An Impractical Philosophy." *Aryan Path* 3 (May 1932): 342–47.

"The Chaos of Modern Psychology." *Aryan Path* 3 (June 1932): 399–403.

"The Development of Consciousness." *Aryan Path* 3 (July 1932): 486–90.

"Old Thames." *Spectator* 149 (23 July 1932): 105–6.

"Determination and Free Will." *Aryan Path* 3 (August 1932): 540–44.

"Supping with the Poets." *Spectator* 149 (27 August 1932): 256–57.

"The Evolution of Religion." *Aryan Path* 3 (September 1932): 632–36.

"Tranquility." *Spectator* 149 (17 September 1932): 337–38.

"John Bunyan and Women." *Spectator* 149 (22 October 1932): 532.

"Philosophy and Mysticism." *Aryan Path* 3 (November 1932): 766–70.

"Reflections on Bacon." *Spectator* 149 (25 November 1932): 748–49.

"The Problem of Consciousness." *Aryan Path* 3 (December 1932): 816–20.

"Evolution." *Aryan Path* 4 (January 1933): 22–26.

"Throcking." *Spectator* 150 (6 January 1933): 10.

"Nature is Alive: Human Ego is Supreme." *Aryan Path* 4 (January 1933): 408–12.

"D. H. Lawrence: The Man of Kama-Manas." *Aryan Path* 4 (February 1933): 93–95.

"The First Article of Belief." *Aryan Path* 4 (March 1933): 176–79.

"The Next Step Forward." *Aryan Path* 4 (May 1933): 294–98.

"Equality." *Aryan Path* 4 (July 1933): 474–78.

"Old and New England." *Spectator* 102 (25 August 1933): 246–47.

"Man and His God." *Aryan Path* 4 (September 1933): 602–6.

"Evolution and Redemption." *Aryan Path* 4 (October 1933): 689–92.

"The Sin of Retaliation." *Aryan Path* 4 (December 1933): 802–5.

"A Letter from London." *Aryan Path* 5 (February 1934): 119–22.

"I—Influence of Indian Thought." *Aryan Path* 5 (April 1934): 241–45. Article continued in the same issue by Max Plowman.

"The Artist and the World Today." *Bookman* (London) 86 (May 1934): 94.

"A Letter from London." *Aryan Path* 5 (August 1934): 537–42.

"Will and Wish." *Aryan Path* 5 (October 1934): 629–33.

"The Philosophy of A. N. Whitehead." *Aryan Path* 5 (November 1934): 683–87.

"A Reasonable Doctrine But—!" *Aryan Path* 6 (March 1935): 130–34.

"On Teaching." *Aryan Path* 6 (April 1935): 235–39.

"The Faculty of Research: A Staff but not a Sign Post." *Aryan Path* 6 (September 1935): 547–51.

"The Heresy of Separateness." *Aryan Path* 7 (January 1936): 25–28.

"The World is One: Western Religion and Internationalism." *Aryan Path* 7 (February 1936): 82–86.

"The Storehouse of Memory." *Aryan Path* 7 (June 1936): 264–68.

"The One in the Many." *Aryan Path* 7 (September 1936): 421–25.

"New Books and Old: Reviews." *Aryan Path* 7 (October 1936): 481.

"New Books and Old: Reviews." *Aryan Path* 7 (November 1936): 532–33.

"The Phenomena of Jesus: I.—Temptation of Jesus." *Aryan Path* 7 (December 1936): 539–42.

"Human Relations." In *The Root of the Matter, Essays by J. D. Beresford and Others.* Edited by H. R. L. Sheppard. London: Cassell, 1937, 4–47.

"Christian Asceticism." *Aryan Path* 8 (July 1937): 324–28.

"New Books and Old: Reviews." *Aryan Path* 8 (September 1937): 431–32.

"The Reproof of Righteousness." *Aryan Path* 8 (December 1937): 571–74.

"The Author's Dream." *Manchester Guardian,* 7 June 1938, 18.

"The Law of Love." *Aryan Path* 9 (September 1938): 442–44.

"The Future of Religion: I. The Inevitability of a World-Religion." *Aryan Path* 9 (November 1938), 535–38; continued as "The Coming of the Forerunners" (December 1938): 596–601.
"New Books and Old: Reviews," *Aryan Path* 10 (February 1939): 114–15.
"Ways of Knowledge." *Aryan Path* 10 (June 1939): 304–7.
"The Meeting Place of East and West." *Aryan Path* 10 (July 1939): 355–59.
"Political Thought." *Aryan Path* 10 (August 1939): 403.
"Indian Nationalism." *Aryan Path* 10 (November 1939): 546–48.
"New Books and Old: Reviews." *Aryan Path* 11 (July 1940): 368–69.
"Recent Developments in Spiritualism." *Aryan Path* 13 (April 1942): 160–64.
"The Nature of Man." *Aryan Path* 13 (July 1942): 317–19.
"Max Plowman." *Aryan Path* 14 (August 1943): 367–68.
"Needed: A Living Faith." *Aryan Path* 14 (November 1943): 512–14.
"The Federation of the World." *Aryan Path* 15 (January 1944): 14–19.
"Moral Theology of Today." *Aryan Path* 15 (May 1944): 220–21.
"Man and the State." *Aryan Path* 15 (July 1944): 305–9.
"Towards Totalitarianism." *Aryan Path* 15 (November 1944): 431–32.
"New Books and Old: Reviews." *Aryan Path* 16 (April 1945): 147.
"Telepathy." *Aryan Path* 16 (August 1945): 301–3.
"The Demand for Justice." *Aryan Path* 17 (May 1946): 184–86.
"New Books and Old: Reviews." *Aryan Path* 17 (July 1946): 275–76.
"A Statement of Belief." *Aryan Path* 17 (October 1946): 369–73.
"Wisdom as Old as Thinking Man."*Aryan Path* 18 (April 1947): 178–80.

Drama

The Compleat Angler. A Duologue. With Arthur Scott Craven. London: Samuel French, 1915.
The Perfect Machine. With A. S. Craven. *English Review* 26 (May 1918): 393–408.

Verse

Poems by Two Brothers. With Richard Beresford. London: E. Macdonald, 1915.

Miscellaneous Works

W. E. Ford: A Biography. With Kenneth Richmond. London: Collins, 1917.
Introduction to *From the Unconscious to the Conscious,* by Gustave Geley. Translated by S. De Brath. New York and London: Harper, 1920, v–vi.
"The Psychical Researcher's Tale: The Sceptical Poltergeist." In *The New Decameron.* Vol. 3. Oxford: Basil Blackwell, 1922.
Writing Aloud. London: Collins, 1928.
Introduction to *The Unity of Being,* by Esmé Wynne-Tyson. London: Dakers, 1949, 9–13.

SECONDARY SOURCES

Bibliography

Gerber, Helmut E. "J. D. Beresford: A Bibliography." *Bulletin of Bibliography* 21 (January–April 1956): 201–4. Short description of Beresford's work and significance as well as extensive but not complete bibliography.

Books and Parts of Books

Adcock, A. St. John. "John Davys Beresford." In *Gods of Modern Grub Street.* London: Sampson Low, Marston, 1923. Seven-page biographical sketch and critical assessment that argues that the *Jacob Stahl* trilogy is Beresford's highest achievement to date.

Chevalley, Abel. "J. D. Beresford." In *The Modern English Novel.* 1924. Reprint, New York: Haskell, 1973. Sympathetic and perceptive, though not completely accurate, eight-page assessment of Beresford's early work, focusing on *Goslings* and *Housemates.*

Frierson, William C. "J. D. Beresford." In *The English Novel in Transition 1885–1940.* Norman: University of Oklahoma Press, 1965. Considers Beresford the earliest of the "life-novelists" of 1910–1917 who protested the English social ideal.

George, W. L. *A Novelist on Novels.* 1918. Reprint, Port Washington, N.Y.: Kennikat Press, 1970. Predicts that Beresford will be among future leading novelists. Very brief discussion of early novels.

Gerber, Helmut E. "J. D. Beresford: The Freudian Element." *Literature and Psychology* 6 (1956): 78–86. Discusses psychological influences in Beresford's work with the aim of encouraging more detailed studies.

Gould, Gerald. *The English Novel of To-Day.* 1924. Reprint, New York: Books for Libraries Press, 1971. Recognizes Beresford's diversity and considers Beresford's novels under the headings of psychological and biographical fiction.

Hamilton, Mary Agnes. *Remembering My Good Friends.* London: Jonathan Cape, 1944. High praise of Beresford's personality coupled with unjust assessment of the "perils" limiting his fiction.

Hoops, R. *Der Einfluss der Psychoanalyse auf die Englische Literatur.* Heidelburg: Carl Winters Universitatsbuchhandlung, 1934. Discusses Beresford's treatment of psychology and psychoanalysis in his fiction to 1920. Partly based on correspondence with Beresford.

Hungerford, Edward A. "Mrs. Woolf, Freud, and J. D. Beresford." *Literature and Psychology* 3 (August 1955): 49–51. Uses Woolf's review of *An Imperfect Mother* to demonstrate her knowledge of Freudian ideas, but disagrees with Woolf's appraisal of the novel as a "failure."

Johnson, George M. "J. D. Beresford." In *British Short-Fiction Writers, 1915–1945.* Edited by John H. Rogers. Vol. 163 of *Dictionary of Literary Biography.* Detroit: Gale Research, 1996.

Johnson, Reginald Brimley. "J. D. Beresford." In *Some Contemporary Novelists (Men)*. 1922. Reprint, Freeport, N.Y.: Books For Libraries Press, 1970. Astute 22-page assessment of Beresford's work to 1922. Highly praises *God's Counterpoint* and *Revolution*; does not find *The Hampdenshire Wonder* convincing.

Kunitz, Stanley J. and Howard Haycraft, eds. "J. D. Beresford." In *Twentieth Century Authors: A Biographical Dictionary of Modern Literature*. New York: H. W. Wilson, 1942. Short biographical sketch, with Beresford's commentary.

Mansfield, Katherine. *Novelists and Novels*. London: Constable, 1930. Reprints a short and critical review of Beresford's *An Imperfect Mother*.

Marble, Annie Russell. *A Study of the Modern Novel, British and American Since 1900*. New York: Appleton, 1930. Brief description of Beresford's life, literary significance, and selected novels, notably *The Tapestry*.

Shanks, Edward. "Reflections on the Recent History of the English Novel." In *First Essays on Literature*. 1923. Reprint, Freeport, N.Y.: Books for Libraries Press, 1968. Beresford discussed briefly as "an experimental and changing author."

Stableford, Brian. "*The Hampdenshire Wonder*." In *Survey of Science Fiction*. Vol. 2. Edited by Frank W. Magill. Englewood Cliffs, N.J.: Salem Press, 1979. Contextualizes and assesses *The Hampdenshire Wonder*. Concludes that it should be better known than it is.

———. "*The Riddle of the Tower*." *Survey of Science Fiction*. Vol. 2. Edited by Frank W. Magill. Englewood Cliffs, N.J.: Salem Press, 1979. Discussion of Beresford's World War II speculative fiction, with focus on *The Riddle of the Tower*.

———. "J. D. Beresford 1873–1947." In *Supernatural Fiction Writers. Fantasy and Horror*, vol. 1. Edited by E. F. Bleiler. New York: Scribner's, 1985. Critical assessment of Beresford's visionary fantasies to show that Beresford deserves to be remembered for them.

———. *Scientific Romance in Britain 1890–1950*. London: Fourth Estate, 1985. Most serious recent assessment of Beresford's speculative fiction in context.

Swinnerton, Frank. "Oliver Onions and J. D. Beresford." In *The Georgian Literary Scene 1910–1935*. 1935. Reprint, London: Hutchinson, 1969. With some admiration presents Beresford as a novelist of current ideas, but also makes unjustified claims about biographical influence on Beresford's work.

———. *Swinnerton: An Autobiography*. Garden City, N.Y.: Doubleday, 1936. Describes the literary milieu of, and his friendship with Beresford, one of the reflective lights of his generation.

Ward, R. H. "J. D. Beresford: Artist in Living." *Aryan Path* 18 (May 1947): 212–14. Moving but honest tribute to Beresford the man and the artist. Points out that Beresford's work falls between popular appeal and appeal to an intelligentsia. Nevertheless, he made a number of his contemporaries and juniors think.

Unpublished Dissertation

Gerber, Helmut E. "J. D. Beresford: A Study of His Works and Philosophy." Ph.D. diss., University of Pennsylvania, 1952. The most comprehensive study of Beresford's ideas and works.

Index

The Author

George M. Johnson was born in 1961 in Waterdown, Ontario. He received his Honours B.A. in English and psychology from the University of Western Ontario in 1984. He received an M.A. and Ph.D. from McMaster University, where he held a S.S.H.R.C. doctoral fellowship. Since 1991 he has taught English literature at the University College of the Cariboo in Kamloops, British Columbia. In addition to contributing to volumes of the *Dictionary of Literary Biography,* Johnson is the editor of *Late-Victorian and Edwardian British Novelists,* First Series (1995) and Second Series (forthcoming), and *British Novelists Between the Wars* (forthcoming). His articles on literary history, Virginia Woolf, and Gerard Manley Hopkins have appeared in *Textual Studies in Canada, Twentieth Century Literature,* and *Biography.* He currently holds a Government of Canada S.S.H.R.C. grant that he is using to research the influence of psychical research on British novelists of the transitional period.

The Editor

Kinley E. Roby is professor emeritus of English at Northeastern University. He is the twentieth-century field editor of Twayne's English Authors Series, series editor of Twayne's Critical History of British Drama, and general editor of Twayne's Women and Literature Series. He has written books on Arnold Bennett, Edward VII, and Joyce Cary, and edited a collection of essays on T. S. Eliot. He makes his home in Naples, Florida.